TEN
MASTERPIECES
OF MUSIC

OTHER BOOKS BY HARVEY SACHS

Toscanini: Musician of Conscience

The Ninth: Beethoven and the World in 1824

Rubinstein: A Life

Reflections on Toscanini

Music in Fascist Italy

Virtuoso

AS EDITOR AND TRANSLATOR

The Letters of Arturo Toscanini

TEN
MASTERPIECES
OF MUSIC

HARVEY SACHS

LIVERIGHT PUBLISHING CORPORATION

A Division of W. W. Norton & Company

Independent Publishers Since 1923

NEW YORK   LONDON

For information about permission to reproduce selections from this book,
write to Permissions, Liveright Publishing Corporation, a division of
W. W. Norton & Company, Inc., 500 Fifth Avenue, New York, NY 10110

For information about special discounts for bulk purchases, please contact
W. W. Norton Special Sales at specialsales@wwnorton.com or 800-233-4830

Manufacturing by Lakeside Book Company
Book design by Ellen Cipriano
Production manager: Anna Oler

Library of Congress Cataloging-in-Publication Data

Names: Sachs, Harvey, 1946– author.
Title: Ten masterpieces of music / Harvey Sachs.
Other titles: 10 masterpieces of music
Description: First edition. | New York : Liveright Publishing Corporation, 2021. |
Includes bibliographical references and index.
Identifiers: LCCN 2021033585 | ISBN 9781631495182 (hardcover) |
ISBN 9781631495199 (epub)
Subjects: LCSH: Music—History and criticism.
Classification: LCC ML193 .S23 2021 | DDC 780.9—dc23
LC record available at https://lccn.loc.gov/2021033585

Liveright Publishing Corporation,
500 Fifth Avenue, New York, N.Y. 10110
www.wwnorton.com

W. W. Norton & Company Ltd.
15 Carlisle Street, London W1D 3BS

1 2 3 4 5 6 7 8 9 0

In memory of

Maurice Wolfson (1912–2007),

who brought me to great music.

CONTENTS

PREFACE

WHY DO SOME PIECES OF MUSIC survive while others fall into oblivion?

According to credible estimates, about two hundred residents of Vienna in the year 1800 were making at least part of their living as composers, but most music lovers today can name only two of them: Haydn and Beethoven. Similarly, in the 1850s dozens of Italian composers were writing operas for a national and international public that enthusiastically followed the latest trends in the lyric theater, yet how many non-specialists in our time can think of any of them except Verdi?

I once raised this matter with Gianandrea Gavazzeni (1909–1996), an Italian conductor whose literary, historical, and philosophical interests were wide-ranging. "I don't know whether *Pagliacci*, for instance, is beautiful or ugly, great or not great," Gavazzeni said. "But I know that it is alive—that it has what Bergson called *élan vital*"—the life force. "Many works may be well-made and highly interesting, but if that *élan vital* isn't bursting out of them, they won't last."

The ten extraordinary works that I have chosen to write about in this book all possess that life force. They have endured over decades and, in some cases, centuries, because they were created by people who had a gift for pulling music out of their deepest wellsprings. These composers absorbed experience and then transformed and communicated it through music. And through music they universalized the intimate—because, after all, music grows out of an impulse to express what we sense about who and what we are. By heightening and sharpening our perceptions, music can stimulate or disturb our inmost being, just as it can bring us feelings of joy or solace. Sometimes it does all of these things and more within a few seconds.

I am not, however, proposing these works as candidates for classical music's Top Ten or because I love them more than I love many dozens of other pieces. My favorite piece by each of the composers featured here, and by many others as well, is usually the one that I'm listening to or thinking about at any given time, whether it's Alban Berg's *Lyric Suite*, the sextet from Donizetti's *Lucia di Lammermoor*, or Bach's keyboard Partita in B-flat major. I've chosen these ten pieces partly by chance—because I happened to be thinking about them when I was deciding on this book's "repertoire"—but primarily because I thought that I had something useful to say about them, about their composers, about how each piece fits into its composer's life, and about how each of these lives fits into its time and place and into the continuum of Western musical history.

Difficult decisions had to be made, and I imagine that some readers will ask, "Why didn't you include Composer X or Y or Z?" In some cases, my reasons for those decisions were personal. For instance: I love the music of Monteverdi, Bach, Handel, and many other Baroque and earlier composers, but I feel too distant from the dominant mentality of pre-Enlightenment Europe to attempt the sort of mini-portrait that I will try to draw for each of the people represented in the following pages. In other cases, the reasons for my choices were practical: I excluded Chopin, Debussy, and Bartók, among others, in order not to exceed this volume's prescribed dimensions. And I wanted to avoid settling on one of the most often-performed works of each composer: no *Eine kleine Nachtmusik* of Mozart, no Beethoven Ninth Symphony (about which, in any case, I had already written a book), no Schubert "Unfinished" Symphony, no Verdi *Aida*, no Stravinsky *Firebird*. Most of the pieces I chose are well known, but not all of them are necessarily works with which most music lovers will be familiar.

Another important criterion was my wish to choose pieces in ten different genres. Thus, there are works for various numbers of performers: one (a piano sonata), two (a song cycle for solo voice plus piano), three (a piano-violin-cello trio), four (a string quartet), five (a string quintet), a symphony orchestra, and an orchestra plus one solo instrument. Also included are a religious work for orchestra plus chorus and vocal soloists, an opera, and a composition that defies categorizing, although it is sometimes performed as an oratorio and sometimes as an opera.

Many outstanding scholars have devoted their professional lives to the study of each of the composers discussed in the following chapters, and I am not attempting in any way to compete with their work. What I offer here is a glimpse of certain aspects of each of these ten musicians, with emphasis on a specific work in each one's output. Descriptions of those works form the centerpieces of the various chapters.

SINCE THE CHOICES I HAVE MADE for this book are personal, I want to say a few things about myself. For me and people like me, born into white, middle-class families in Middle America (in my case, Cleveland, Ohio) in the middle of the twentieth century, life seemed pretty good, on the whole, when we were children. Most of us did not experience war or famine, and our parents, whether they were white-collar or blue-collar workers, had jobs that paid at least enough to keep us housed, fed, clothed, and schooled. But in my early teens, just as I was beginning to question received opinions on religion, politics, race, and nearly everything else, and just as I was becoming aware of the Cold War and of the effects that a nuclear conflict would have on humanity, my desultory interest in piano lessons turned into a real passion for great music. My parents were encouraging but they were not involved with music, and it was thanks to Maurice Wolfson (to whom this book is dedicated), a family friend and a violinist in the Cleveland Orchestra, that I was able, from the age of twelve onward, to attend the rehearsals and performances of that magnificent ensemble under its then music director, George Szell. Somehow the simultaneous emotional and intellectual superimposition of art on all the other things that were rattling around in my brain created a sort of explosion in the adolescent me.

At the time, I didn't recognize, let alone understand, this conjunction; I knew only that I *needed* great, complex music—that that music spoke to me, personally and directly. Only in my late teens, when I came across Nietzsche's statement that beauty exists in order that we not perish through truth, did I grasp what had happened to me a few years earlier. Art provides, among much else, important methods for deceiving ourselves, for pretending that humanity counts for something in the cosmos, and for lightening and beautifying our awareness of our mortality. On the other hand, the most profound works of music, in particular, are complicated but direct communications that allow, or perhaps even constrain, our subconscious mind to *explore* our mortality. They are labyrinths in sound. This book begins with the elegantly inviting opening bar of Mozart's G major Piano Concerto and ends with the chilling "chord of Death" of Stravinsky's *Requiem Canticles*, yet I maintain that every one of these works, including those that bring us face to face with our existence's bleakest aspects, is life-giving and affirmative.

We necessarily make distinctions between interests and loves. In music, my interests are wide-ranging; my loves are more restricted and steady. These loves already overwhelmed me in my teens, were consolidated by my mid-twenties, and have changed little since then. I have examined and continue to examine—often thoroughly and with great pleasure and fascination—the works of many other composers of the past and present, but the real, intense loves remain what they were half a century ago. All of the ten composers represented in this book are among those whom I came to love early on, although they are not the only ones. My hope is that I will be able to communicate that love not only to people who are already receptive to this music but also to others, especially young people, whose lives could be as immeasurably enriched by music as mine has been.

SOME NOTES:

1) All of the pieces discussed in this book can easily be found on compact discs and vinyl as well as via the Internet, and I have listed some recordings toward the end of this book. A few chapters also contain relevant mentions of specific recordings. I suggest that readers listen to each piece at least twice: once before reading about it and once after. (Some may also like to listen while they are reading; I myself like only to listen when I'm listening and only to read when I'm reading.)

2) I have provided what I call descriptive analyses, rather than technical ones, of the music that I discuss. A certain amount of basic technical language—about keys, tempi, harmonic movement, and the like—could not be avoided, but lay readers may skim over these references and get on with the meat of the matter.

3) The translations of quotations that were originally in Italian, French, and German are my own, except where otherwise noted, although with some of the German translations in the

first three chapters I have had valuable assistance from my kind and patient friends Mark Ebers and Yola Schabenbeck-Ebers. Another friend, Claire Catenaccio, generously corrected my embarrassing mistranslations from Latin in the final chapter. For translations from other languages I have relied on preexisting versions.

PART I

1789: BEFORE AND AFTER

Mozart and Beethoven, who dominate this book's first and second chapters, respectively, were not even fifteen years apart in age but reached their artistic maturity under very different social and political conditions. In 1784, when Mozart composed his profoundly moving Piano Concerto in G major—the focal point of the first chapter—Europe's various "divine right" monarchs seemed unshakeably enthroned. The storming of the Bastille was still five years in the future, and by the time the French Revolution reached its climax Mozart was dead. Although he had disliked kowtowing to aristocrats, the system that they personified was the only one he knew.

Beethoven, on the other hand, was only eighteen when the Revolution began, and he would live through and beyond the quarter-century-long epoch of the Revolutionary and Napoleonic Wars. In 1811, when he composed his "Archduke" Trio (on which the second chapter is centered), millions of Europeans were either welcoming or trying to repel Napoleon's armies. Beethoven was of two minds on the matter: he believed in the Revolution's basic principles, which those armies were supposedly bringing with them, but he feared Napoleon's hegemonic aims. Besides, Beethoven's finances in Vienna, where he lived most of his adult life, were kept afloat in part by aristocratic patrons who were mightily opposed to both the Revolution and Napoleon. As we shall see, his life unfolded on the dividing line between the old order and the new.

1

"IL CATALOGO È QUESTO"

Wolfgang Amadeus Mozart: Concerto No. 17 in
G Major for Piano and Orchestra, K. 453 (1784)

SHORTLY AFTER HIS TWENTY-EIGHTH birthday, Wolfgang
Amadeus Mozart began to make entries in a notebook that he
labeled *Verzeichnüss aller meiner Werke* (Catalogue of all my works).
After he had finished a composition, he would open the notebook and
write, on a left-hand page, the date of the work's completion plus its
genre and instrumentation. On the opposite right-hand page, which
contained five pairs of five-line musical staves, he would notate each
piece's first few bars, to remind himself of the music proper. The *Catalogue*'s first pair of pages begins with the three piano concerti that
are now known as numbers fourteen, fifteen, and sixteen (in E-flat
major, K. 449; B-flat major, K. 450; and D major, K. 451); it continues
with the Quintet in E-flat major, K. 452, for piano, oboe, clarinet,
horn, and bassoon; and it ends with the Piano Concerto No. 17 in G

major, K. 453.* All five pieces were completed between February 9 and April 12, 1784—an average of one major work approximately every twelve and a half days. The last of them, the G major Concerto, is, in my opinion, the most exquisitely beautiful member of the group, and it will be the focus of this chapter.

But why had Mozart not begun his catalogue sooner? By 1784, the former child prodigy had already composed well over four hundred pieces, so why was he only now beginning to keep track of his output? One answer to that question seems fairly obvious but requires a bit of background. Three years earlier, Mozart had made the bold decision to move from provincial Salzburg, his home town, to Vienna, the capital of the vast Hapsburg Empire—and the musical capital of German-speaking Europe—where he hoped to find a steady position at the court of Emperor Joseph II; otherwise, he would have to work as, in effect, a freelance, at a time when most professional composers were employed by church prelates or noble families. As the court position was not forthcoming, Mozart's initial difficulties were considerable, but his brilliance as both keyboard virtuoso and composer gradually brought him popularity and a comfortable income, at least for a while. He was a much-sought-after piano teacher who charged top fees for instructing the children, talented or otherwise, of the aristocracy and the growing bourgeoisie, and he participated in series of concerts, known as "academies," during which his latest compositions were performed. Some of these events took place in the homes or palaces of people who paid

---

* The "K." indications in the titles of Mozart's works refer to the numbers assigned to each piece by Ludwig Köchel (1800–1877), an Austrian musician, musicologist, and scientist, who, in 1862, published a thematic and chronological catalogue of Mozart's works that was amazingly accurate for its day. It has since been revised, but it remains the basis of our knowledge of when the hundreds of pieces that predated Mozart's own catalogue were composed, and the same for those later works that Mozart did not include in his catalogue. In German, instead of "K." the indication is usually given as "KV"—Köchel-Verzeichnis (Köchel catalogue).

Mozart and his collaborators for their services; others—sponsored by Mozart himself, who kept the profits—were held in theaters and were subscribed to by substantial numbers of the Austrian capital's wealthiest music lovers.

Most of the subscribers, like other music enthusiasts of the day, were not particularly interested in hearing multiple performances of music that they had heard before; as a result, Mozart was under constant pressure to compose new works. Solo keyboard pieces that he wrote for himself to perform could be written at the last moment, but compositions that required a chamber ensemble or an orchestra had to be completed at least far enough in advance to allow sufficient time for copyists to transcribe the various parts and for a basic rehearsal or two to be held before the concert. Often, after a few new works had been performed, Mozart would send the manuscript scores via mail coach to his father and sister—both of them accomplished musicians—back in Salzburg, for their perusal, after which the scores would be returned to him in Vienna. This constant flow and transport of his manuscripts, as well as worry about having his works plagiarized by other composers in those pre-copyright days, meant that he needed a method for remembering what he had written. Thus the *Catalogue* came into existence.

But there may well have been another, less obvious answer to the question of why someone who had been a composer since childhood waited so long to keep track of his works. Not until 1784, perhaps, did he deem himself fully mature as a practitioner of his art. It's true that numerous pieces written during his teens and early-to-mid-twenties were not only accomplished but extraordinarily beautiful: the A-list from those years includes the stunning motet *"Exsultate, jubilate,"* for soprano (originally castrato) and orchestra; the golden third, fourth, and fifth violin concerti, which remain staples of most concert violinists' repertoires; the Piano Concerto No. 9 in E-flat major, K. 271, with its unusual juxtaposition of orchestra-piano-orchestra-piano in its very

first bars; the "Coronation" Mass—thus nicknamed because it was performed (after Mozart's death) at the coronation of Francis II as Holy
Roman Emperor; the *Sinfonia Concertante* for violin, viola, and orchestra, for which Mozart wrote a sun-drenched first movement, a profoundly moving second movement, and a playful finale; the masterly
operas *Idomeneo* and *Die Entführung aus dem Serail* (The Abduction from
the Seraglio); and many string quartets, songs, symphonies, and sonatas
for various instruments. Nevertheless, as he reached his late twenties
Mozart must have realized that he had arrived at a higher plateau in his
musical development.

"My brother appreciated his older works less and less, the more he
advanced in composition," Wolfgang's sister, Maria Anna, wrote in a
letter, several years after his death.[1] He must have known that he was
achieving greater richness and depth in his most important works, and
that the wellspring from which his ideas poured forth was producing
masterpieces at a faster rate than before. The decision to create a catalogue may have grown out of pride as well as expediency.

What can we say about that wellspring? Many composers' life stories make us speculate that mental and physical sufferings, professional
tribulations, and, in many cases, character flaws functioned as catalysts
for their creativity. The speculation may be partially or wholly inaccu-
rate, depending on the composer and condition in question, but it gives
us the illusion of being on solid ground. In the case of Mozart's music,
however, the *vexata quaestio*—"Where does it come from?"—presents
itself with particular insistence and no plausible answer. Much of it
seems to emerge out of nowhere. His music takes us by surprise, holds
us lovingly but firmly within its temporal borders without exercising
any apparent external power or authority, and leaves us feeling amazed,
moved, sometimes disturbed, yet somehow always satisfied.

"How deeply (beyond words) he speaks to us about the mysteries
of our common human nature," wrote Saul Bellow—a man who loved

and lived by words. "We can't speak of Mozart without wondering 'where it all comes from,' without touching on certain 'eternal,' 'mysterious' questions. Many have credibly argued that he is 'modern' ('one of us'), and yet it is the essence of the 'modern' to demystify. How is it that our 'modern Mozart' should *increase* mystery? We are inclined to think of mystery as woolly or amorphous, yet Mozart, working in the light, openly, is all coherence." Mozart's music, Bellow wrote, expresses "our sense of the radical mystery of our being."[2]

THE PERSON WHO EXPRESSED that radical mystery in so many of his works was born in Salzburg on January 27, 1756, to Leopold and Anna Maria (*née* Pertl) Mozart. Wolfgang was the last of the couple's seven children but only the second to survive infancy; the other survivor was his sister, Maria Anna, four and a half years his senior, known in the family and to posterity by her nickname, Nannerl. Leopold Mozart was a noted violinist who also composed music and who, in the year of Wolfgang's birth, published a treatise on violin playing that attracted considerable attention and that is consulted even today by musicians and musicologists interested in instrumental techniques of the past. When Leopold realized that both of his children had musical talent, he made sure that they were given excellent training.

By the age of five, Wolferl, as he was called at home, was learning to play the violin and keyboard instruments and was beginning to write music—simple music, to be sure, but pieces that nevertheless brought tears to his father's eyes. Barely a year later, the Mozart family undertook a series of tours, with the aim of showing off the children's keyboard virtuosity, to the astonishment and delight of crowned heads and musical connoisseurs in Munich, Vienna, and, eventually, western Germany, Brussels, Paris, and even London, where, at the age of eight, Wolfgang composed his first symphony. (Nannerl also composed, but the fact that none of her compositions has survived makes any judgment of her accomplishments in that area purely conjectural; whether she decided on her own to stop composing or was discouraged from continuing by her father, because she was a girl, can no longer be determined. Her brother praised her compositions and encouraged her to stand up to their father on various matters, but she seems to have been completely submissive to Leopold's will.) When Wolfgang was thirteen, a decision was made, within the family, to have Leopold take his son on an extended tour of Italy. In December 1769 the two male Mozarts set out on their journey.

For eighteenth-century musicians, Italy was Europe's conservatory, and Milan, Venice, Bologna, Florence, Rome, and Naples were famous centers of musical activity, for opera first and foremost but also for ecclesiastical and instrumental music. Leopold's purpose was twofold, as he crossed the Alps with his son: to show him off, so that Wolfgang's public and private appearances would garner the fame and the funds that would enable the tour to continue, and to expose him to some of the leading musicians of the day and the latest compositional trends.

Leopold's gamble paid off. In Rome, Pope Clement XIV awarded Wolfgang the Order of the Golden Spur; in Bologna, the fourteen-year-old prodigy was made a member of the much respected Accademia Filarmonica; and in Milan, he composed an opera, *Mitridate, re di Ponto* (Mithridates, King of Pontus—a three-act work consisting almost entirely of solo arias and recitatives), and conducted, from the keyboard, its successful premiere at the Regio Ducal Teatro, the city's main opera house.* *Mitridate* ran for twenty-one subsequent performances.

All in all, the fifteen-month-long tour was a great success, and it led to other such journeys during the following decade—return trips to Italy as well as tours elsewhere, all at a time when travel was slow,

---

* La Scala, which later became Milan's and Italy's most famous opera theater, was not constructed until 1776–78, after fire had destroyed the older house.

extremely uncomfortable, often dangerous, and always costly. As a side benefit, Wolfgang became reasonably fluent in Italian and learned some French and English, too. (He had already studied Latin and arithmetic— all under Leopold's tutelage, as far as we know.)

Another side-effect of Mozart's cosmopolitan upbringing proved to be negative at first but positive in the long run, and it can be summed up with the words of a post–World War I popular American song: "How ya gonna keep 'em down on the farm after they've seen Paree?" As a young adult, Wolfgang—who had seen not only "Paree" but also London, Rome, and Vienna—regarded beautiful Salzburg as backward and provincial. According to a legend among some of today's students at the Mozarteum, the town's international music academy, the composer was heard to say: "After a year in Salzburg, you're a fool. After two years, you're an idiot. After three years, you're a true Salzburger." Whenever he returned home after a period spent abroad, he felt overrestricted and underappreciated. He had to face the fact that, like his father, he was in the employ of Salzburg's secular and religious ruler, Prince Archbishop Hieronymus von Colloredo, who, although a reformist with regard to church practices, was dictatorial in his methods and disliked by the citizenry in general and by Mozart in particular. "Opportunities in the Salzburg musical establishment were limited, and the archbishop was ungenerous over leave," according to musicologist Stanley Sadie; "feeling his talent stifled . . . , Mozart pined for the larger musical world where since childhood he had won so much applause."

In September 1777, at the age of twenty-one, Wolfgang set off on yet another tour—this time with his mother as chaperone—in an attempt to find an alternative to Salzburg by securing steady employment in one of the places he visited: Munich, Mannheim (where he fell in love, unrequitedly, with a sixteen-year-old aspiring soprano), and Paris. But he was not offered any of the jobs that interested him. To make matters much worse, during his stay in Paris his mother became ill and died. When he returned home, after nearly a year and a half abroad, he resigned himself to accepting Colloredo's offer to make him Salzburg's court organist, at a higher pay than he had previously received as a violinist in the court orchestra, but still as barely more than a lackey within the hierarchy of the local archiepiscopal court.

Toward the end of 1780, Mozart went to Munich to complete an Italian opera that he had been commissioned to write for the Bavarian capital's Residence Theater and to supervise and lead rehearsals and performances of the new work. *Idomeneo, re di Creta* (Idomeneus, King of Crete) was successful at its first performance on January 29, 1781, two days after its composer's twenty-fifth birthday, and it is now recognized as Mozart's first thoroughly great opera, extraordinary in its solo arias, ensemble pieces, and dramatic orchestral writing.

Six weeks after *Idomeneo*'s premiere, Archbishop Colloredo ordered his court organist to Vienna, where the prelate was temporarily in residence. Mozart was happy to be in the imperial capital but extremely unhappy to have to live with Colloredo's entourage. In Munich he had been the object of admiration and esteem; now, his position at table was below that of the valets. More irritating still was his employer's refusal to allow him to accept invitations to perform for others, including even the emperor. He requested and was granted a meeting with Colloredo—a meeting during which the young musician had the audacity to talk back to his master. In a letter to Leopold Mozart, Wolfgang described the incident. The archbishop, he said, had ranted on in one mighty stream.

> [He said] I was the most obnoxious fellow he knows—no one serves him as badly as I—he advises me to leave right here today, otherwise he will write home to have my salary stopped—one couldn't get a word in edgewise, he was going on like a fire—I heard him out patiently—he lied in my face that I was being paid 500 gulden—called me a scoundrel, a rascal, a fool—oh I don't want to write you all [of it]—Finally,

when my blood was made to boil, I said—so Your Highness is not satisfied with me?—[He said:] what, you want to threaten me, you fool, oh
you fool!—there is the door, look there, I won't have anything more to
do with such a despicable brat—at last I said[,] nor I with you either—
[He said:] so go—and I [said], in leaving: this will be upheld; tomorrow
you will receive it in writing.[3]

Mozart did indeed make a formal request to be dismissed from Colloredo's service, and the archbishop eventually told his steward, Count
Arco, to let the musician go because he no longer needed him. Arco
summoned Mozart, called him a "lout" and a "knave," and—as Wolfgang wrote to Leopold—"he threw me out the door with a kick in the
ass . . . that may have been ordered by our High Prince [Colloredo]."[4]

Owing to one of history's many ironic twists and turns, the then-
powerful Prince-Archbishop Colloredo is remembered today mainly
for having mistreated a man he regarded as one of his servants.

MOZART REMAINED IN VIENNA, trying to establish himself as a
keyboard virtuoso, composer, and teacher of piano and composition
while hoping to be granted an official post as a musician in the imperial court. His Vienna years (1781–91) coincided mainly with the reign
(1780–90) of Emperor Joseph II, who was only fifteen years older than
the young composer. As a young man, Joseph had read the works
of Voltaire and other Enlightenment luminaries, and as emperor he
quickly began to activate some of his mentors' principles. He severely
restricted the temporal power of the Roman Catholic Church and
instituted religious tolerance throughout the empire; moved to eliminate serfdom—although in that area he succeeded only in part; imple-
mented tax and land reforms; supported the arts, which he loved;
made elementary education compulsory for boys and girls of all social

classes; provided funds for the higher education of poor but deserving students; and imposed German instead of Latin as the language of instruction—a move that today might be considered negative, given that the empire included so many non-Germanic ethnicities, but that, at the time, was meant not only to simplify communication but also to insure equal social and political opportunity for all citizens, regardless of their origins. Joseph believed in absolute monarchy—he was no radical in that sense, and indeed many of his reforms were carried out by decree and created much controversy, especially among his more conservative advisers and administrators—but he also believed that monarchs existed to serve the people over whom they ruled.

Nearly all of these radical reforms were being carried out during Mozart's Viennese decade and were widely discussed by the citizenry, but they are not mentioned in the composer's correspondence. Like many another child prodigy before and since, he had been brought up to focus entirely on developing his talents, and the fact that those talents had brought him adulation from an early age made the continuation of that focus not only natural but virtually inevitable. Music had been his world since before he could remember; everything else in that world revolved around this very particular and peculiar sense of identity. Making and performing music were not merely what Mozart did for a living: they were what and who he was. His letters contain some acute observations about the people he encountered, but there is almost nothing in his correspondence about politics *per se* or even about the lands, landscapes, and landmarks that he saw on his myriad travels. For Mozart, Emperor Joseph II and every other important personage whose path crossed his over the years existed only in relation to what that person did or could do, or did not or could not do, to further Wolfgang Amadeus Mozart's career. This was not conscious egoism: it was a reflex—a way of life that had been inculcated in him since his early childhood.

Still, there were occasions when personal, nonprofessional crises arose in his life, and he had to learn to deal with them. Although Mozart was indisputably a rare genius, his many surviving letters to his father (whom he always addressed with the formal *Sie*, never the familiar *Du*) reveal that he communicated with Leopold in much the same way as millions of other young people communicate with their parents: he usually tried to shine the best possible light on his doings by emphasizing the good things that were happening to him and downplaying, omitting, or occasionally even lying about negative occurrences. Once in a while, however, he could not avoid head-on confrontation on a subject that he knew would cause parental disapproval—and one such occasion arose when, as he approached his twenty-sixth birthday, he expressed his wish to marry. On December 15, 1781, he wrote to Leopold:

> Nature speaks as loudly in me as in any other, and maybe louder than in some big, strong oaf. I can't possibly live like most of today's young folk.—First, I have too much *religion*, second I have too much love for my neighbor and too honest a disposition to lead an innocent girl astray, and third too much terror and disgust, dread and fear of diseases, and too much love of my health to play around with whores; therefore I can even swear that I have never had anything to do with a female of this sort. . . . But my *temperament*, which is more disposed to calm and domestic life than to roistering—I who from my youth onward have never been used to looking after my things, like linen, clothes, etc.—can think of nothing more necessary to me than a wife.[5]

Wolfgang then proceeded to his main point, although he knew that Leopold would disapprove. His choice had fallen upon nineteen-year-old Constanze Weber, one of the three sisters of Aloysia Weber, the singer he had fallen in love with in Mannheim four years earlier and who had rejected him. Contemporary portraits show Constanze as a pretty girl, with large eyes, dark brown hair, a straight nose, and a small mouth, but neither her appearance nor any of her other qualities would have counted for much with Leopold, who held a low opinion of the Weber family, although many of its members were involved in music in one way or another. Constanze's father made his living mainly as a music copyist; Aloysia had become a professional soprano and had married Joseph Lange, a painter and amateur singer; and Constanze and her other two sisters also sang, sometimes professionally. (Constanze's as-yet-unborn cousin Carl Maria von Weber [1786–1826] would become the most famous and influential German opera composer between Mozart and Wagner.) But in Leopold Mozart's not entirely unwarranted view, Constanze's parents were unscrupulous schemers—thus Wolfgang's task was to try to change his father's opinion.

"But who then is the object of my love?" he continued, in his letter. "Don't be startled there as well, I beg you;—don't tell me one of the Webers?—Yes, a Weber—but not *Josepha*—not *Sophie*—but *Costanza* [*sic*]; the middle one.— . . . my good, beloved konstanze [*sic*] is—the martyr among them, and perhaps for that reason the kindest, most capable and in a word the best of them all."[6]

Wolfgang's attempt to persuade his father didn't work: Leopold remained firmly opposed to his son's choice. Not until the following summer, when Wolfgang informed him that Constanze had come to live with him, that her honor was therefore compromised, and that if he did not marry her the Webers would insist that she be paid damages, did Mozart *père* sourly give in. As a matter of fact, the wedding took place in St. Stephen's Cathedral on August 4, 1782, one day before Leopold's letter of consent arrived.

The marriage seems to have been a happy one, and we know from Mozart's letters that sexual activity played an important part in their conjugal life. The facts speak even louder than the letters: between June 1783 and July 1791 Constanze gave birth to six children (an average of one every sixteen months), of whom only the second and the sixth survived infancy.

NINETEEN DAYS BEFORE the Mozarts' wedding, *Die Entführung aus dem Serail* (*The Abduction from the Seraglio*), Wolfgang's latest opera, had been produced at Vienna's Burgtheater; by coincidence, the name of the work's heroine is Constanze.* Apart from the beauty of its music, the composition is remarkable for the humanity of its story: In a sixteenth-century Muslim land, a pasha displays clemency toward a group of Spanish Christians who have betrayed his trust; although he holds life-and-death power over them, he allows them to return, unscathed, to Spain. Within a few years, the *Seraglio*—which includes comic scenes that involve the pasha's curmudgeonly servant, Osmin— became popular throughout German-speaking Europe.

And yet Wolfgang and his flesh-and-blood Constanze struggled financially during their first two years together. They tended to live somewhat beyond their means, and Wolfgang, who had always depended on his father to handle economic matters, now developed the unfortunate habit of borrowing money from this or that friend or patron, then borrowing from another in order to pay off the first loan when it was called in. Gradually, however, he established himself as a major figure in Vienna's musical life, performing not only in concerts but also at balls and other events. In March 1783, the venerated, sixty-eight-year-old composer Christoph Willibald Gluck, a giant in the history of opera and, at the time, the occupant of a sinecure position as the Hapsburg court's Kapellmeister (music director), attended a concert during which Mozart performed some of his own music; Gluck was so

---

* Technically, the work—a setting of a libretto by Gottlieb Stephanie is not an opera at all but a *Singspiel*, a German-language opera in which musical pieces are interspersed with spoken dialogue. The *Seraglio* had been commissioned by the Nationalsingspiel, a project that Emperor Joseph himself had initiated and was financing as part of his project to encourage German culture. But Mozart himself referred to this and similar works as operas, and the *Seraglio* is usually described as such today.

delighted with his young colleague's works that he invited Wolfgang and Constanze, along with Joseph and Aloysia Lange, to dinner the following Sunday—a gesture that would not have passed unnoticed. Sure enough, less than a week later the emperor himself attended and enthusiastically applauded a concert in which all the pieces on the program were not only composed by Mozart but also played, accompanied, or conducted by him. It was, according to musicologist H. C. Robbins Landon, "a tremendous achievement and the high-point of Mozart's career in Vienna to date."[7]

His reputation in the imperial capital rose higher and higher, and before long he was the city's musical man of the hour. This popularity was not the result of revolutionary breaks with the music of the time, on Mozart's part. On the contrary: his music was a culminating point in a style—the so-called Classical style—that had been evolving for over a generation, as, to some extent, a counterfoil to the densely contrapuntal late Baroque style of Bach and his contemporaries. Through the extraordinary qualities of his genius, Mozart brought that style to its summit. This is why the popular Joseph Haydn, who was nearly a quarter-century older than Mozart, was able to tell Leopold Mozart that Leopold's son was the greatest composer he knew of—because Wolfgang Amadeus Mozart was composing music in a style with which Haydn was entirely familiar and indeed had in part created, but with more astonishingly beautiful results than anyone else had managed to do. Some of the city's best-known aristocrats, including Prince Dmitri Mikhailovich Galitzin, the Russian ambassador to the Austrian court, and Count Johann Baptist Esterházy, a scion of one of the Hapsburg empire's wealthiest families, vied with each other to have Mozart give concerts at one or another of their palaces. Often, they would send their coaches and coachmen to bring him to their residences and to take him back to his home after his performances.

As word of Mozart's status with the aristocrats spread, his other private and public appearances multiplied. In a letter dated March 3, 1784, he told his father how he was spending his days:

> You must excuse me for writing so little, but it is impossible for me to find time, as I am giving 3 *subscription concerts* in Trattner's hall* on the last 3 Wednesdays of Lent, beginning on the 17th of this month, for which I already have 100 *subscribers* and will easily get another 30. The price for all 3 *concerts* is six gulden: [I] will probably give 2 *academies* in the theater this year—so you can easily imagine that I necessarily must play some new works—thus one must also write [i.e., compose]. The whole morning is dedicated to pupils. And in the evening I have to play nearly every day. Below you will read a list of all the *academies* at which I have to play for sure.[8]

That list, which covers a six-week period, from late February to early April, indicates nine performances at Count Esterházy's palace; five at Prince Galitzin's; three private concerts—presumably those given at the Trattnerhof; three more at the studio of Georg Friedrich Richter, a well-known keyboard virtuoso; and two concerts in theaters: altogether, an average of a performance every second day. Vienna was a fast-growing city in the 1700s (its population increased by nearly fifty percent through that century), and the demand for public entertainment grew more than proportionally, thanks to the evolution of the bourgeoisie. During Lent alone, in 1784, Mozart is known to have given twenty-three performances of various piano concerti, and there may have been more such performances that we don't know about. No won-

---

* Wolfgang and Constanze were then living in the Trattnerhof, a six-story building in the Graben, in central Vienna; the house's owner was their friend Johann Thomas von Trattner (1717–1798), godfather to three of the Mozarts' sons (all three died in infancy) and husband of one of Wolfgang's pupils. Evidently there was a large enough hall in the Trattnerhof to accommodate a small orchestra plus fortepiano and an audience of at least one hundred thirty.

der that he added, in the same letter to his father—perhaps anticipating Leopold's usual admonishments: "Don't I have enough to do? I don't think that I can get out of practice this way."[9]

Later in March, Wolfgang sent Leopold a list of the one hundred seventy-five people, most of them members of the highest Viennese society, who had subscribed to his concerts, and he gleefully announced that the total was thirty higher than the combined number of subscribers to the concerts of two other virtuosi. "The first *academy* on the 17th of this month came off favorably—the hall was full to overflowing," he wrote. "And the new *concerto* [probably K. 449] that I played was extraordinarily well liked. And wherever one goes one hears this *academy* being praised."[10]

On April 10, Mozart informed his father that he had "written two grand concerti"—presumably K. 450 and K. 451—as well as the Quintet for Piano and Winds, K. 452, which he deemed "the best [work] I have yet written in my life," and which he played on the same program as the two concerti. "By the way (to confess the truth) I got tired of late—after playing so much—and it is not a little to my credit that this never happened to my listeners."[11] He added, almost as an afterthought, that he had just finished another concerto "for Fräulein Ployer." That piece was none other than the Concerto in G major, K. 453, which, according to Mozart's own catalogue, was completed on the twelfth, not the tenth, of April; it was the last item on the catalogue's first page.

In Mozart's day, more and more young women were beginning to play musical instruments, and Barbara (known as Babette) Ployer, the eighteen-year-old niece of Court Councilor Gottfried Ignaz von Ployer, studied both piano and composition with Mozart. He was pleased with her accomplishments. On June 12, he wrote to tell his father that the following day there would be a concert at Herr Ployer's country home in the village of Döbling—now part of the city of Vienna—where Babette would play the Concerto in G that he had written for her; he would then play the piano part in the Wind Quintet; and he and Babette would perform together his "grand *Sonata* for 2 *pianos*" (D major, K. 448). As the famed Italian opera composer Giovanni Paisiello was visiting Vienna, Mozart arranged to bring him along in his carriage "so that I can let him hear my *Composition* and my pupil."[12] (Paisiello's opera, *Il Barbiere di Siviglia*, written two years earlier, was immensely popular in Vienna and across much of Europe at the time, and would remain so until it was eclipsed, more than thirty years later, by the young Gioacchino Rossini's opera of the same name.)

WHAT PAISIELLO AND THE OTHER GUESTS present at that private concert in Döbling heard, on June 13, 1784, was, in my opinion, Mozart's finest piano concerto to date—a work of exceptional beauty and depth even by his extraordinary standards. Just over two weeks earlier, he had sent to Salzburg manuscript copies of this and some of his other newest concerti, along with a letter in which he asked Leopold and Nannerl which of the works they preferred: "I am eager [to know] whether your opinion coincides with the *general* one here and *my own*, of course it is necessary that all 3 be heard with all the parts and well *performed*."[13] And nearly two months later, he repeated to Nannerl that he was "eager to learn from you, when you will have heard all 3 grand *concerti* [K. 450, K. 451, and K. 453], which one you like best."[14]

Unfortunately, we do not know either Nannerl or Leopold's response to Wolfgang's queries, nor can we be sure of his own opinion. But the G major Concerto seems to be a cut—maybe even several cuts—above its immediate predecessors, at least as far as expressive power is concerned, and Mozart's eagerness to have Paisiello hear it may indicate that he attached special value to it. If we judge by the frequency of its appearances on today's concert programs and in recordings, it seems to be the most admired of all the piano concerti that he wrote before the great D minor Concerto, K. 466, and its seven magnificent successors. Between *The Abduction from the Seraglio* in 1782 and *The Marriage of Figaro* in 1786, Mozart completed no full-length operas, but the fourteen wordless piano concerti that he wrote during the intervening period spoke to contemporary listeners—and speak to us, nearly two and a half centuries later—as clearly and directly as his operas were and are able to do.

The opening bars of most of K. 453's predecessors are either joyful or playful, but this concerto's first movement (Allegro, 4/4) begins in an atmosphere of intimate charm. Perhaps this has something to do with the fact that this is the only one of Mozart's twenty-three original piano concerti* that is in the key of G: there are two in A; three in F; four each in B-flat, E-flat, and D (including the one in D minor); and five in C (including one in C minor); but no others in G. Something about the neutral "color" of the tonality of G—a sort of *tabula rasa* quality— seems to inspire in some composers a particular intimacy of expression or even a confessional character.[†]

This first movement, like the rest of the concerto, is scored for a typical, small orchestra of the day: one flute, two oboes, two bassoons, two horns, and strings (first and second violins, violas, cellos, and double basses playing the cello line one octave lower), plus the piano, of course.

---

* For the sake of convenience, the piano concerti retain their old numbering of 1 through 27, but we now know that Nos. 1 through 4 were the very young Mozart's arrangements of sonata movements by other composers. His first original piano concerto is the one called No. 5 (D Major, K. 175), which he composed at the ripe old age of seventeen.

† Well after I had made my choices for this book's contents, I noticed that three of the ten pieces I had chosen are in the key of G major, out of thirty possible major and minor keys. I have always thought of G major as a "neutral" key (as opposed to—for instance—"bright" D major, "warm" F major, and "tragic" E minor), onto which almost any expressive character can be imprinted. Whether or not that notion makes sense, the fact remains that G major is the basic key chosen by Mozart for his Piano Concerto, K. 453; by Schubert for his String Quartet, D. 887; and by Brahms for his String Quintet, Op. 111. And each of these pieces, as well as some G major works not included in this book (Beethoven's Fourth Piano Concerto comes immediately to mind), counts as one of its composer's most intimate musical statements.

It begins with a conventional, extended orchestral *tutti* that sets out all of the thematic material. But the material itself is anything but conventional. An entire solo bar for the first violins serves as a sort of elegant, elongated upbeat to the movement as a whole, and Mozart, instead of following a pattern of regular, four-bar phrases as he presents his first theme, gives us the following series of bar groups: 4–4-4–3-3–3-3–2-2–2-4. This is because the gently lyrical opening passage, marked *piano*, is brusquely interrupted early on by a *forte* passage during which the long, melodic line played by the first violins, flute, and oboes is supported by the propelling motor-energy of the second violins and violas and repeated notes in the bassoons, cellos, and basses. And that long, melodic line soon gives way to fast notes that seem to tumble over themselves, with phrases barging in on each other in a sort of extroverted, beautifully organized mayhem. Each of the theme's fragments shoves the previous fragment into the background, until at last the calmer second theme arrives.

Altogether, the first theme consists of fifteen quiet bars followed by fifteen loud bars and then by a quiet, four-bar transition into the second theme. But the brief second theme has its own strange pattern—four bars, then three bars, then four, then three—and is brought to a halt by four very short, dramatically contrasting motivic groups that are actually mini-themes, each of which will reappear, transformed, in the course of the movement. And in the last bar of the orchestral *tutti*, the solo piano enters with a flourish that leads back into the first theme.

I promise not to count bars through this whole concerto; my intention in the two previous paragraphs was only to point out that although standard compositional procedures served Mozart as a useful framework, he bent those methods to his imagination's will—and his imagination did seem to have a will of its own. The adage "Necessity is the mother of invention" applies to Mozart only because he needed to keep composing in order to survive; when he was at work, invention became a necessity in itself, a sort of self-engendering organism, with respect not only to formal norms but also to common harmonic, melodic, and rhythmic practices. He did not want to shock his listeners: his job, he seems to have believed, was to move, delight, and even astonish them through music that was immediately comprehensible to his contemporaries within the boundaries of their common musical culture. Yet, intentionally or not, he led them into previously unexplored regions. He couldn't do otherwise.

Luminescence and good humor characterize almost all of the G major Concerto's first movement. There are fleeting shadows—little more than a grayish musical brushstroke or two here and there, as in the first bars of the second theme—but as a whole the movement expresses an elegantly Apollonian cheerfulness, which perfectly aligns with the literal definition of its tempo indication: in everyday Italian, *allegro* means cheerful.

The second movement, on the other hand, is one of the great examples of musical chiaroscuro—the frequent, sometimes flickering alternation of light and darkness, or the superimposition of one on the other—of which Mozart was and remains the unequaled master. More than the concerto's two other movements, brilliant though they are, this Andante, in C major and 3/4 time, exemplifies the increased depth and maturity that the composer reached in the year in which he began his catalogue.

The movement begins with a subdued melody played by the first violins over a quiet, moderately paced accompaniment provided by the rest of the strings. The Italian word *andante* means "going" or "moving along," and Wolfgang, in a letter, asked Leopold to tell Nannerl that "in none of the concerti" (referring to this one and its three predecessors) "should there be Adagios, but just Andantes."[15] Not too slow, in other words. Oddly, however, after only about fifteen seconds the theme stops and a pause of several seconds is indicated, as if a speaker were to stop in mid-sentence and stare into space for a moment. Then the second part of the theme begins, with the woodwinds, accompanied by horns and strings, presenting gently intertwining melodic lines. When the piano enters, alone, it restates the opening phrase, including the pause, but then, all of a sudden, it embarks on some startlingly dark passages of new thematic material, in the key of G minor and accompanied by the strings. The piano part then trails off; the winds reenter, bringing us gently into G major; the piano takes over again, embellishing the melody that the winds were playing; and, finally, winds, strings, and piano join forces to bring this whole opening section (exposition) to a close.

After another pause of several seconds, we enter a dark place. First, the piano, alone, in D minor, plays a somber phrase; then, over a quiet string accompaniment, the woodwinds carry on a stark conversation with the piano in a bar-by-bar segment reminiscent of Orpheus's dialogue with the Furies in Gluck's *Orfeo ed Euridice*—except that Gluck's dialogue is vehement, whereas Mozart's is spectral, blood-chilling. The flute and first oboe softly but firmly declare "No" to whatever the piano is asking of them; the piano then pleads eloquently; the flute and oboe rebuff the piano; and the piano's plea becomes more elaborate. The flute and first bassoon repeat their "No"; the piano's insistence grows stronger; the flute, oboe, and bassoon try, together, to push the piano's request away; but the piano extends its demand over five whole bars—all but the first of them unaccompanied—until at last the entire orchestra reenters and, through a series of bold harmonic modulations, gradually brightens the sound-picture, allowing the piano to bring us back to the tranquil, opening C major theme.

This time, however, after the pause at the end of the first phrase, Mozart jolts us with a *forte* chord in E-flat major—an enlivening intake of fresh air—played by piano and strings. But after only a dozen or so seconds of this refreshing openness, the piano, hovering around C minor and accompanied by a tissue-paper-thin sound from the violins, warns us not to be so easily consoled. This dark statement is in turn almost immediately canceled out by the reentry of the woodwinds, with inter-twining lines similar to those that the same instruments had offered near the beginning of the movement, but joined now by the piano.

Mozart uses the strings and piano to bring the recapitulation nearly to a close, but he then gives the piano a subtly brilliant solo cadenza (written by the composer himself, as are this concerto's other caden-zas) within which most of the music's variegated building blocks are once again heard and transformed. Finally, a coda—played first by the woodwinds, then by the piano, then by full orchestra and piano together—brings the movement to an end with a quietly ambivalent, extraordinarily touching mixture of darkness and light.

This entire, eventful, profoundly moving Andante lasts only about ten minutes and is followed by a delightful finale—an Allegretto in G major and 2/2 time—that consists of a theme and five brilliant varia-tions plus a playfully virtuosic coda, marked "Presto." A starling that Wolfgang and Constanze kept in a cage would "sing" a somewhat eccentric version of the first four bars of the finale's opening theme, and when the bird died Wolfgang wrote a poem in memory of it. But for us non-avians, the concerto's middle movement, the Andante, remains the part of the work that makes the most profound impression. Its tragic elements—sometimes subtle, sometimes dramatic—insinuate them-selves into our consciousness, and they are set within, or even insulated by, music that consoles us by its very existence.

SEVENTEEN-EIGHTY-FOUR CONTINUED to be a magnificent year for Mozart in Vienna. Landon quotes the critic J. F. Schink's report on one of the young composer's concerts that year: "Oh, what an effect!—magnificent and grand . . . Mozart. That's a life here, like the land of the blessed, the land of music."[16] The popularity of Mozart's performances brought him a degree of financial success, and he and his family moved into a large, elegant apartment in the Grosse Schulerstrasse (today called, simply, Schulerstrasse), near the cathedral square; the rent was more than three times what they had been paying at the Trattnerhof. Before the year was over, Wolfgang wrote two more piano concerti—one in B-flat major (No. 18, K. 456), and one in F major (No. 19, K. 459)—as well as a Sonata for Piano and Violin in B-flat major (K. 454); the dramatic Piano Sonata in C minor (K. 457)—which, when it was published the following year, was preceded by an equally dramatic Fantasy in C minor (K. 475); and the String Quartet in B-flat major (K. 458, nicknamed the "Hunt"). And, in December, Mozart began his initiation into the Freemasons' Lodge *Zur Wohlthätigkeit* (Charity or Benevolence).*

Mozart's popularity in Vienna underwent various ups and downs during the remaining years of his short life, and during some of the down periods he found himself in dire financial straits. The result of one such gap was that he and his family had to abandon their ample lodgings in the Grosse Schulerstrasse and move into more modest quarters. But he continued to create masterpieces: the operas *Le nozze di Figaro* (The Marriage of Figaro), *Don Giovanni* (completed in Prague, where its premiere took place), *Così fan tutte* (Thus Do All Women), *La clemenza di Tito* (Titus's Clemency), and *Die Zauberflöte* (The Magic Flute); his last three symphonies; his last eight piano concerti; many extraordinary pieces of chamber music; and works for piano and for the voice.

He went on making entries in his *Catalogue*, and I imagine him

---

* As early as 1738, Freemasonry had been banned by Pope Clement XII, yet in Mozart's day membership was legal in Austria—mainly owing to Emperor Joseph II's interest in the Masons' declared dedication to the virtues of humanity, tolerance, brotherhood, and the Enlightenment ideal, Reason. Numerous Austrian Catholics, including members of the intelligentsia and the nobility, were attracted to the Masonic Order, as were many of Mozart's friends in Vienna, and during the remaining years of his life Mozart would write several works connected with Freemasonry, both directly (the *Masonic Funeral Music*, for instance) and indirectly (*The Magic Flute*).

smiling or even laughing aloud as he began to set to music the opening words—written by his brilliant rapscallion of a librettist, Lorenzo
Da Ponte—in Leporello's first-act aria in *Don Giovanni*: "Madamina, il
catalogo è questo / delle belle che amò il padron mio"—"Little lady,
this is the catalogue of the beautiful women my master loved." That
opera—by the way—is listed on the thirteenth of the *Catalogue*'s pairs
of pages, and bears the date of October 28, 1787, one day before the
work's premiere. The *Catalogue*'s final, twenty-eighth pair of filled-
in pages lists two entire operas—*The Magic Flute* and *La clemenza di
Tito*—as well as a separate entry for *The Magic Flute*'s March of the
Priests and Overture, written after Mozart had finished the rest of the
work. These last pages also list the astonishingly beautiful Clarinet
Concerto in A major (K. 622) and the Masonic cantata, *Laut verkünde
unsre Freude* (Loudly be our joy proclaimed, K. 623). But of course
the catalogue does not include the incomplete Requiem Mass, which
Mozart was working on at the time of his death—probably from kid-
ney failure—on December 5, 1791, at the age of thirty-five years, ten
months, and eight days.

The fourteen remaining pairs of the *Catalogue*'s pages stare at us
blankly, to remind us of our irretrievable loss, and we may be touched,
today, to see the title on the cover of this artifact. It reads, in the composer's hand:

Verzeichnüss
aller meiner Werke
vom Monath febraio* 1784 bis Monath
Wolfgang Amadé Mozart[17]

---

* Here, for February Mozart wrote *febraio* in Italian (it would be *febbraio* in modern Italian
orthography), whereas on the first page of the catalogue proper he used the now obsolete
German *Hornung* instead of the modern German *Februar*.

Catalogue
    of all my Works
    from the Month of February 1784 to the Month of
Wolfgang Amadé Mozart

The trailing off of the third line—"to the Month of"—demonstrates that he intended to fill this catalogue completely, perhaps by 1795 or 1796, and then to start a new one.

On the other hand, Mozart was always aware of life's brevity. "I have made a habit of always imagining the worst in all things," he wrote to his father in 1787, when Leopold was gravely ill. "Since death (strictly speaking) is the true goal of our life, I have become so familiar in the last couple of years with this true, best friend of mankind that its image not only no longer horrifies me but is actually very calming and comforting! and I thank my god that he has granted me the joy of giving me the opportunity (you understand me) of learning that to get to know him is the key to our true bliss."[18] Leopold had more or less secretly joined the Masonic Order during his visit to Vienna two years earlier, thus Wolfgang's parenthetical "you understand me"—because his statement is a mixture of Christian beliefs and Masonic precepts. The letter continues: "I never lie down in bed without thinking that perhaps (as young as I am) I may not see another day—and yet no one of all my acquaintances can say that I am morose or sad among friends—and for this blessing I thank my Creator every day and wish it from my heart for each of my fellow men."

Leopold Mozart died, at the age of sixty-seven, not quite two months after having received Wolfgang's letter. Had Wolfgang lived as long as his father, he would have died in August 1823. Beethoven, age fifty-two at the time, was completing his *Missa Solemnis* and working hard on his Ninth Symphony; the operas of the thirty-one-year-old Rossini were tremendously popular, in Vienna as elsewhere in Europe; Franz Schubert, twenty-six, was writing his song cycle *Die schöne Müllerin*; the young Gaetano Donizetti, Vincenzo Bellini, and Hector Berlioz were starting or preparing to start their careers; and the even younger Richard Wagner and Giuseppe Verdi were beginning their musical education. But would any of this have happened in the same way had Mozart lived three decades longer than he actually did? Would his musical evolution have pushed Beethoven's development in different directions and influenced the work of all the other composers as well?

These questions are unanswerable, of course—just as unanswerable as the question of how the history of European music would, or would not, have changed if Beethoven, Schubert, and numerous other outstanding composers (for instance: Purcell, Mendelssohn, Chopin, Schumann, Mahler, Debussy, and Berg) had survived into their sixties or beyond. All of us who love music must simply consider ourselves extraordinarily lucky for the vast number of great works that Mozart and the others did manage to leave behind.

DURING MOZART'S LIFETIME, relatively little music was published; performers usually played or sang music as they read it from manuscripts written out by the composers themselves or by copyists. On January 15, 1783, for instance, the *Wiener Zeitung* (Vienna Journal) announced that people could buy one of Mozart's latest works, "beautifully copied and revised by him personally," for four ducats, simply by going to his apartment "on the High Bridge in the small Herberstein House No. 437, on the third floor."[19] Thus, at the time of Mozart's death most of his works existed only in manuscript. By 1800, however, the publication of music was becoming common in Europe, thanks in part to improvements in printing techniques but above all to the growth of the middle classes and their desire to emulate the aristocracy by making musical instruction part of their children's education. Constanze Weber Mozart, who outlived her husband by over fifty years, worked hard to preserve and publish Wolfgang's works, and so did her second husband, the Danish diplomat Georg Nikolaus von Nissen, whom she married in 1809, when she was forty-seven; Nissen wrote one of the earliest biographies of Mozart. Constanze died in 1842, at the age of eighty, and was survived by her—and Wolfgang's—sons, Carl Thomas Mozart (1784–1858) and Franz Xaver Wolfgang Mozart (1791–1844); Franz Xaver was a composer in his own right, albeit a minor one.

The *Catalogue* passed through several hands after Wolfgang Amadeus Mozart's death: Constanze sent it to the German publisher Johann Anton André, who issued as many of Mozart's works as he could, and one of André's children eventually inherited it. In 1935, the popular Austrian novelist Stefan Zweig—an avid collector of musical and literary manuscripts—acquired it from the Leo Liepmannssohn auction house in Berlin, and half a century later Zweig's heirs presented the *Catalogue* and the rest of his collection to the British Library, where it remains to this day. A facsimile edition of the *Catalogue* was published in 1990.

Mozart's music also remains to this day, and it presumably will remain in the repertoires of most performers of Western art music, and in the ears and minds and hearts of most of the people who love that music, as long as our civilization endures. Many of his works particularly influenced a musician who, in 1787, at the age of sixteen, went to Vienna from his home town of Bonn, in western Germany, in the hope of studying with Mozart. That youngster developed into quite a master in his own right.

2

HIS IMPERIAL HIGHNESS'S
SORE FINGER

Ludwig van Beethoven: Trio in B-flat Major for Piano,
Violin, and Cello, Op. 97, "Archduke" (1811)

L UDWIG VAN BEETHOVEN TURNED forty in December 1810, but
he didn't know it. More than three decades earlier his father,
Johann van Beethoven—an alcohol-soaked singer and music teacher
at the court, in Bonn, of the archbishop-elector of Cologne—had
arbitrarily knocked two years off Ludwig's age. This was part of
Johann's plan to create an income-generating musical prodigy who
could be shown off around Europe, as Leopold Mozart had done
with his son, Wolfgang, only a few years earlier. The stratagem did
not work, but Ludwig had grown up thinking that he was born in
1772 instead of 1770.

To us in the twenty-first century, thirty-eight or forty seems barely
the beginning of middle age, but in Beethoven's day, when the average
life expectancy of a European male who had survived infancy and early

childhood hovered around fifty-five, forty or thereabouts was likely to be the onset of a man's declining years. "What shall I tell you about myself?" the composer wrote in February 1811 to Bettina Brentano, a young cultural gadfly from Frankfurt whom he had met the previous summer. "'Pity my fate' I shout with Joan [of Arc]." He was quoting *Die Jungfrau von Orleans* (The Maid of Orleans), a popular drama by Friedrich Schiller, who—a case in point—had died at the age of forty-five, just six years earlier. "If I am spared a few more years of life," Beethoven wrote, "I shall also give thanks for this, as for all other goodness and woe, to the All-Perceiving, the Highest One."

Beethoven's pitiable fate included, especially, deafness, which had begun to afflict him in his mid-twenties, had gradually become grave, and was making social interaction—including his often expressed desire to marry—more and more difficult for him. But the condition had not cut him off entirely from human society, as is clear from a later passage in the same letter to Fräulein Brentano, sister of the poet Clemens Brentano and fiancée of another poet, Achim von Arnim. "I did not come home until four o'clock this morning from a bacchanal" in one of Vienna's taverns, Beethoven wrote, "where I even had to laugh a lot, so that today I have to cry almost as much; noisy glee often drives me violently back into myself."[1]

Goodness and woe; laughing and crying . . . In setting up these contrasts Beethoven could also have been describing his artistic work at that exact time in his life. During the previous fall he had composed a terse string quartet in F minor, known as the "Serioso," Op. 95—a piece characterized by violence, anguish, and resistance. But in March 1811, shortly after he had written the just-cited letter to Bettina Brentano, he created a work of Olympian calm and expansive good humor: a trio in B-flat major for piano, violin, and cello. The latter work came into being when the Archduke Rudolph—Beethoven's pupil and one of his most devoted patrons—had had to cancel some lessons. Rudolph was the younger brother of Austrian emperor Francis I, and the cancelation was caused in part by the imperial family's celebrations in honor of a royal visitor, but mainly by a finger infection that had evidently prevented Rudolph from playing the piano. Beethoven had taken full advantage of his unanticipated free time: "During the festivities for the Princess of Baden and when Your Imp[erial] Highness had a sore finger I began to work rather hard," he wrote to Rudolph at the end of March; "one of the fruits of which among other things is also a new trio for the piano."[2] Thus the "Serioso" Quartet and the work that became known as the "Archduke" Trio have come to encapsulate the two expressive poles of the entire previous decade of Beethoven's musical explorations. They may be considered a sort of *summa* of his work up to that time, but they also hint at what was to come, as he moved gradually onto previously uncharted terrain.

BEETHOVEN HAD FIRST ARRIVED in Vienna as a sixteen-year-old, hoping that the thirty-one-year-old Mozart would take him on as a pupil. He had been well trained in his native Bonn, especially by his principal teacher, Christian Gottlob Neefe, chief court musician of Archbishop-Elector Maximilian Franz, the local ruler, and by the age of thirteen Neefe's star pupil had published a set of variations and was working as assistant court organist. Nevertheless, Neefe believed that the unusually gifted boy needed to venture out into the wider world, and he persuaded someone—probably Maximilian Franz himself—to provide funds to enable young Ludwig to make the five-hundred-mile journey from the Rhineland to the Austrian capital on the Danube.

No amount of research has yet been able to confirm or deny the story of Beethoven's audition for Mozart, during which the initially inattentive master is said to have perked up when he heard his young visitor improvise brilliantly at the keyboard. Beethoven may have had a few lessons with Mozart, and he probably heard Mozart play, but when a letter from Bonn informed the boy that his beloved mother was dying of consumption, he returned home as hastily as the poor traveling conditions of the time allowed.

Maria Magdalena Keverich Beethoven died a few weeks later, "after a great deal of pain and suffering," as Ludwig wrote to a friend. For five more years he remained in his home town, working as a court musician in order to support himself and his two younger brothers, since their dipsomaniacal father had become unfit for work. Once Ludwig turned eighteen, the elector's court granted him official head-of-household status; his father was dismissed from service and half of his salary was added to Ludwig's pay. Finally, in 1792, when his brothers were old enough to fend for themselves, Ludwig once again set out for Vienna, with funds provided by the elector. Mozart had died a few months earlier, but arrangements were made for Beethoven to study with the sixty-year-old Joseph Haydn, the most famous composer in Europe. Count Waldstein, one of Beethoven's admirers in Bonn, exhorted the young musician: "With assiduous labor you will receive *Mozart's spirit through Haydn's hands.*"

Mozart's spirit was nontransferable, of course, and Haydn's relations with his touchy, independent-minded pupil were not always easy. Besides, only a year after Beethoven's arrival in Vienna Haydn departed for an eighteen-month sojourn in England, and young Ludwig turned to other mentors to help him complete his already advanced training; these included the much-respected Johann Georg Albrechtsberger and probably also Antonio Salieri, Mozart's former rival. Beethoven quickly made an excellent reputation for himself as a keyboard virtuoso, performing solo works and chamber music and improvising brilliantly on themes of his own or others' invention. In 1795, at the age of twenty-four, he published three magnificent trios for piano, violin, and cello and dubbed them, collectively, his Opus One—the first of his compositions that he deemed worthy of his burgeoning creative abilities. By the turn of the nineteenth century he would complete and give individual or collective opus numbers to thirteen piano sonatas, two cello and piano sonatas, three violin and piano sonatas, six string quartets, two concerti for piano and orchestra, and his first symphony, among many other works.

But as 1800 passed into 1801 and then 1802, and despite an unimpeded creative flow (including the Second Symphony, Third Piano Concerto, seven more piano sonatas, two more violin sonatas, and music for Salvatore Viganò's ballet, *The Creatures of Prometheus*), his worsening deafness led him to contemplate suicide. "O ye men who consider or declare me hostile, obstinate, or misanthropic, how greatly you wrong me," he wrote in October 1802, in a letter nominally addressed to his brothers but in fact intended for everyone he knew, or even for posterity.

> You do not know the secret cause of what seems thus to you. . . . For six years I have been afflicted with an incurable condition. . . . It was not possible for me to say to people: speak louder, shout, for I am deaf; ah, how would it be possible for me to reveal a weakness in the *one sense* that should be perfect to a higher degree in me than in others[?] What a humiliation when someone stood next to me and heard a flute from afar and *I heard nothing* or someone *heard the shepherd* sing, and I again heard nothing; such experiences brought me almost to despair, little was lacking to make me put an end to my life.—Only *art* held me back, ah it seemed to me impossible to leave the world before I had brought forth all that I felt destined to bring forth, and so I muddled on with this wretched life.[3]

Beethoven never gave this document—which was written in the village of Heiligenstadt, near Vienna, and which came to be known as the "Heiligenstadt Testament"—to his brothers or to anyone else; it was found among his possessions after his death. But the very act of writing it seems to have helped him to face his situation head-on, and the effect was liberating: he would proceed along his musical path, wherever it might lead him and notwithstanding deafness and the increasing social isolation that accompanied it.

The following decade proved to be not only the most prolific phase in his creative life but also a period that would change the course of Western music. The extraordinary originality that was already unmistakable in Beethoven's previous works now reached full, glorious maturity, and it began to lead the art of music into the realm of self-referential Romanticism. Beethoven, suffering or triumphant or in any intermediate state, became the unnamed but ever-present protagonist of his own creations. His Third ("Eroica"), Fifth, and Sixth ("Pastoral") symphonies; his opera *Leonore* (a hymn to human freedom but also to the conjugal love that he sought but never found; the opera was later revised and renamed *Fidelio*); his Fourth and Fifth ("Emperor") piano concerti; his Violin and Triple concerti; his "Waldstein" and "Appassionata" piano sonatas; his "Kreutzer" Violin Sonata; his Third Cello Sonata; his three "Razumovsky" string quartets, Op. 59—all of these brilliant works and many others as well opened new paths of musical communication.

By early 1811, when Beethoven composed the "Archduke" Trio, deafness had forced him to eliminate all but a very few public appearances as a pianist, while, as a creative artist, he was nearing the close of the extraordinary decade that many music historians refer to as his "middle" or "heroic" period. Although his fame was rapidly spreading beyond the German-speaking world into much of the rest of Europe, his rate of productivity began to slow down, at least with respect to immediate results. The personal and professional causes were many, but external events, too, took their toll on him as on millions of other Europeans. In particular, Napoleon's continent-conquering troops had defeated Austria for the second time in 1809, and by the following year the Austrian treasury was verging on bankruptcy—a fact that contributed in no small way to feelings of dire uncertainty throughout the empire.

Only a few months before the French occupation of Vienna, Beethoven had received a flattering invitation from Jérôme Bonaparte, Napoleon's youngest brother, who had been installed as King of Westphalia, in northwestern Germany: Jérôme had offered to make Beethoven his court Kapellmeister at a substantial annual salary of 600 ducats. The idea of moving from brilliant Vienna to the relatively remote, provincial town of Kassel, Westphalia's capital, could not have filled Beethoven with joy, but he made sure that word of Jérôme's offer got around. When Vienna's music lovers learned that the most famous composer in their midst (with the exception of the aged Haydn, who was no longer professionally active and who died a few months later) was thinking of leaving them, they formulated a plan to keep him *in situ*. Archduke Rudolph persuaded two of the composer's other aristocratic admirers, Prince Ferdinand Kinsky and Prince Franz Joseph Lobkowitz, to join him in offering the composer an annual stipend that would provide him with financial stability for life, even if he were to become ill or otherwise disabled, and that would therefore allow him to remain in Vienna. Perhaps these members of the Viennese nobility felt some guilt over the fact that Mozart—whose genius was now recognized, even worshiped, all over Europe—had been left to fend entirely for himself barely two decades earlier. They could not allow such a thing to happen to Beethoven!

Beethoven would have liked the agreement to include a position for himself as the Austrian imperial court's music director, as well as a guarantee that his patrons would sponsor a public concert of his music once a year, but in the end he accepted the purely financial offer. On March 9, 1809, the composer and the three noblemen signed an agreement that stated that whereas Herr Ludwig van Beethoven was constantly giving proof of "his exceptional gifts and genius as musician and composer"; and whereas he was likely to "exceed the highest expectations," which were "quite justified, considering what he has achieved so far"; and whereas he needed to be able to dedicate himself to creating "grand and outstanding works," the noble signatories committed themselves to paying him a lifetime annuity of 4,000 florins: 1,500 from Rudolph, 700 from Lobkowitz, and 1,800 from Kinsky.[4] Beethoven, for his part, agreed to continue to live in Vienna as long as the agreement remained in force and to renounce the contract if he were to accept regular employment elsewhere or from other sources. In short, unlike Mozart, who, during his last decade, had been a freelance musician without any guarantee of support, Beethoven would be a freelance musician with a regular, dependable basic income.

Unfortunately, the two princes' finances suffered almost immediately from the fivefold devaluation of Austria's currency—a result of the country's military and territorial losses. By the time relative stability returned, the 4,000-florin annuity had lost approximately eighty percent of its original value. Kinsky died in a riding accident in 1812 and Lobkowitz went bankrupt the following year, but the Kinsky estate and Lobkowitz himself eventually settled their accounts with Beethoven, and in the meantime Rudolph was able to increase his support, which remained a lifeline for the composer. Beethoven never again found himself in dire financial circumstances, although he never ceased to worry about money.

Amid all the political and economic turbulence of 1810, the only complete major works to emerge from Beethoven's pen were the intensely dramatic "Serioso" String Quartet and the incidental music to Goethe's five-act tragedy, *Egmont*, of which the wonderful overture remains a staple of the orchestral repertoire. (Beethoven and Goethe would meet at the spa town of Teplitz in Bohemia—present-day Teplice in the Czech Republic—in the summer of 1812, and would duly impress each other, although Beethoven was displeased by Goethe's deferent behavior toward the aristocrats who were present at the resort, and Goethe found Beethoven's unrefined social behavior off-putting.) Beethoven produced more lieder (songs) than usual that year, plus a number of smaller instrumental pieces, including the memorable "Für Elise," which young piano pupils around the world still play with varying degrees of fluency and accuracy, but his output remained far below the quantitative level that he had achieved from 1802 through 1809. He must have known, or at least sensed or suspected, that he was gradually exhausting the specific creative vein that he had been mining so assiduously and successfully. Still, that vein would yield a few more astonishing masterpieces before Beethoven's artistic explorations and aspirations led him in new directions.

COINCIDENTALLY OR NOT, the *Egmont* Overture and the "Serioso" Quartet both begin in F minor and end in F major. But there is a fundamental difference of intent between the two works. The overture is a musical representation of the steadfast courage of Lamoral, Count of Egmont and Prince of Gavere, a martyr in the Flemish struggle for liberation from Spain in the sixteenth century (see this book's sixth chapter for further references to that struggle), whereas we may assume that the quartet communicates the acute psychological distress of Ludwig van Beethoven. Perhaps Beethoven saw himself reflected in Egmont's story—the story of an achievement that was only partially recognized in the hero's lifetime—yet the divergences between the overture and the quartet are stronger than their similarities.

In modern Italian, the word *serioso* generally implies a sort of self-dramatizing or even tongue-in-cheek seriousness (as opposed to just plain *serio*: serious), but there can be little doubt that Beethoven, who actually called this work *Quartett Serioso* in his autograph score, meant "serious" in the strict sense. In a letter to a correspondent in England—

written out in English for him by a trusted friend, but signed by the composer himself—Beethoven declared outright: "N.B. The Quartett [*sic*] is written for a small circle of connoisseurs and is never to be performed in public." He must have considered this piece—shorter and more compact than any of his previous ten string quartets or than any of the five that would follow—too intimately confessional and too terrifyingly harsh to entertain casual listeners. But now that we human beings have lived through two further centuries of global horrors, we can face the onslaught head-on: the "Serioso" appears frequently in the programs of most of today's professional string quartets. I want to take a paragraph to discuss it because I see it as an opposite-side-of-the-coin piece to its close successor, the "Archduke" Trio.

The first movement, *Allegro con brio*, of the "Serioso" begins violently, *forte*, in 4/4 time. It contains moments of respite, including a lyrical second theme, but an undercurrent of unrest—an accompanying figure made up of groups of repeated, snarling sixteenth notes—creates an uncertain climate throughout. By far the longest segment of the work is the second movement, *Allegretto ma non troppo* (somewhat quick but not too much so), in 2/4 time; it is nominally in D major but in fact goes back and forth between D major and D minor, with many sorties into other tonal areas and with a densely contrapuntal middle section. The following movement is a scherzo in F minor marked *Allegro assai vivace ma serioso*: very fast [and] lively but serious. *Scherzo* means joke, in Italian, but this scherzo is no joke: it tosses us back and forth between violence and mystery. And the finale, which begins slowly and expressively in 2/4 time, quickly transforms itself into a sort of fatal waltz, *Allegretto agitato*, in 6/8 time. Oddly, however, Beethoven closes the proceedings with a very fast (*Allegro*, 2/2), high-spirited coda, in F major, that appears to have nothing in common, content-wise, with anything that has preceded it, as if he were saying, "This may be a 'serious' quartet, but after all, don't take it (or me) too seriously." Yet despite this incongruity, the quartet as a whole is a hyper-dramatic and highly disturbing work, poles apart from the trio that would follow it and that would be dedicated to Archduke Rudolph.

RUDOLPH JOHANN JOSEPH RAINIER von Habsburg-Lorraine, archduke of Austria, was the youngest son of the Austrian and Holy Roman Emperor Leopold II and his consort, the Spanish Infanta Maria Louisa. (He was also a nephew of Beethoven's boss from his Bonn days, the archbishop-elector of Cologne, Maximilian Franz.) As a child Rudolph was epileptic and generally sickly, clearly unfit for the military career for which he had been intended; thus he was allowed to develop an apparently innate love of, fascination with, and talent for music. At the age of fifteen or sixteen, in 1803 or 1804, he became one of Beethoven's piano pupils and, more significantly, his only student of composition. The master would betake himself from his notoriously dirty and disorderly lodgings (he was constantly giving up one apartment and moving to another) to one of Vienna's magnificent imperial palaces, where he would instruct his royal pupil. Yet however important this contact was for him, he would try to squirm out of giving lessons to Rudolph whenever he could come up with a reasonably believable excuse—usually ill health, which did indeed frequently plague him. "I am feeling better and in a few days I shall again have the honor of waiting upon you and of making up for the absence," he wrote in a typical letter to Rudolph:

> I am always terribly worried if I cannot be as assiduous as often as
> I would like for Your Imperial Highness. It is certainly true if I say

that I suffer very much from this, but very soon things will no longer be so bad for me—Kindly keep me in your thoughts. The time will come when I shall doubly and triply show that I am worth it.

Your Imperial Highness's faithful devoted servant

Ludwig van Beethoven[5]

Yet despite Rudolph's sense of divinely inherited privilege and Beethoven's difficult character and anti-monarchic beliefs, the relationship seems to have been one of mutual respect, even affection, and it endured for nearly a quarter-century, until the end of the composer's life. By 1811, Beethoven had already dedicated to Rudolph his Fourth and Fifth ("Emperor") piano concerti and his Piano Sonata in E-flat major ("Les Adieux")—this last piece written specifically to commemorate the archduke's departure and absence from Vienna at the time of the imperial family's escape, as Napoleon's armies advanced on the city, and to celebrate Rudolph's return when the danger had passed. But the new Trio in B-flat major, Op. 97, is the piece that musicians and music lovers all over the world have long associated with Rudolph, through its nickname, the "Archduke." It is a work of great breadth and considerable length: a complete performance, if all of the repeat passages indicated by Beethoven are respected, lasts between thirty-five and forty minutes—which makes it roughly twenty percent longer than the next-longest among the composer's piano trios.

Late in March 1811, shortly after Beethoven had informed his pupil of the new trio's existence, Rudolph wrote to ask for a copy of it, which he must have been eager to learn. This proved to be easier said than done. "Since despite all my practical efforts I could get no copyist to write in my house, I am sending you my manuscript," Beethoven replied. "You need only be so kind as to send for Schlemmer[,] a competent copyist[,] who must however copy the trio only in your palace, because one can otherwise never be sure about theft."[6] This may have been a money-saving ploy on Beethoven's part: if the archduke wanted to see the trio, he could pay the copyist! But it is also true that copyists disliked working directly under the frequently ill-tempered composer's hypercritical eye and in his chaotic lodgings.

A whole book could probably be written on the subject of Beethoven and his copyists. His manuscripts were the messy battlegrounds of his creativity, and they often showed the scars of those battles, in the form of cross-outs, insertions piled atop previous insertions, and other changes large and small. Since many of his compositions contained bold new harmonic and melodic patterns, the musicians who eked out a miserable living by making fair copies of other musicians' works were frequently hard put to understand what Beethoven wanted. When they misinterpreted his indications he severely berated them.

In the previous chapter, I touched briefly on the subject of music publication—a business that had not yet come into its own in Mozart's day but that seemed to be growing exponentially during the early decades of the nineteenth century. Ever-increasing quantities of printed music were being disseminated across Europe, especially in the German-speaking countries, and *Hausmusik*, music in the home, was quickly becoming the home entertainment system of the day, thanks above all to the rapid growth of the bourgeoisie. These middle-class families—imitating, to some extent, the nobility—yearned to enjoy "the finer things in life." Thus, for Beethoven, the publication of his works was not merely a symbolic form of recognition, as it had been for his predecessors, but rather a significant and growing source of income. Copyright laws and the concept of royalties were in their infancy or nonexistent at the time; publishers paid flat fees to composers, which meant that composers had to negotiate as substantial a payment as possible for each work offered, since no further money was likely to be forthcoming, no matter how well a piece might sell.

Once Beethoven and a publishing house had agreed upon a fee

for a given piece, he would send off either his original manuscript or a copyist's transcription, but the proof sheets that came back to him were often strewn with errors, many of them the result of the compounded mistakes of copyists and typesetters. Shortly after Beethoven had completed the "Archduke" Trio, for instance, the Leipzig-based publishing house of Breitkopf & Härtel sent him the first proofs of his "Emperor" Concerto, Choral Fantasy (for piano, chorus, and orchestra), and "Les Adieux" piano sonata. Beethoven was appalled. "Mistakes—mistakes! You yourself are one big mistake!" he wrote indignantly and with characteristic tactlessness to Gottfried Christoph Härtel, the firm's director.

> So, I must send my copyists there, I myself must go there, if I don't want my works to appear as nothing but mistakes. It seems that the musicians' guild in Leipzig can't produce a single respectable proof-reader; furthermore you publish the works before you receive the corrections. . . . My warmest thanks for having so greatly shaken me up over such an interesting matter. . . . Make as many mistakes as you like, have as many mistakes made as you like.—I hold you in high esteem, [because] it is of course customary among people to esteem each other for not having made even worse mistakes.[7]

A month earlier, Beethoven had offered to sell his new piano trio (it had not yet acquired its archducal nickname) to Härtel, who, however, had postponed a decision on the matter. The composer replied that he was in no hurry to see the piece in print, and shortly thereafter his relations with the company broke off, not to be resumed for several years. The house of Sigmund Anton Steiner finally published the "Archduke" in Vienna in July 1816, more than five years after the trio's composition (although in the meantime Beethoven had made some changes in the score), and in December of the same year the London-based publisher Robert Birchall brought out an English edition.

Well before that—indeed, soon after its creation—the trio in its original form must have been played privately at the archduke's palace and elsewhere,* but its first public performance did not take place until April 11, 1814, during a benefit concert in the lobby or ballroom of Vienna's Hotel zum Römischen Kaiser. Beethoven's friends Ignaz Schuppanzigh and Joseph Linke took the violin and cello parts, respectively, and the composer himself played the piano. The famed violinist and composer Louis Spohr, who attended a rehearsal in Beethoven's apartment, reported:

> It was not a treat, for, in the first place, the piano was badly out of tune, which Beethoven minded little, since he did not hear it; and secondly, on account of his deafness there was scarcely anything left of the virtuosity of the artist which had formerly been so greatly admired. In *forte* passages the poor deaf man pounded on the keys till the strings jangled, and in *piano* he played so softly that whole groups of notes were omitted, so that the music was unintelligible unless one could look into the pianoforte part.[8]

In Beethoven's day, pianos were being constructed all over Europe in widely, sometimes wildly, different ways, but in none of its incarnations did the piano have a cast-iron internal frame, which came into being only after the composer's death and made it much more robust than any of the instruments available in 1814. We don't know which instrument Beethoven was playing, either at the rehearsal that Spohr heard or at subsequent public performances. Was it the French Erard that he had owned since 1803; or perhaps an instrument by the Viennese piano builder Nannette Streicher, who was also a good, patient friend

---

* According to Angus Watson, in his book, *Beethoven's Chamber Music in Context* (2010), the trio was given a read-through at the home of a Baron Neuwirth only two days after Beethoven had completed it.

of the composer; or a different instrument altogether? In any case, Beethoven's hearing was by then so badly impaired that the first public performance, when it finally took place, often teetered on the brink of disaster.* And yet, the pianist Ignaz Moscheles, who was present, noted in his diary:

> In the case of how many compositions is the word "new" misapplied! But never in Beethoven's [case], and least of all in this [work], which again is full of originality. His playing, aside from its intellectual element, satisfied me less, being wanting in clarity and precision; but I observed many traces of the *grand* style of playing which I had long recognized in his compositions.[9]

A second performance by the same musicians took place a few weeks later at a matinee concert presented by Schuppanzigh at a hall in the Prater, Vienna's public park; we may assume that it was not much better, and may even have been worse, than the first performance, but audiences in those days were unaccustomed to thoroughly rehearsed concerts. That performance proved to be Beethoven's last major public appearance as a pianist. Yet as for the "Archduke" Trio itself: once it was published, it was well received wherever it was performed, and for two centuries it has been one of the most frequently played works, worldwide, in its genre.

---

* For nonmusicians, Beethoven's ability to compose music despite his advancing deafness is the most remarkable element in his biography, but the truth is that deafness made a much worse impact on his personal life than on his musical career. Many well-trained musicians can "hear" a piece of music in their mind's ear simply by reading a score, and many composers write their music without trying it out on a piano or any other instrument. It is possible, maybe even likely, that his deafness was a major factor in leading him into previously unexplored regions of musical creativity, but composing despite being deaf was not in itself as extraordinary a feat as many nonmusicians believe.

WITH NO PREAMBLE, THE PIANO LAUNCHES into the broad, lyrical main theme of the "Archduke" Trio's first movement, *Allegro moderato* (moderately quick, in 4/4 time), solidly in the tonic key of B-flat major. But after only ten or eleven seconds the violin and cello slip in with a commentary that almost immediately turns itself into a recitative-like passage; the string instruments seem almost to be remonstrating with the piano: "You've had your say; now it's our turn!" They restate the first part of the theme while the piano docilely accompanies them for a short spell, until all three instruments unite in a friendly, back-and-forth conversation. Extended melodic lines characterize most of this minute-and-a-half-long first theme, although the piano often embellishes the strings' legato phrases (notes connected to each other in sequence, without separations) with short, explosive triplet figurations (three-note groups). In the G major second theme, on the other hand, a staccato opening section (separated notes) alternates with a more lyrical follow-up segment, marked *dolce* (sweet). This theme's layout echoes that of the first theme: the piano speaks first, the strings then take over, and, finally, the three instruments combine forces. An ascending, energetic closing theme leads into a repetition of the entire first part (exposition) of the movement; once that repetition is concluded, the extraordinary development section begins.

In keeping with his usual practice, Beethoven used this movement's development to splinter his thematic material into its various elements and to transform the resulting fragments in surprising ways. In some works, he intentionally pulverized some of the elements into such tiny molecules that only the most attentive listeners can identify them, but in the development of the "Archduke"'s opening movement he presents the fragments in six easily recognizable segments, most of them sunny in character. The longest and most celebrated of the six is a sort of back-and-forth game between the piano, playing staccato, and the strings, playing pizzicato (plucking the strings)—alternately at first, then together, in joyous cohesion. The last of these segments (the retransition) leads into a recapitulation of the themes in approximately their original forms. Finally, an increasingly excitable and exciting coda, based almost entirely on the main theme, ends the movement in a tremendous sunburst of sound.

In the great majority of Beethoven's four-movement works—symphonies, chamber music, and piano sonatas alike—a typically fast-paced first movement is followed by a slow, or at least slow-ish, second movement, which is followed in turn by a fast-tempo scherzo and then by a finale. But in the "Archduke" Trio as in some other pieces (the String Quartet in F major, Op. 59, No. 1, for instance, and, most notably, the Ninth Symphony) the composer switched the positions of the two inner movements. After the "Archduke"'s high-flying first movement, a quietly playful scherzo appears—an *allegro* in B-flat major and 3/4 time. And whereas the piano makes the first movement's opening statement, in the second the strings begin—the cello alone, then the violin and cello together; the piano doesn't start to put its two cents'-worth in until the sixteenth bar. The movement follows the traditional scherzo form: main section, trio section (thus named whether it is in a trio, quartet, sonata, symphony, or other structure), and repetition of the main section.

Perhaps "quietly playful" is too bland a descriptor, because the movement includes many sparkling forte passages as well as numerous crescendos, diminuendos, and sudden outbursts on individual chords. Nor does the word "playful" work at all if, as often happens, performers play the movement's main body in a bar-by-bar manner instead of in sweeping, four-bar phrases that propel the musical material forward, pulling the listener into the irresistibly jaunty rhythmic motion.

And then comes the amazing trio section, which is considerably longer than the main section—one hundred sixty-one bars as opposed to one hundred twenty-five. For listeners, be they musically trained or not, this segment is a delight, but for musicians it is also an erudite wisecrack—a *scherzo* in the literal, joking sense of the term. It begins as the musical equivalent of someone groping around in the dark, trying to find a mislaid object; in this case, the object being sought is the right tonality—the right key. First the cello enters, quietly, almost stealthily, feeling its way chromatically upward, from B-flat to C-flat, forward and back again, then from C-flat to C-natural, forward and back again, and so on up to D-flat, D-natural, and E-flat. Then, as the cello sinks back downward, the piano enters, slithering gradually upward in the same manner, from F all the way to B-flat. The violin adds its voice to the search, and after about half a minute the three instruments crescendo to a "Eureka!" moment—an explosion that lands us firmly in the key of D-flat major—D-flat being the lowered third of B-flat major, our basic key. Firmly—but only for about twenty seconds. Then the groping in the dark resumes and leads to another explosion—this time in the "wrong" key of E major, which is harmonically very distant from B-flat major. An extended, rhythmically fraught passage brings us back to B-flat and a transition into a repetition of the scherzo proper. Toward the end, the "groping" trio section seems to be starting up again, but Beethoven is only teasing us: the chromatic motion gradually subsides until, with a seconds-long "coda to the coda," the movement comes to an abrupt, high-spirited close.

FROM THE FIRST BAR of the third movement, or even from the piano's very first chord, we realize that Beethoven is taking us into a different world, still solar but far from the fundamentally extroverted nature of the two previous movements. This extraordinarily beautiful *Andante cantabile*, which lasts about twelve minutes, consists of a twenty-eight-bar theme followed by four variations—each variation also exactly twenty-eight bars in length—and an extended, fifty-three-bar-long variation-coda. Even the internal structure of the theme and the four initial variations remains constant: an eight-bar phrase (let's call it A1) is followed by what is essentially a repetition of the same material (A2) but with the three instruments trading their dominating or subordinate positions back and forth; this repetition also lasts eight bars. At the end of a new, different eight-bar phrase (B1), there is a repetition (B2) of only the last four bars of B1, again with the instruments exchanging places.

Beethoven's choice of D major for this broad, warm, consolatory piece of music is atypical: he more often used this key for extroverted works—the bright opening and closing movements of his Second Symphony, Violin Concerto, and the third of his Opus 18 string quartets, for instance—just as Mozart had used D major for the rambunctious first and last movements of his "Haffner" and "Prague" symphonies and the joyous beginning and ending of *The Marriage of Figaro*. Nevertheless, the key choice for this altogether different type of piece works magnificently.

Beethoven evidently wanted his theme to convey a sense of serenity, of calm contemplation, because he indicated that it is to be played *piano* and *semplice* (simply): no posturing or showing off, he tells his potential interpreters—just state the material warmly but directly, and not too slowly! This is easier said than done, since simplicity is much harder to achieve than brilliance. Many performers tend to ignore the *semplice* indication and to set an excessively slow basic tempo, thereby exaggeratedly inflating the musical material. And if the serenity is properly established in the theme, it prepares the path into the first variation—a dream world in which the piano weaves continuous, light triplet figurations around the simple, stable notes of the cello and violin.

In complete contrast, the second variation begins lightheartedly, with staccato notes tossed back and forth between the piano and the strings; later, the tone becomes more lyrical, but then the lighter character of the opening segment returns. The third variation acts almost as an extension of the second—an alternatingly dramatic and playful variation on a variation, in which the piano's quick, often nervous triplet figurations move the action forward while the violin and cello second, or punctuate, the piano's activity.

The atmosphere changes completely in the fourth variation, which is marked *Poco più adagio* (a little more at ease). Through this segment's entire duration, the pianist's left hand never stops playing groups of flowing and, for the most part, gentle thirty-second notes: six-hundred-seventy-two notes in roughly two minutes! For half of that time span, the strings play a quiet but solidly anchored version of the movement's original theme while the pianist's right hand produces a series of soaring, syncopated echoes of the theme. For the other half, the right hand plays thirty-second notes an octave above the left hand's notes, while the strings take care of the soaring syncopations. We, the listeners, should feel as if we are defying the laws of gravity, floating high above the rest of humanity and all its agitations.

The return of the main theme in the original tempo brings us gently back to earth, but only for a while. Roughly one minute into this extended final segment, Beethoven again loosens the moorings, as if he were about to attempt the musical equivalent of what the Mongolfier brothers, his older contemporaries in France, had done some years earlier with their hot-air balloons. In a series of two-bar phrases, the piano plays ascending groups of triplets* while the strings sing a slow, legato melodic line, and the whole piece begins once again to hover in air. The volume level is mostly *pianissimo*, with an occasional *crescendo-diminuendo*, a tiny accentuation, an *espressivo* indication, or

---

* A natural, flowing tempo for these triplets can also serve as an indication for an approximate, basic tempo for the entire movement, excepting the fourth variation. It will help players avoid the tendency to turn *andante cantabile* into a slow-moving *adagio*.

a rise to a simple *piano*. And then, following a few long, leave-taking phrases played by the strings, the piano, subsiding, interrupts its trip-let chords and ends, together with the violin and cello, on the sole, *pianissimo* note of D.

But now, still in 3/4 time, within the *Andante cantabile* tempo indi-cation, and still *pianissimo*, a chord—B-flat, D, F, and A-flat (musicians call it a dominant seventh chord in the key of E-flat major)—appears out of nowhere, played by all three instruments. And all of a sudden, *bang!*—the chord is repeated, *forte*, again by all three instruments, but in 2/4 time and with the tempo indication *Allegro moderato*. An inattentive listener who may have been lulled into a reverie by the nearly forty bars of repeated triplets at the end of the third movement will be rudely—and no doubt intentionally—awakened by this startling beginning to the "Archduke"'s boisterous finale. But where are we? Shouldn't we be back in B-flat major? After all, last movements in Beethoven's day were meant to be in the same key as first movements. Are we instead in E-flat major? This is the same trick that Beethoven played in the opening bars of his First Symphony, written more than a decade earlier: what sounds like a dominant seventh chord is actually a tonic seventh chord, and not until we're about half a minute into this finale can we be one hundred percent certain that, yes, we are indeed in B-flat major, where we're supposed to be.

The composer and conductor Franz Lachner (1803–1890) recounted that once, when he was very young, he was studying the piano part of the "Archduke" Trio together with Nanette Streicher, the aforemen-tioned Viennese piano manufacturer, at her home, where Beethoven was often a guest. At the beginning of the finale, Beethoven himself "suddenly entered the room," Lachner recalled. "He listened for a few moments, using the ear trumpet he always carried with him, but soon indicated that he was not in agreement with the too-tame performance of the principal motif of the finale, but rather leaned over the pianist

[Frau Streicher] and played it for her, after which he immediately left."[10] In short: the movement is meant to be played brilliantly.

The high-stepping main theme of this lighthearted movement in rondo form is followed by a second theme, in F major, which begins delicately but then gets roughed up. The main theme comes back but transforms itself, toward the end, into a half-dramatic, half-joking third theme, in E-flat major, which is followed by another return of the main theme in a slightly extended, very much altered, and even more exuberant incarnation. A reprise of the second theme transitions into . . . well, not exactly the anticipated, "proper" return of the main theme. Instead, that theme is transmogrified into a wild dance, *Presto*, in 6/8 time and, initially, in the distant key of A major—from which Beethoven gradually, slyly brings us back to B-flat major. This whirlwind—a sort of manic coda that lasts over one hundred forty bars—eventually begins to subside in speed and volume, and we expect the movement to end gently. But then, as at the very end of the "Emperor" Concerto's finale, Beethoven jolts the players back into action with an outburst of higher-than-high spirits: in this case, fifteen super-fast (*Più presto*) bars of pure joy.

AN INDIVIDUAL ARTISTIC CREATION may have little to do with how the artist is feeling, mentally, physically, or spiritually, while the work is being created. A tragic piece of music, for instance, may have been gestating for a long time in its composer's mind, and the composer may be in a much happier psychological state by the time he or she actually sets down the score's dark-hued notes. Yet in the case of the "Archduke" Trio, one can hardly help imagining that Beethoven was in an expansive mood during much of the compositional process. Perhaps he was simply enjoying his temporary release from giving lessons to Rudolph while the archduke's sore finger was healing, or maybe he was remembering or reflecting on some past or recent happiness. Or maybe I am completely wrong. But whatever the reason, or lack thereof, the "Archduke" is undeniably one of the sunniest of all of Beethoven's major works. It makes us feel that we are alternately observing human existence from high above it and diving down to enjoy life's most delightful moments.

ILL HEALTH CONTINUED to beset Beethoven, off and on, through the spring and well into the summer of 1811, after he had completed the "Archduke" Trio, and he spent most of August and the first half of September taking the mineral baths at Teplitz. There had been a lull in the Napoleonic conflicts, and Beethoven was thinking of writing an opera based on a new French melodrama, *Les Ruines de Babylone*, by Guilbert Pixerécourt. But he soon discarded that idea and set to work instead on three future masterpieces: the Seventh and Eighth symphonies and the Tenth (last) Sonata for violin and piano—the one in G major, Op. 96.

By 1813, the relatively fallow period that had begun three years earlier was becoming even less fruitful—perhaps even to the point of worrying the composer himself, although we don't know whether this was so. His biggest accomplishment that year was an orchestral potboiler, *Wellington's Victory*—a musical depiction of the Iron Duke's triumph over Napoleon at Vitoria in Spain—which received considerable attention, thanks to its timeliness, but which certainly does not qualify as a major work. Nevertheless, when, years later, the critic Gottfried Weber published an article in which he declared the piece to be unworthy of its composer, Beethoven wrote, in a marginal note that betrays both his sense of self-worth and his ability to combine anger with humor: "Oh you miserable rogue, what I shit is better than anything you ever thought."

An important achievement of 1814—the year in which the "Archduke" Trio was first performed in public—was the heavy revision of *Leonore*, which, under its new name, *Fidelio*, would remain Beethoven's sole completed opera; another was the composition of his touching Piano Sonata in E minor, Op. 90. Eighteen-fourteen also saw the opening of the Congress of Vienna, which determined how Europe would be carved up in the aftermath of Napoleon's defeat. Beethoven, despite his republicanism, enjoyed the attention he received from the assembled crowned heads and their ministers: this was the moment of his greatest celebrity—until after his death. Throughout 1815, his only major works were the last two of his five sonatas for cello and piano, and by the end of that year he was caught up in a legal battle over the guardianship of his nephew, Karl, the only child of his deceased brother, Caspar Carl van Beethoven; that contentious struggle would preoccupy him for years.

Beethoven continued to produce a fair number of short pieces through the mid-eighteen-teens, along with a few more significant works: the song-cycle *An die ferne Geliebte* (To the Distant Beloved) and the Piano Sonata in A major, Op. 101, were composed for the most part in 1816—the same year in which the "Archduke" Trio was finally published. But only toward the end of the decade did the fertility of earlier years begin to return, blossoming into what we now describe as the composer's "late" (third) period. The masterpieces that he completed between 1819 and 1826—his final active year—included his last four piano sonatas, the "Diabelli" Variations for piano, the *Missa Solemnis*, the Ninth Symphony, and the last five string quartets. Four of these works—the monumental "Hammerklavier" Piano Sonata; the final Piano Sonata in C minor, Op. 111; the *Missa Solemnis*; and the Great Fugue for string quartet, Op. 133 (originally intended as the finale of the String Quartet in B-flat major, Op. 130)—were dedicated to Rudolph. The *Missa*, in particular, was composed in honor of the archduke's elevation to the title of Cardinal Archbishop of Olmütz (present-day Olomouc, in the Czech Republic). With these compositions, Beethoven stretched the boundaries of musical expression and radically altered the future of his art.

Rudolph, whose health remained delicate, died of a cerebral hemorrhage in 1831, at the age of forty-three. He is remembered today not so much for having been the Austrian emperor's brother or a prelate in the Roman Catholic Church as for having helped to support one of Western civilization's most extraordinary creative artists—and, in particular, for having been *the* archduke from whom Beethoven's Trio, Op. 97, got its nickname.

BEETHOVEN HAD DIED FOUR YEARS before his imperial patron— on March 26, 1827, in Vienna, at the age of fifty-six. So great was the esteem in which he was held, even by people who knew his works only by reputation, that his funeral cortège, three days later, was followed by more than a thousand people. Columns of black-clad, black-gloved torch-bearers walked on either side of the coffin, with bouquets of white lilies pinned to their left sleeves. A funeral oration, written by the poet Franz Grillparzer, declared that Beethoven's successors would have to "begin anew, for he who went before left off only where art leaves off."

One of the torch-bearers was a thirty-year-old composer who had idolized Beethoven but was nevertheless determined to "begin anew" and to make a mark of his own. His name was Franz Schubert.

PART II

THE ROMANTIC CENTURY

Of the five composers who dominate this section of the book, the oldest was born three years before the nineteenth century began, the youngest died three years before that century's end, and one of them even survived into the twentieth century. These five, together with a dozen or so others, are the Romantic-era composers whose works have remained staples of concert halls and opera houses the world over.

What constitutes Romanticism in the arts is a much debated question. In my opinion, the movement—if such one may call it—was rooted in politics. Napoleon's final defeat at Waterloo in 1815 put an end not only to the French emperor's personal dreams but also to the democratic aspirations, realistic or otherwise, of vast numbers of Europeans. The old monarchs, once again firmly installed on their thrones, wanted to insure that there would be no further uprisings in the name of *liberté, égalité, fraternité,* and that the re-established Establishment would maintain its regained status quo.

Chief architect of this new-old situation was Prince Clemens von Metternich, foreign minister of Austria's Emperor Francis I. Francis had been brought up to believe in and practice the Enlightenment ideals of his uncle, Joseph II, and father, Leopold II; the latter had written that his many sons (who, as we have seen, included Beethoven's patron, Archduke Rudolph) must be "convinced of the equality of man" and that they must understand "that their entire existence must be subordinate to their duties. They must regard it as their highest duty to listen to and to comfort" their subjects. In other words, monarchs had to be obeyed, but they also had to keep in mind the "fact" that God had given them their authority in order to aid their subjects, not to exercise unbridled power over them.[1]

Nevertheless, after a quarter-century of continent-wide revolution and counter-revolution, conquest and counter-conquest, Francis—who, by 1815, had already occupied the throne for twenty-three of his forty-seven years—seems to have persuaded himself that he could not carry out his duties without also restricting his citizens' freedom of action and expression. In order to do this, he put Metternich in charge of guaranteeing obedience throughout the Austrian Empire, which, at the time, included not only present-day Austria but also most or all of present-day Hungary, the Czech Republic, Slovakia, Slovenia, Croatia, and Serbia, as well as large portions of present-day Germany, Italy, Romania, Poland, and Ukraine. Metternich used his power to create what was, in effect, a prototype of the modern police state. Under his watch, student associations were outlawed, as were publications that expressed political dissent; paid spies and amateur informants were abundantly strewn throughout the imperial domains; and common citizens were kept in line through fear of imprisonment, exile, or worse, simply on suspicion of disloyalty. "Many eras witnessed tyrannical governments," wrote the cultural historian E. H. Gombrich, "but what gave a special characteristic to life under Metternich was the sense of deep and widening disappointment."[2] Freedom of expression had for a while been seen as attainable; now it was denied.

In an earlier book (*The Ninth: Beethoven and the World in 1824*), I considered the possibility that what we know as Romanticism in the arts was created by a mixture of relief over the end of the quarter-century of revolutionary and Napoleonic Wars, regret over the loss of the sense of possibility that those wars had brought to the young generations of the day, and despair over the political repression that followed. Together, these conditions or states of being led artists to internalize their modes of expression and to make their creations self-referential—a path that Beethoven had already explored while Napoleon's armies were advancing across Europe. The writer E. T. A. Hoffmann declared music to be "the most romantic of all the arts," because "its sole subject is the infinite." And in post-revolutionary, post-Napoleonic Europe, the ability to lose oneself in the infinite was a practical necessity for artists, because the contemplation of political reality led only to depression.

Thus music became, among much else, an escape route. And Schubert, with whom this section of the book begins, is a stellar example of the Romantic flight into music.

3

A QUARTET THAT'S ABOUT NOTHING

Franz Schubert: String Quartet No. 15 in
G Major, Op. posth. 161, D. 887 (1826)

"I'M NOT WORKING AT ALL. The weather here is really horrible, the All Highest One seems to have completely abandoned us, the sun won't ever shine. Even in May you can't sit out in the garden. Terrible! horrible!! awful!!! for me the cruelest thing that can be!"[1]

Franz Schubert, waiting out the rain in Vienna in the spring of 1826, would have liked to join his friends Eduard von Bauernfeld and Johann Mayrhofer in a rural area near what are now Austria's borders with Italy and Slovenia, but the twenty-nine-year-old composer had no money for travel, or for anything else beyond bare survival. He had, however, managed to attend the Schuppanzigh Quartet's premiere performance of Beethoven's astonishing new String Quartet in B-flat major, Op. 130, with its original "Great Fugue" finale, and this may have prodded him to get back to work on a long-planned quartet of his own. Whether or not his state of mind had improved in the meantime, however, is open to question, because the String Quartet in G major—the masterpiece that he wrote out during the last ten days of June—is anything but sunny, and much of it seems to be an open-eyed confrontation with the Abyss on the part of a man who, despite his youth, knew that he probably did not have long to live.

VIENNA BOASTS OF THE GREAT COMPOSERS who lived in its midst, and indeed Haydn, Mozart, Beethoven, Bruckner, Brahms, and Mahler all spent substantial portions of their creative lives in the Austrian capital. But the only native Viennese among the famous Classical- and Romantic-era composers was Franz Peter Schubert*—and even he was born outside Vienna's old city walls, in the Himmelpfortgrund district, to parents who hailed from elsewhere in the Austrian Empire. Still, he counts as authentically Viennese. His father, Franz Theodor Schubert, a schoolteacher, and his mother, Elisabeth (née Vietz), a former servant, had fourteen children, of whom only five reached adulthood; Franz, born on January 31, 1797, was the fourth of those five. The Schubert family was poor, but within the household there was a strong emphasis on education in general and on music-making in particular. As a child, Franz was taught to play the piano, violin, and organ and was instructed in singing and harmony. Michael Holzer, one of his principal music teachers, later said of his pupil: "If I wished to instruct him in anything fresh, he already knew it. Consequently I gave him no actual tuition but merely conversed with him, and watched him with silent astonishment."

At the age of eleven, Franz was admitted to the Imperial-Royal

---

* The city was also the birthplace of Arnold Schoenberg, Anton Webern, and Alban Berg, the three leading protagonists of what we now know as the Second Viennese School, but those births took place only in the latter decades of the nineteenth century.

Chapel as a choirboy; the Chapel was part of the Imperial-Royal City Boarding School, and for the following five years Franz's general and musical education continued under what were excellent conditions for a boy of his meager economic means—especially since his room and board, however austere, were covered by the Crown. Among his many instructors, the best known was none other than Antonio Salieri, whose name was linked with Mozart and Beethoven as well.* But at sixteen, Schubert turned down another scholarship in order to devote himself to composing music.

The path he chose was a difficult one, and so it would remain for the rest of his life. It was one thing for the adult Mozart, a former child prodigy, to become a freelance musician when his name was already known throughout Western Europe, or for Beethoven to opt for a similar course in his twenties, when he could rely on his abilities as a keyboard virtuoso to help support himself. It was quite another thing for a poor boy in his mid-teens to feel sure enough of his talents to renounce a guarantee of sustenance from the imperial government, at least for a few more years, and to focus instead on developing his skills as he himself saw fit. Under pressure from his family, he trained as a teacher and then took a job as an assistant schoolmaster, but he simultaneously applied himself with great diligence to his craft. Between his sixteenth and seventeenth birthdays he composed about sixty items, including numerous lieder—the genre in which he would become the most celebrated master—as well as various piano pieces and liturgical settings, three string quartets, a wind octet, and his First Symphony. The following year, 1814, was somewhat less productive quantitatively, but in 1815

---

* In the 1780s, Salieri (1750–1825) had succeeded Gluck as the Hapsburgs' imperial music director and had been Mozart's rival at court; in the 1790s, he had probably been one of Beethoven's teachers; in the 1810s, Schubert studied under him; and in the 1820s, Salieri, by then in his seventies, would give lessons in composition to a child prodigy named Franz Liszt. Thus his name is associated with famous musicians who lived over a stretch of one hundred seventy-two years, from the birth of Gluck (1714) to the death of Liszt (1886).

he composed over two hundred pieces, or parts or sketches of pieces, and the flow of music continued through the following years.

Although Schubert would struggle throughout his adult life to receive recognition from Vienna's musical establishment, he did enjoy the attention and admiration of many friends and supporters for his prodigious accomplishments, and eventually a number of artists, writers, and musicians would gather in the evening at the home of one or another of them for private performances of some of the young man's latest compositions. Many of these soirees, which they called Schubertiades, were held at the home of the young composer's lifelong friend and sometime financial supporter Joseph von Spaun. At these gatherings Schubert was often merry and loquacious, but at other times he could be withdrawn. Short, chubby, nearsighted, bespectacled, but with an open, naïve-looking face, he was teased and treasured by friends and family alike. One friend—the previously mentioned Johann Mayrhofer—described Schubert's character as "a mixture of tenderness and coarseness, sensuality and candor, sociability and melancholy."[2]

The melancholy, perhaps even depressive, facet of his nature increased in his mid-twenties, and with good cause. First, there was the general, repressive, post-revolutionary Metternichian political situation. Schubert himself was arrested in 1820, at the age of twenty-three, on the charge of having insulted the police. But the underlying reason for his arrest was his friendship with an ex-schoolmate, the politically suspect poet Johann Senn, who was apprehended at the same time, imprisoned, subsequently exiled, and forbidden ever to return to Vienna; he and Schubert never met again. Schubert is not known to have been jailed or otherwise punished by the police, but he must have been mightily frightened by the episode.

And then there was the shattering personal course of Schubert's life. By 1823, when he was twenty-six, he had contracted syphilis, for which there was no effective cure at the time, and he was often seriously ill with the disease. During one long bout, in May of that year, he wrote verses that seem to express his state of mind at the time; translated into prose, the lines read: "Behold, vast, unprecedented grief, my life's tormented path lies annihilated in the dust, nearing eternal demise. Kill it and kill myself, plunge everything into Lethe, and then, o Great One, let a pure, strong being flourish."* And three months later, in a letter to a friend, he commented, more matter-of-factly: "Whether I shall ever again be completely healthy I rather doubt."[3] The illness frequently caused him to withdraw from the company of friends—company he had always enjoyed; even Beethoven's nephew, Karl, wrote, in one of the notebooks that he used for communicating with his deaf uncle: "People praise Schubert a lot, but they say that he should hide himself away."[4]

In short, Schubert in his mid-twenties was aware that what Vladimir Nabokov, in another century, would call the "brief crack of light between the two eternities of darkness" would probably not illuminate him much longer. And yet his anguish was probably not so much an abstract fear of death as an immediate horror of dying before he could reach his zenith as a creator of music. In the previous chapter, we observed Beethoven, at the age of thirty-one, declaring that although his increasing deafness had brought him to the verge of suicide, "it seemed to me impossible to leave the world before I had brought forth all that I felt destined to bring forth, and so I muddled on with this wretched life." Schubert, too, felt destined to bring forth great music, but he was constantly aware of the extreme fragility of his own life; at times he wished that his suffering would simply end forever. On March 31, 1824, during another severe bout of illness, he wrote to his friend Leopold Kupelweiser.

---

* "Sieh, vernichtet liegt im Staube / Unerhörtem Gram zum Raube, / Meines Lebens Martergang / Nahend ew'gen Untergang. / Tödt' es und mich selber töte, / Stürz' nun Alles in die Lethe, / Und ein reines kräft'ges Sein / Lass', o Grosser, dann gedeih'n."

I feel that I am the unhappiest, most wretched man in the world. Think
of a man whose health will never again be right, and who, out of despair
over it always makes the thing worse instead of better; think of a man,
I say, whose most brilliant hopes have become nil, for whom the happiness of love and friendship offers nothing but pain at best, for whom
enthusiasm (at least the inspiring sort) for the Beautiful threatens to
dwindle away; and I ask you whether this isn't a wretched, unhappy
man?—"My heart is heavy, my peace is gone, I shall never, ever find it
again,"* I can surely sing this every day now, for every night when I go
to bed I hope that I'll never wake up, and every morning only tells me
of yesterday's grief.[5]

Yet during the same month in which he wrote this terrible confession to his friend, Schubert noted in a private diary: "Pain sharpens the
mind and strengthens the disposition; on the contrary, joy seldom troubles itself over the former and makes the latter softer or frivolous." In
other words, he was determined to take advantage of his suffering and
to use it for creative purposes. In a poem written the following September, he apostrophized: "To thee alone, o sacred Art, is it still given to
portray those times of strength and action, to ease a little the great pain
that can never reconcile [Art] with Destiny."[†]

A COUPLE OF ASIDES ARE NEEDED at this point—one on the question of Schubert's attitude toward religion, the other about his sexuality. Several Schubert specialists have described him as an agnostic,

---

* The quotation, slightly turned around, is from Goethe's *Faust*: "Meine Ruh' ist hin, /
mein Herz ist schwer, / ich finde sie nimmer / und nimmermehr." Schubert had set those
words to music in his song "Gretchen am Spinnrade."
† "Nur dir, o heil'ge Kunst, ist's noch gegönnt / Im Bild, die Zeit der Kraft u. That zu schil-
dern, / Um weniges den grossen Schmerz zu mildern, / Der nimmer mit dem Schicksal
sie versöhnt."

and we can be fairly certain that he did not regularly practice either Roman Catholicism, the state religion of the Austrian Empire and the religion in which he was brought up, or any other -ism. This did not preclude his writing a great deal of Catholic liturgical music—much of it extraordinarily beautiful—on commission or in the hope of receiving a *post facto* commission—but it is noteworthy that in some of his settings of the mass he excised, from the Credo, the words "Et unam sanctam catholicam et apostolicam Ecclesiam" (And one holy catholic [i.e., universal] and apostolic Church), as well as, in some cases, "Et exspecto resurrectionem mortuorum" (And I await the resurrection of the dead).

From what I have gleaned from Schubert's relatively sparse writings and from writings about him, I would describe him as a Goethean freethinker who believed in the fundamental moral principles enunciated by Christ, according to the Gospels, without believing in any of the dogmas offered by specific Christian doctrines—doctrines that Goethe had described as a "hodgepodge of error and violence."* Some of Schubert's statements, however, could lead one to surmise that he was a theist who considered divine intervention in human affairs, and perhaps even some form of life after death, as possibilities, if by no means certainties. But we do not know for sure.

The question of Schubert's sexual orientation has vexed a number of late twentieth- and early twenty-first-century musicologists. We know that Schubert was attracted to quite a few girls and women and that in his youth he had been deeply in love with and had proposed marriage to one of them—Therese Grob, a neighbor and friend. She had accepted his proposal, but her parents had forbidden the marriage on the grounds that her would-be fiancé could not support her—or himself, for that

---

* "Ein Mischmasch von Irrtum und Gewalt," in "Zahme Xenien" IX, *Goethes Gedichte in Zeitlicher Folge* (Berlin: Insel Verlag, 1982).

matter. But some researchers have theorized that Schubert was also attracted to men, that he may have had homosexual relationships, and that circumstantial evidence pointing in that direction can be found in letters and elsewhere. Happily, in today's arts world few people care much whether their colleagues are hetero-, homo-, bi-, or even asexual, but in Schubert's day homosexuality would have been something to keep hidden, and it could have created profound feelings of guilt or even self-loathing—feelings that could then have influenced his work as an artist. Schubert scholars John M. Gingerich and Christopher Gibbs have stressed the impossibility of providing an answer to this question based on the evidence currently available; all in all, we know even less about Schubert's sexuality than we know about his religious beliefs.[*]

DESPITE THE PHYSICAL AND EXISTENTIAL sufferings that afflicted Schubert in 1824, he managed, before the year was over, to create his exuberant Octet for winds and strings and the great string quartets in A minor ("Rosamunde") and D minor ("Death and the Maiden"), among much else. He intended to compose a third quartet, too, and the work that would become the String Quartet in G major, D. 887,[†] may already

---

[*] For those interested in a thorough investigation of both subjects, I recommend John M. Gingerich's excellent essay, "'Those of us who found our life in art': The Second Generation Romanticism of the Schubert-Schober Circle, 1820–1825," which occupies pp. 67–113 in the important volume *Franz Schubert and his World*, edited by Christopher H. Gibbs and Morton Solvik and published (in conjunction with the Bard College Music Festival) by Princeton University Press in 2014.

[†] This and other "D." numbers refer to the chronological list of Schubert's works prepared by the Viennese musicologist Otto Erich Deutsch (1883–1967), to whom all modern students of Schubert's life and work owe their gratitude, and whose own life story was dramatic. In 1938, Deutsch—a Jew and a widower with two young children—had to flee Nazi Austria. His son did not escape but managed to survive; his fourteen-year-old daughter, Gitta, escaped to England thanks to the *Kindertransport*; and Deutsch himself likewise ended up in wartime England, where he continued his work, at Cambridge. Father and daughter both returned to Vienna in the 1950s; he produced a revised version

have begun to take shape in his mind. Not until 1826, however, did he get around to setting down on paper what would remain his last—and greatest, in my opinion—work in the genre. And once he had taken up his pen, he quickly set down the entire, vast, four-movement G major Quartet: the first page of the manuscript bears the date June 20; the last page, June 30.

At the time, Schubert was staying in the suburb of Währing (now part of the city of Vienna) with his friend Franz von Schober and Schober's mother, because he could not afford to live on his own. Two months earlier, he had applied to the imperial court for the position of deputy court music director, but the request was still pending during the summer of 1826 and was eventually turned down. Likewise, Schubert's plan to write an opera based on a libretto that his friend Bauernfeld had prepared for him came to naught because the imperial censors had balked at the plot, which included a bigamous marriage. Bauernfeld invited him to spend part of the summer at a resort in Upper Austria, but Schubert wrote to him, on July 10: "I can't possibly go to Gmunden or anywhere else, I have no money at all, and things are generally going very badly for me. [But] it doesn't bother me, and I'm cheerful."[6] Perhaps he was continuing to go over the new quartet, since the manuscript shows many changes and insertions: the fact that he was working on something he loved might have made him cheerful, even though that adjective cannot properly be applied to the quartet itself. Some of the alterations to the score may have been made much later, around the time when Schubert offered it, along with the "Death and the Maiden" Quartet and various other works, to the Mainz-based publishing firm of B. Schott's Sons. Schott, however, in replying to Schubert, did not even mention the two quartets

---

of his Schubert catalogue; she became a well-known translator and was the life partner of the Austrian naturalist Engelbert Broda, who had also fled to England in 1938.

According to John Reed, one of Schubert's biographers, the G major Quartet "has been comparatively slow to establish itself in the affections of the general public, perhaps because it lacks those metaphorical associations which contribute to the popularity of its two great predecessors. The A minor ['Rosamunde'] Quartet is 'about' disenchantment, and the loss of innocence. The D minor ['Death and the Maiden'] Quartet is 'about' death. But what is the G major Quartet about?"[7]

I propose the hypothesis that the G major Quartet is "about" nothing. Or rather, it is "about" trying to accept the nothingness of death—a concept that Schubert stares down here, with some fear but also with remarkable honesty. The work can feel loose-limbed and loquacious: its first movement alone may last twenty minutes or more, if the repeat of the exposition is observed and the tempi chosen by the players are on the slow side, and a complete performance of the entire quartet takes at least three-quarters of an hour. Yet the whole work communicates intense, concentrated drama, virtually nonstop.

Had Schott or another publisher undertaken to bring out an edition of the quartet within Schubert's lifetime, the composer would almost certainly have provided a fair copy of his manuscript, with changes that would probably have included further refinements. But it was not published until twenty-three years after Schubert's death, and music editors from that day to ours have had to deal with the messy "working" manuscript. Although the basic text is clear, one can't help wondering whether Schubert might not have intended to give performers a little more help, especially with tempo indications in the first movement.

The opening fourteen bars of that movement, which is in 3/4 time, constitute a sort of introduction—an introduction that is a mixture of terrifying despair and blood-chilling dread. Until Schubert wrote this quartet, he had never used the key of G major for any large-scale instrumental work, and before any performance of the first movement is more than five or six seconds old, attentive listeners may legitimately wonder whether that tonality is going to hold. Musicians know that the third note of the traditional Western diatonic scale is the main element in establishing in a listener's ears whether a piece is in a major or a minor key—and this is true even for lay listeners who may not know what the terms "major" and "minor" mean in a musical context: the difference is heard, felt, experienced. In this quartet's opening bars, we hear B, the third note of the G major scale, immediately lowered to B-flat, the third note of the G minor scale, and we are disoriented, exactly as Schubert wished: that first chord begins as a faint glimmer of light in G major but immediately crescendoes into a shattering explosion of darkness in G minor. The aggression continues for two more bars but is followed, barely more than a second later, by a sad whimper, still in G minor. And the pattern immediately repeats itself, this time in D major and D minor.

Schubert is telling us something, but what is he saying? What are we to make of those devastating first four bars, which lead not only from major into minor but also from vagueness into violence, or of the subsequent modest little chords, which seem to apologize for the initial outburst? Are we observing someone waking up suddenly from a horrendous nightmare—a nightmare of hopelessness, of gazing into the maw of approaching death and trying to assimilate the image? These questions are, of course, unanswerable. And, in any case, the introductory bars, which last only about half a minute and resemble nothing else in the quartet literature, are followed by a modest glimmer of hopefulness, or perhaps even a smidgen of resistance, in what appears to be the first part of the main theme, which establishes itself *almost* solidly in G major.

What the basic tempo of this noble theme ought to be, however, is a thorny issue, and the issue becomes even thornier if performers ask themselves—as they should—whether they ought or ought not to attempt to integrate this theme's basic tempo with that of the preceding introduction and the succeeding second theme. These and related questions make this movement one of the most difficult pieces in the entire eighteenth- and nineteenth-century string quartet repertoire—not technically (although it is by no means easy in that area either), but interpretively. Throughout the movement, the level of emotional intensity fluctuates every few seconds, and the music seems to demand tempo flexibility—but to what degree? Schubert gives no verbal assistance: his tempo indication, *Allegro molto moderato*—very moderately fast—is maddeningly ambiguous, and he alters it only once, minimally, during the movement's entire four hundred forty-four bars (not counting the one hundred seventy-one-bar repeat of the exposition). That one small change is a *stringendo*—quickening—indication toward the end of the development section, and even there Schubert failed to mark the point at which he wanted the previous tempo to be resumed, although the character of the music itself makes the approximate return point clear.

The result of this ambiguity is a wider than usual variety of approaches and solutions to the tempo question on the part of performing ensembles. In a classic 1938 recording by the esteemed Busch Quartet, the tempo of the introductory bars hovers around one hundred quarter-note beats per minute on the metronome; the main theme begins much slower, at about eighty, but sometimes rushes back up to one hundred; and the second theme stays mainly in the nineties. Tempi are generally slower, sometimes considerably so, in the Belcea Quartet's 2009 recording: the introductory bars are played at about eighty quarter-note beats per minute; the main theme is sometimes as slow as sixty-six and at other times well into the nineties; and the second theme is usually in the eighties. Of the recordings with which I am familiar, only the Hungarian Quartet's 1968 recording, which to my ears sounds somewhat perfunctory, and the Emerson String Quartet's much more effective 1988 version, stay within more restricted tempo ranges—the former, from the low nineties to under one hundred ten; the latter, from the low eighties to the mid-nineties.

I have used the word "noble" to describe the first part of the main theme, but "questing" may be a better adjective. Or, better yet, "questing plus questioning"—because there is something hesitant, tentative, insecure, full of wonderment yet simultaneously full of fear within this segment, which consists of thirty-five or forty seconds of tremolos—tremulous, quickly repeating notes. The tremolos are played initially by the second violin, viola, and cello while the first violin hovers above them with a quietly intense melodic line, and then by the two violins and viola while the cello digs deeper and deeper into a similar line, all the way down to its lowest note, as much as three-and-a-half octaves below the first violin's preceding phrases. Schubert's only dynamic indication for this entire, eighteen-bar stretch is *pianissimo*, but he begins the following segment with a sudden *fortissimo*. And—surprise!—we discover that the second part of the main theme is actually a variant of the movement's very first, introductory bars.[*] So: should we continue to think of those introductory bars as a separate statement, or should we consider them to be the first part of the main theme? Or both?

In the end, these questions are nothing but brainteasers for those of us who spend a lot of time analyzing musical compositions. What counts most for lay listeners—and what should count most for professionals, too—is the dramatic effect made by the return of those powerful introductory chord-patterns, especially when we realize, or at least sense, that the rhythmic kernels of both of the theme's basic motifs are closely intertwined. This dramatic portion of the main theme holds the listener in its

---

[*] Those interested in a much more detailed, technical analysis of this movement, especially as regards Schubert's use of thematic variation within sonata form, should read Carl Dahlhaus's essay "Sonata Form in Schubert: The First Movement of the G-Major String Quartet, Op. 161 (D. 887)" (translated from the German by Thilo Reinhard), in Walter Frisch, ed., *Schubert: Critical and Analytical Studies* (Lincoln and London: University of Nebraska Press, 1987), pp. 1–12.

grip for the better part of a minute; there is much anguish in it, but also a subsequent, short-lived sense of triumph over the anguish. (Some readers may recall that the introductory bars and first theme of this movement were used by Woody Allen in his 1989 film *Crimes and Misdemeanors*. The material is used twice—just before and soon after the murder of Dolores Paley, played by Anjelica Huston.) Schubert then brings the whole theme to a close with a *fortissimo* chord in F-sharp major. Musical conservatives of his day would have prescribed a chord nearer to G major—D major, for instance—as a lead-in to the second theme, but Schubert plays a neat trick at this point: using a deft harmonic sleight-of-hand, he manages to begin his second theme immediately in D major, just as the textbooks of the day would have prescribed, and with a complete change in emotional tone, at least for the time being. This is because the second theme starts off, *pianissimo*, as a lilting, slightly melancholy ländler—an Austrian and south German dance in 3/4 time that was among the immediate ancestors of the waltz. We seem to have moved far away from the high intensity of the first theme.

This assumption proves to be false. The new theme undergoes multiple transformations, often with the first violin playing a lighthearted, folklike descant of sixteenth-note triplets over the melodic line, but at other times with violent, military-sounding chords, also made up of sixteenth-note triplets, fired off by the second violin and viola or by the first violin and cello. Sometimes the cello plays the melodic line gently while the other instruments punctuate with even gentler pizzicato notes, like a guitar accompaniment for a serenading baritone. But the love song never lasts long: *Sturm und Drang*—storm and stress—always intervene. Second themes are often referred to as "subordinate" themes, but that is certainly not the case in this movement: the first theme is forty-seven bars long; the second is one hundred three bars long and runs all the way to the end of the exposition. The subordinate has become the commanding officer.

A lot more *Sturm und Drang* await us in the substantial development section, which, as is normal, makes use of and transforms the
melodic, harmonic, and rhythmic elements of the exposition—the two
contrasting principal motifs of the first theme and the multiple variet-
ies of the second. But the great surprise comes at the very beginning of
the recapitulation, when the sonic and emotional characteristics of the
introduction—those first, hyper-dramatic fourteen bars with which the
movement began—are reversed. Instead of a faint glimmer of light in
G major crescendoing into a shattering explosion in G minor (followed
by a repetition in D major/D minor), we hear a faint glimmer of darkness in G minor, played by the second violin and viola, leading into a
sweet resolution in G major, capped by tender pizzicati from the first
violin and cello (with a repetition in D minor/D major). And for most
of the rest of the movement, Schubert seems almost to be assuming an
attitude that later generations of Europeans came to associate specifically with his native city: Ach, all that high drama—what does it matter? Things will either work out or they won't, so why worry?* After the
parallel passage to the movement's introductory bars, the first violin,
in its middle register, seems to improvise an embellished version of the
first theme's main motif while the rest of the instruments provide a gentle accompaniment—like a mezzo-soprano embellishing the melodic
line in the repeating passages of "Una voce poco fa" in Rossini's *Barber
of Seville*, which was immensely popular in Vienna in Schubert's day.
Even as the drama builds up, during the lead-in to the second theme,
the original anguish is mitigated by a softening of the harmonics. And
within the second theme itself, passages that were at first violently martial now have the joyful aspect of a parade by tin soldiers who will never
go to war.

----

* "Glücklich ist, wer vergisst, was doch nicht zu ändern ist" (Happy is the person who
forgets what can't be changed anyway), sing some of the principal characters in the most
Viennese of all operettas, Johann Strauss II's *Die Fledermaus* (1874).

Schubert, like Beethoven, loved extended codas that turned into second development sections, but in this case he wrote a conclusion that lasts less than a minute—a conclusion in which the recollection of the darkest moments of the piece's opening are repeatedly beaten back by joyous, triumphant chords in G major. The shadows have been thrust into the background—at least for a while.

"FOR A WHILE" IS A GOOD TERM to use also in stating that the quartet's second movement is in E minor, because Schubert is constantly weaving in and out of his basic key—sometimes subtly, sometimes startlingly. The tempo indication—*Andante un poco mosso*—although not quite as ambiguous as the *Allegro molto moderato* marking for the first movement, isn't much of a help, either. *Andante un poco mosso* could be translated as (believe it or not) "moving along with a little motion," by which Schubert presumably meant a little faster than a regular *andante*. Some ensembles intentionally or unintentionally ignore the *alla breve* (2/2) time signature and play the movement as if it were a slowish *andante* in 4/4 rather than 2/2 time; others move the tempo forward a little more expeditiously. If I could suddenly play one of the instruments that make up a string quartet, I would try to persuade my three colleagues to take a tempo at about half note = 60—a little faster than the tempo that most groups adopt, but the same sort of "natural" pace that works for each half-bar of the *Andante con moto* second movement of Schubert's "Great C Major" Symphony. Otherwise, the gentle opening theme can become somewhat stretched out, even maudlin. The half note = 60 tempo works, with only subtle modifications, for the entire movement.

The movement begins with two mysterious, curiosity-provoking introductory bars that lead directly into the main theme (in an extended three-part form), which is stated by the cello in its middle-high register, accompanied by the other three instruments. The lovely, somewhat somber, mildly melancholy melody is simple, folk-tune-like—highly original but not shocking. But then, after three bars of even simpler transitional unison notes and chords, we find ourselves in a nightmarish horror scene, complete with shrieks from the first violin and fearful trembling from all four instruments, first in G minor, then in harmonically distant F-sharp minor. More unison notes and chords bring us back to the main theme, stated this time in B minor. Now, however, the somber, mildly melancholy melody feels a little more threatening—and sure enough, the nightmare returns, this time in D minor. It is followed by a final, extended reprise of the main theme—an embellished reiteration that sometimes feels unconvincingly reassuring; at other times the subtly menacing quality dominates, as if to warn us that the nightmare could come back. But it does not come back, and the movement's coda ends with four unconvincingly prettified E major bars. What could be coming next?

As it happens, the third movement is a scherzo of Mendelssohnian fleetness, although Schubert in 1826 would probably not have heard of Felix Mendelssohn, a seventeen-year-old who lived in distant Berlin. (The prodigious Mendelssohn had already composed his brilliant Octet for strings, which contains a dazzling scherzo movement, as well as the equally impressive Overture to *A Midsummer Night's Dream*, but neither of these works had been published or performed in public.) The main body of Schubert's scherzo is in B minor and 3/4 time, with the very definite tempo marking *Allegro vivace*, which means that it is to go very fast indeed; most ensembles adopt a metronome speed of roughly one bar = 100. Nervously dramatic segments, with lightning-like flashes, alternate frequently with more cheerful moments. The trio section (G major) remains in 3/4 time but is marked *Allegretto*, thus it is clearly meant to be paced several notches slower than the scherzo itself. Just how slow, however, is open to question: like the second theme of the first movement, the trio's theme is, in essence, a gentle ländler, but it ought to be taken somewhat faster than the first movement's ländler—otherwise the melody becomes too inflated for its own good. Some ensembles milk every bar for emotional effect, as if to tell listeners, "Poor Schubert—he never wrote another quartet after this one! He died so young!" But poor Schubert didn't know, at the time, that he would never write another quartet, and the lovely, gentle little tune that he provided for this trio suffers from hyperbolic interpretations.

The trio is followed by a reprise of the scherzo proper, and the movement ends forcefully. The quartet's members, who have been playing for thirty-five or forty minutes, are now faced with a more than ten-minute-long, eight hundred fifty–bar (if the repeats are observed) marathon of a finale—a tarantella-like *Allegro assai* (very fast) movement in 6/8 time, with frequent, sudden changes in rhythm, dynamics, and overall expressive character. Thus, in addition to its musical problems, this movement presents challenges of sheer physical endurance to all four musicians. And there are psychological challenges, too, because the entire finale is an emotional roller-coaster ride. Within the piece's first four seconds, performers and listeners alike are confronted with the same major-minor quandary that greeted them at the beginning of the first movement, but with the action sped up so that the sound-images flash by almost faster than the ear can comprehend. The first movement opened with a G major chord that transformed itself into G minor; now, it's the other way around: the first half of that four-second-long opening is in G minor, the second half in G major. Declaration and response, declaration and response, declaration and response—this bifurcation dominates the entire movement, sometimes rapidly, as in these first instants, and sometimes with more extended passages in either major or minor. Nominally, the movement is in G major—the key signature, a single F-sharp, never varies—but in reality we bounce back and forth between major and minor, from the start almost to the finish.

This schizophrenic movement verges at times on complete madness—and, like the opening of the first movement, it is unlike anything else in the repertoire. The basic motivic and thematic elements are simple, but they constantly dissolve and recompose themselves at a tremendous speed. There are many brief, lighthearted interstices to keep us wondering whether, after all, Schubert meant this finale to be *allegro* in the literal, cheerful sense of the word, but strident, frantic, disoriented and disorienting passages constantly interrupt the pleasantries. Twice in the course of the movement the onward rush is stopped by firm, steady passages that Schubert marked *ben marcato* (well emphasized), but at the end of each of these roughly twenty-second-long interludes the crazed, headlong charge resumes.

In the chapter on Mozart, I referred to that composer's unparalleled mastery of musical chiaroscuro—his extraordinary ability to combine and counterbalance light and darkness within the briefest time spans. One might describe Schubert's major-minor ricocheting in this finale as another example of chiaroscuro—major being the light, minor the darkness. But Mozartean chiaroscuro, no matter how intensely dramatic it may be, is always beautifully balanced—Apollonian, one might say—whereas Schubert's back-and-forth in this movement explodes into Dionysian wildness. Or neurosis, as Sigmund Freud might have said two or three generations later. Only during the last half-minute does the piece find itself solidly in G major, with a pleasant smile painted onto its face. Given the frenzy of the previous ten minutes, the smile seems false, out of place, wrong—which, I choose to believe, is precisely what Schubert wanted. It's true that as I write these words I am two and a half times as old as Schubert was when he wrote this String Quartet in G major, and that I may well be superimposing my septuagenarian mind-set onto his youthful, albeit much tormented, one. On the other hand, all of us superimpose our mind-sets, our individual essences, onto every piece of music that we listen to.

———————

SCHUBERT'S LAST THREE STRING QUARTETS were written during the same years in which Beethoven was completing what would prove to be his final masterpieces: the *Missa Solemnis*, Ninth Symphony, and, above all, last five string quartets. Schubert was in awe of Beethoven, yet he did not try to emulate, much less to continue, what Beethoven had achieved, especially in the quartet repertoire. As for Schubert's G major Quartet, I take issue with the claim of the groundbreaking Schubert scholar Maurice J. E. Brown that although there are "isolated moments" in this work that are "of greater value than the corresponding ones in the D minor ['Death and the Maiden'] Quartet," the G major is not, "as a whole, so sustainedly great."[8] That the D minor Quartet is more immediately attractive than the G major is undeniable: the G major is more elusive, more complex, and on a first or casual hearing it can seem long-winded. As a matter of fact, it *is* long-winded. But it also seems to emerge from a deeper source within Schubert's subconscious and to point toward virgin territory that he would not live to explore, unfortunately for him and for us.

SCHUBERT, AS WE HAVE ALREADY OBSERVED, was among the torch-bearers at Beethoven's funeral, on March 29, 1827. After the burial, he and two acquaintances—the aspiring young composers Franz Lachner (who made a cameo appearance in the previous chapter) and Benedict Randhartinger—made their way to a tavern and ordered wine. Schubert proposed a toast: "To the memory of our immortal Beethoven!" The three musicians drank to the master. Then Schubert refilled the glasses and said, "This one is for the one of us three who will be the first to follow Beethoven!"[9]

Lachner became a famous composer and conductor in his day and lived to be nearly eighty-seven; Randhartinger, known in his time as a composer, conductor, and singer, survived to the even more extraordinary age, for the time, of ninety-one. Both lived into the 1890s, thus outlasting Schubert by more than six decades. Schubert, however, was not only the first of the three to follow Beethoven to the grave but also the first (and only) one of them to achieve ever-growing musical fame and admiration. Just a little over a year and a half of life remained to him after Beethoven's funeral: he died on November 19, 1828, two months and twelve days short of his thirty-second birthday. His death was officially attributed to typhoid fever, but other causes, including tertiary syphilis, have been hypothesized.

Most of Schubert's works remained little known or entirely undiscovered until years or even decades after his death, which is one of the reasons why the poet Franz Grillparzer, who had known him, provided a somewhat ambiguous epitaph for the composer's grave: "The art of music buried here a rich possession, but also far more beautiful hopes."* Like Schubert's other acquaintances, and even the composer's intimate friends and family members, Grillparzer had no idea of the quantity and quality of the young man's achievements. Yes, had Schubert lived longer and maintained at least the delicate level of health that he had had in his last years, he would have developed in directions that we cannot imagine. But how could his subsequent works have been "more beautiful" than those he had already given the world?

Among the many compositions that remained unpublished and unperformed at the time of Schubert's death, a particularly significant one was his final symphony—the "Great C Major." Ten years later, in 1838, a twenty-eight-year-old Saxon musician visited Schubert's brother Ferdinand in Vienna and asked to see some of Franz's manuscripts. When he came upon and read through the score of the symphony, he

---

* "Die Tonkunst begrub hier einen reichen Besitz aber noch viel schönere Hoffnungen."

could hardly believe what he held in his hands. He persuaded Ferdinand to allow him to have it copied, and he sent the copy to Mendelssohn, who conducted the work for the first time with the Gewandhaus Orchestra in Leipzig on March 21, 1839. In describing the symphony, the Saxon musician wrote that it "reveals something more than mere fine melody, mere ordinary joy and sorrow . . . it leads us into a region we never before explored. . . . Here we find, besides masterly musical composition, life in every vein, coloring down to the finest grade of possibility, sharp expression in detail, meaning throughout . . . while over the whole is thrown that glow of Romanticism that everywhere accompanies Franz Schubert."[10]

Schubert was beginning, at last, to be understood. And the young Saxon—one of the first musicians to recognize the greatness of Schubert's achievement and the terrible loss that his early death had brought to the world of music—was Robert Schumann.

4

IN THE WONDROUSLY DISTURBING MONTH OF MAY

Robert Schumann: *Dichterliebe* (Poet's Love), Op. 48 (1840)

THE GERMAN WORD *Schadenfreude*—a combination of *Schaden* (misfortunes) and *Freude* (joy)—is usually translated as "malicious glee" or "gloating." It communicates the notion of taking pleasure in the misfortunes of others. But among artists, misfortune sometimes provides a stimulus to creativity; in such cases, *Schadenfreude* could be translated more literally as "joy in misfortune"—an artist's own misfortune. There are those for whom instability is a precondition for productivity, and in such cases a degree of misfortune can function as a basic work-tool.

Robert Schumann lived most of his life in alternating states of instability—financial, professional, physical, or mental instability—and those states fed and stoked his imagination through most of his lifetime. For instance: when Schumann was in his late twenties, trying to establish himself as a composer, the father of the young woman he was aiming to marry engaged in a lengthy legal battle against his own daughter and Schumann to prevent the marriage. (She was under twenty-one and required parental consent.) During the same period, Schumann's mother and older brother died, and the family's financial situation was imperiled. Yet these crises seem to have ignited in the young composer a burst of creative energy that produced a number of extraordinary works for the piano as well as an outpouring of lieder that comprised several enduring masterpieces in the genre. *Schadenfreude* indeed!

The opening line of one of those lyric masterpieces—*Dichterliebe* (Poet's Love), a cycle of sixteen lieder—translates as "In the wondrously beautiful month of May," a phrase that goes a long way toward characterizing Schumann's entire compositional output. Even in its darkest moments, his work displays a fresh, youthful, springlike quality, a quality that is entirely his. Compare his music, for instance, with that of Mozart or Schubert: both composers died young, but I don't hear youthfulness or any other specific age-related characteristic in their music. They seem to have been born all-knowing, like the veiled woman portrayed in Raphael's *La velata*. She, too, is very young, but her eyes reveal that she is complete, of no age and all ages. I hear this innate agelessness in the music of Mozart and Schubert, but not in Schumann's music. In nearly all of his major compositions and in many of the smaller ones as well, he communicates a new beginning, a curiosity, a need to try something different, notwithstanding his psychological upheavals and the encroaching darkness that would afflict his later life. As a result, when we listen to Schumann, we almost always seem to be in the month of May, but the undercurrent of instability in his music makes his May a wondrously disturbing one.

DICHTER—THE GERMAN WORD FOR POET—probably derives from the Latin *dicere*: to say, to tell, to speak. Beethoven had described himself as a *Tondichter*—a tone-poet, a speaker in musical sounds—and the Romantic-era composers who followed him held onto the notion that through music they were speaking directly to listeners' minds and hearts and creating poetic speech in music. Schumann certainly thought in those terms, as is clear from the title that he gave to the last piece in his piano suite *Kinderszenen* (Scenes from Childhood), which he composed two years before *Dichterliebe*; it's called "Der Dichter spricht" (The Poet Speaks)—he himself being the poet, of course. And in Schumann's case, the title of poet is doubly appropriate, because his passion for literature was as strong as his immersion in music, especially in his early years.

Robert Alexander Schumann was born on June 8, 1810 in the town of Zwickau in the Kingdom of Saxony, in eastern Germany, during the reign of King Frederick Augustus I. (Saxony was then part of the German Confederation, Metternich's brainchild, but Germany, as a unified political entity, did not come into existence within Schumann's lifetime.) Robert was the youngest of the five children of August Schumann, who owned and ran a small publishing firm, and Johanna, *née* Schnabel, a surgeon's daughter. The family was not wealthy, but it fitted squarely into Central Europe's rapidly expanding, moderately comfortable bourgeoisie. The Schumanns, however, also had a history of mental and psychological disorders. Robert's only sister, Emilie, was mentally and emotionally handicapped; she died, possibly a suicide, when Robert was fifteen, and the event gave him an enduring and portentous fear of insanity. August Schumann, the paterfamilias, was also described as suffering from "nervous disorders," although his ailments evidently were not serious enough to impede him from achieving success in his work or from taking a lively interest in his children's education.

Robert, an intelligent boy, became reasonably adept at Greek, Latin, and French during his early school years, and he demonstrated a precocious interest in literature. Unlike Mozart, Beethoven, and Schubert, however, and unlike his near contemporaries Mendelssohn, Chopin, and Liszt, Schumann did not have parents who were capable of recognizing and fostering his musical talents. As a result, his initial education in that area was haphazard. He later envied the hothouse musical atmosphere in which Mendelssohn, for instance, had been raised: "If I had grown up in the same circumstances as he did, and been destined for music from childhood, I should now beat every one of you," he wrote, in his late twenties, to another musician. But he added, more philosophically, "Well, everyone's life has something peculiar about it, and I will not complain of mine."[1] He did begin to take piano lessons at about the age of seven, and by the time he reached his early teens he was dreaming up grandiose musical and literary compositions. He seems to have enjoyed playing the piano at musical evenings at Zwickau's lyceum, which he attended for eight years, starting at age ten, and, thanks to his friendship with a music-loving family, he familiarized himself with the music not only of Haydn, Mozart, and Beethoven but even of Schubert, who was by no means well known.

Robert was sixteen when his father died, leaving a will that stipulated that the boy was to attend university for at least two years, with an appropriate allowance, after he had left the lyceum. Had August Schumann lived a few years longer, he might well have encouraged his youngest son's hopes of pursuing a life in music or literature, or both, but after August's death Johanna Schumann insisted that her son opt for a more secure future by studying law. The boy duly spent a year at the University of Leipzig and another at Heidelberg, but he hardly ever attended lectures at either institution. Instead, he spent his time trying to write fiction in the style of the then-popular novelist Jean Paul (nom de plume of Johann Paul Richter) and improvising at the piano. More fatefully, he also began, during his Leipzig stay, to take piano lessons from Friedrich Wieck, a well-known pedagogue whose nine-year-old daughter, Clara, was already demonstrating prodigious keyboard talent. As Robert's piano-playing improved he became increasingly serious about both performing and composing, and in 1830 his mother allowed him a six-month break from his all-but-nonexistent legal studies in order to discover whether or not he had sufficient talent to become a professional musician. The reprieve became permanent, albeit with ongoing concern on the part of Johanna and her other sons, who ran the family's publishing business. Since Robert's regular allowance from home rarely covered his extra expenses, he often had to beg his mother and brothers for additional funds.

Many private music students lived at their masters' homes, paying for room and board, and Schumann, now in his early twenties, moved into the Wiecks' house in Leipzig. But lessons with Wieck himself proved to be irregular: the professor, eager to display Clara's prowess, took her on long, lucrative concert tours, during which she won the admiration of the likes of Paganini, Goethe, Mendelssohn, and Chopin. Robert turned to other musicians for lessons in music theory, but he was easily distracted, not only by his musical and literary fantasies but also by alcohol, tobacco, and sex—with a girl named Christel (whom he dubbed Charitas) but probably also with prostitutes from whom he contracted syphilis. Although he eventually mastered the elements of harmony and counterpoint, the loss of flexibility in at least two fingers of his right hand made him abandon the idea of becoming a concert pianist.* This handicap, however distressing, almost certainly provided an extra stimulus to his creative impulses.

Schumann began to compose and publish a series of imaginative piano miniatures, including the *Variations on the name "Abegg,"* Op. 1; *Papillons*, Op. 2; Toccata, Op. 7; and *Carnaval*, Op. 9, among other

---

* The debilitating condition may have been the result, in part, of mercury poisoning, since mercury was used in the treatment of venereal diseases. Other causes probably included over-practicing and the use of finger-strengthening mechanical devices that did more harm than good.

works—all completed between his twentieth and twenty-fifth birth-days. Many of these pieces originated in literary ideas or musings, or with symbolic names that he gave to himself and others. The most enduring of these invented characters were Florestan and Eusebius, who, he said, represented the two sides of his own nature: bold and impetuous (Florestan); sensitive and dreamy (Eusebius).

A growing awareness of some of the leading composers of his own generation—the aforementioned Mendelssohn but especially Chopin and, a little later, Berlioz—led Schumann to become the leading force in creating a music journal that would serve, on the one hand, as an alter-native to the somewhat staid and technical *Allgemeine musikalische Zei-tung* (General Musical Newspaper) and, on the other, as a taste-setter in opposition to the then-popular fixation on virtuoso performers, regard-less of the quality of the music they played. The publication, originally called the *Neue Leipziger Zeitschrift für Musik* (New Leipzig Journal for Music) but soon shortened to the *Neue Zeitschrift für Musik*, began publi-cation in 1834; Schumann was its editor from 1835 to 1843. His respon-sibilities with the *Zeitschrift* resulted in a number of advantages: they gave him a small income; forced him to clarify his thinking about the music and musicians of his day; brought his name before a wider public than had previously been the case; and distracted him from some of his numerous phobias, which included fear of cholera (a disease that fre-quently ravaged European cities), fear of tuberculosis (which claimed the lives of several of his family members and close friends), and, above all, fear of mental illness and suicide. This last fixation once became so acute that he moved his residence from an upper-story room to a ground-floor room, to avoid the temptation to jump from a window.

During the summer of 1834, when he was twenty-four, Schumann began courting Ernestine von Fricken, a seventeen-year-old girl who, like her suitor, had moved into the Wiecks' home in order to study with Friedrich Wieck. Ernestine was pretty, but Schumann's attraction to

her was not only physical: Captain Ignaz von Fricken, the man who presented himself as her father, was a wealthy, landowning baron and amateur musician, and Schumann, whose finances still depended largely
on his family's generosity, longed for economic stability. The attraction
was mutual, the relationship intensified through much of the following year, and Robert eventually gave Ernestine an engagement ring.
He also made her a character, "Estrella," in his piano suite *Carnaval*,
and he used a theme of the baron's invention as the basis for his magnificent Symphonic Etudes. But when he learned that the baron was
only Ernestine's godfather and that the girl was the illegitimate, dowry-
less daughter of the baron's sister and an unnamed father, he broke the
engagement. Later, he admitted his motive: had he married a woman of
no economic means he would have had to "work for my daily bread like
a craftsman."[2] The episode did not redound to his glory.

Exit Ernestine, enter Clara. At sixteen, Friedrich Wieck's daughter
was already one of the most celebrated pianists in Europe. Schumann,
at twenty-five, was more than half again her age, but she had been
fond of him since she was eleven, when he had first come to live in
her father's scandal-ridden home: Clara's mother, Marianne, *née* Trom-
litz, a singer, had long since abandoned and then divorced the severe
Wieck and had married her lover, and Wieck, out of spite, had brought
home a wife twenty years his junior. The young Schumann's arrival in
the Wieck household had been a boon to Clara and her two younger
brothers, whom he had entertained with stories and games. Perhaps
Clara saw Robert as the only steady figure (everything is relative!) in
her extraordinarily uncommon life; in any case, her affection for him
had grown during the five years of their acquaintanceship, and a deep
understanding had begun to blossom between them. Before the end of
1835—not more than two or three months after the breakup of Robert's
engagement to Ernestine—Robert and Clara were declaring their love
for each other and considered themselves betrothed.

When Friedrich Wieck grasped what was happening, he decided to put an immediate end to the relationship—and he had plenty of good reasons for his decision. He had observed Schumann closely for years, and what he saw was a young man who had destroyed his chances of becoming a performing pianist, whose compositions went largely unrecognized and earned him next to nothing, and who was still economically dependent on his family. Moreover, Schumann frequently overindulged in alcohol, had behaved abominably toward Wieck's pupil Ernestine, and was prone to stray with other women. Clara was not only Wieck's daughter: she was his protégée. He had invested years of his life in nurturing her talent and her career, and the investment was now paying enormous dividends for both of them. Was all of this hard work, with its resultant success, to be thrown away because of his daughter's infatuation with a ne'er-do-well—an intelligent, gifted, well-meaning ne'er-do-well, certainly, but a ne'er-do-well all the same? Wieck made up his mind to prevent any further contact between Clara and Robert.

For nearly five years thereafter, the two young musicians lived in an emotional limbo. There were periods in which Wieck's preventive measures worked and others in which they did not, and periods in which Robert was angry with or suspicious of Clara—usually unjustifiably—or vice versa—often justifiably. There was even a moment at which, under paternal pressure, Clara threatened to break off the engagement unless Robert could provide assurance of his ability to support her. Robert sometimes succumbed to the temptations of the flesh, possibly with his former lover "Charitas," and flirted with other young women, including two English girls—the nineteen-year-old soprano Clara Novello, who was the inspiration behind his *Novelletten* for the piano, and the eighteen-year-old pianist Anna Robena Laidlaw, for whom he wrote his *Fantasiestücke*, and who gave him a lock of her hair. Yet for the most part, Robert tried hard to demonstrate that he sincerely loved Clara; he also tried not to resent the obvious fact that her pianistic talents were held in much higher regard than his efforts as a composer. In Vienna in 1838, she was named a Royal and Imperial Chamber Virtuoso—the Austrian Empire's highest honor for a musician, rarely bestowed on a woman— which prompted Robert to seek a doctorate in philosophy from the University of Jena; the honor was eventually granted, but thanks more to his work for the *Neue Zeitschrift* than to his compositions. Yet his desire for the degree was not only a matter of male pride; it grew out of his wish to prove to Friedrich Wieck that he was worthy of Clara.

Wieck *père*, however, remained adamant and eventually initiated a lawsuit against both Clara and Robert. His demands became more and more irrational, his accusations increasingly offensive, and his behavior highly erratic. Clara would in any case have been free to marry Robert when she turned twenty-one, but had her father won the lawsuit he could have kept all of her previous earnings and possessions. Early in 1840 the legal tide began to turn against Wieck, and Robert's anticipation of marriage to Clara unlocked a specific vein in his creative nature that had previously been little tapped.

Throughout the years of waiting, Schumann had been writing works for the piano, including some of his finest masterpieces: *Davidsbündlertänze* (Dances of the League of David), *Fantasiestücke* (Fantasy Pieces), *Kinderszenen* (Scenes from Childhood), *Kreisleriana,* the great Fantasy in C major, *Arabeske, Humoreske, Nachtstücke* (Night Pieces), and *Faschingsschwank aus Wien* (Carnival Farce from Vienna). But now, beginning in February 1840, he began to write lieder, partly under the influence of Mendelssohn, with whom he had become friendly and who was himself engaged at the time in composing songs to texts by Goethe and Heine. By the end of the year, Schumann had written over one hundred forty lieder, including many of his, or anyone's, greatest works in the genre. For his biographers from the nineteenth century to the present, 1840 has been known as Schumann's "Year of Song."

EXQUISITE TRANSPARENCY and natural, unembarrassed intimacy: these are the primary qualities of nineteenth-century German lieder that people who love this special art form find most attractive. A lone singer, supported, usually, by a single instrument, stands before us (even if we are listening to a recording) and communicates the most intensely personal states of being, letting us in on emotions and thoughts that are usually kept hidden. Even for people who speak little or no German, or who think of German as an essentially guttural language, the musical and linguistic delicacy that take hold of us when we listen to lieder also pull us back into pre-Hitlerian, pre-Wilhelminian, pre-Bismarckian Germany.

"Until 1870, the Germans were thought of as a nation of spectacled professors, evolving everything out of their inner consciousness, and scarcely aware of the outer world," wrote Bertrand Russell in "An Outline of Intellectual Rubbish," an essay published in 1950, "but since 1870 this conception has had to be very sharply revised." Russell's sly intention was to demonstrate the absurdity of generalizations about nations, peoples, or just about anything else, but the example he used suits our present purposes beautifully. The luminous humanity of Goethe, the quasi-mystical melancholy and nostalgia of Joseph von Eichendorff, and the sometimes bitter lyricism of Heinrich Heine—in short, the characteristics of the Early and High Romantic German poets dear to the likes of Schubert, Schumann, and their contemporaries and successors—are located at an almost unimaginable remove from the stereotypical image of the militaristic, obedient-unto-death Teuton that became all too credible during the first half of the twentieth century.

Schumann never met Goethe or Eichendorff, but he did meet Heine in the spring of 1828, shortly before he turned eighteen. During a trip to Bavaria, and with the help of a letter of introduction from an acquaintance they had in common, he called on Heine in Munich, where the thirty-year-old poet was then unhappily employed in editing a political magazine—a position from which he would soon resign. Heine had already published a number of influential works, including the poem collections *Die Nordsee* (The North Sea) and *Buch der Lieder* (Book of Songs), in addition to prose volumes, notably *Die Harzreise* (Journey in the Harz Mountains), and Schumann, who already adored Heine's poetry, was delighted by their encounter. "Heine—witty conversation—ironic little man—charming mask," he noted in his diary on May 8. "Went with him to the Leuchtenberg Gallery," where they saw, among other things, the armchair that Bonaparte had used as First Consul and two of Antonio Canova's sculptures: the *Three Graces* ("not noble enough," Schumann commented superciliously), and the *Repentant Mary Magdalene* ("pretty").[3]

"I had imagined Heine to be sullen and misanthropic," he wrote to his mother, "but he was completely different from what I thought. He greeted me in a friendly manner and escorted me around Munich for several hours, not with a bitter ironical smile—but a lofty smile at the trivialities of life."[4] One can't help wondering whether Schumann mentioned to Heine that he was about to begin studying law, against all of his inclinations and instincts. (He would not have revealed such an exchange in the letter to his mother!) If so, Heine would surely have told him that only a few years earlier he himself had been virtually shoved and kicked onto a similar path but had eventually rebelled and set out on his own life-course, just as Schumann would do before long. One thing is certain: neither Heine nor Schumann could have imagined at the time that much of the poet's posthumous renown, at least among non-German-speakers, would be connected with the musical settings that this teenager would later create for some of Heine's poetry.

Heine did indeed possess all of the characteristics that the young Schumann had noted: wit, irony, charm, misanthropy, friendliness, bitterness, and loftiness. He was a sharp observer of the world around him and a strong believer that the repression under which most of the Germanic world was living in those Metternichian times would have to collapse before the citizens of that world could evolve into freer, better, stronger individuals. He was a Jew who, as a young boy in Düsseldorf, where he was born in 1797, had enthusiastically welcomed Napoleon's troops as they knocked down the walls of the town's ghetto in the name of liberty, equality, and fraternity, but who then, in the post-Napoleonic era, had felt forced to convert to Christianity in order to be eligible for gainful employment. At various times in his life, Heine became personally acquainted with Goethe, Hegel, Marx (to whom he was distantly related), and Engels, but he seems in many ways the most modern of them all, in his thinking and even in his predictions of the savagery that would eventually befall Germany.* The German Confederation's parliament deemed his prose works and poetry so inflammatory that it included them in a decree that attacked "the wicked, anti-Christian, blasphemous literature that wantonly treads all morality, modesty and decency underfoot."[5] In 1831, three years after his brief encounter with the young Schumann, Heine fled to Paris, where he would live until his death, in 1856. Eighty years later, the English novelist and man of letters Ford Madox Ford would describe Heine as "at once romanticist, realist, impressionist, folksong folk-lore German lyricist, French lost soul, Jewish Christian, and the one man who cannot have been descended from the brute beasts." Heine may have been "the most exquisite of all the world's lyrists since the great Greeks, perhaps the greatest of all the world's realistic-bitter romantics," Ford continued. He was "of no place and of no race," and "there is no poet—there is, indeed, no other man— who resembles him."[6]

Schumann was a very different sort of person. It's true that he wrote

---

* See his *Zur Geschichte der Religion und Philosophie in Deutschland*, published in 1835.

that "everything that happens in the world affects me, politics, literature, people; I think it all over in my own way, and then it has to find a
way out through music."[7] Yet he was never intensely interested in social
and political issues; he seems, for instance, barely to have noticed the
revolutionary uprisings that sprang up across much of Europe in 1830
and that led to the establishment of a constitutional monarchy in Saxony, where he lived. He was a daydreamer and a sensualist by nature,
and the texts that most attracted him as a song composer expressed
direct emotional and dramatic characteristics rather than abstract ideas
or irony. Eric Sams, author of an important book about Schumann's
lieder, pointed out that the composer's "sense of social satire" was "far
from keen" and that his vision was "always that of the lone idealist and
dreamer endlessly questing for new worlds of the spirit, and the universal brotherhood of the outsider's dream."[8]

And yet Schumann's attraction to Heine's poetry produced some
extraordinary results. Altogether, he used Heine's texts for forty-one of
his solo lieder and two of his part-songs for four unaccompanied male
voices. All but three of these pieces date from his "Year of Song," and
those three were written shortly thereafter. In the remaining dozen
years of his active life as a composer, Schumann never again turned to
Heine's poetry for a text, and one can't help surmising that this had to
do with the fact that in 1840, when he sent some of his Heine settings
to the poet himself, Heine did not even reply, let alone demonstrate any
appreciation or enthusiasm for the music.* Schumann may well have
decided to respond to Heine's silence by ignoring the poet's subsequent
works, but his settings of Heine's earlier poems remain among the high-

---

* Heine's favorite musical settings of his poetry seem to have been by one Johann Vesque
von Püttlingen (1803–1883), an Austrian diplomat, lawyer, and amateur musician who
composed under the pseudonym of Johann Hoven. (Perhaps he thought of himself as a
somewhat reduced Beet-Hoven.) Vesque/Hoven set to music the remarkable number of
one hundred-thirty-seven of Heine's poems.

est achievements in the entire European song repertoire, worthy of a place next to Schubert's masterpieces in the form.

THE FIRST SONG THAT SCHUMANN WROTE—apart from some attempts he had made as a teenager—was a setting of Heine's "Du bist wie eine Blume" (You Are Like a Flower); a preliminary version, completed in January 1840, was dedicated to the twenty-five-year-old Antwerp-born mezzo-soprano Elisa Meerti, who had been performing in Leipzig with the Gewandhaus Orchestra under Mendelssohn's direction. (For Meerti's farewell concert, Mendelssohn himself composed a song with the not terribly imaginative title of "Auf Wiedersehen.") But only a month later, Schumann thoroughly revised his piece and dedicated and regifted it to Clara, and in April he re-revised it and made it part of a group of twenty-six songs, three of them on texts by Heine, which he collected under the title *Myrthen* (Myrtles), Op. 25. That work—as the baritone Christian Gerhaher, a dedicated and outstanding Schumann interpreter, has written—was "a kind of metaphorical bridal gift, but obviously also a collection of thoughts, reminiscences and desires that Robert Schumann associated with his marriage, so longed-for and now at last foreseeable."[9] Schumann would present the manuscript of *Myrthen* to Clara on the eve of their wedding, in September.

As a complete entity, however, *Myrthen* was preceded by settings of nine, untitled Heine poems; these lieder, all written in February 1840, were published together under the simple title *Liederkreis* (Song Cycle), Op. 24. In my opinion, few of the songs in either the Heine *Liederkreis* or *Myrthen* reach the heights that Schumann was about to achieve in some of his other works in the genre. The final, untitled song in the Heine *Liederkreis* does make it to that level, and one can hardly help surmising that the composer was particularly inspired by the words of the last verse as he thought of Clara, who was still far away from him: Someday, when the poet's book falls into his distant beloved's hands, the spirit of love will revive the fire that burned in the poet himself, and the "pale letters" that stare up into his beloved's beautiful eyes will whisper to her with the "breath of love." Similarly, the first song of the *Myrthen* series, "Widmung" (Dedication), on a text by Friedrich Rückert, stands out for its passionate call to the woman who is the poet's (or composer's) soul, heart, bliss, pain, whole world, the tomb in which he has buried his sorrow forever, his peace, his better self.

There are many other masterly songs from the early months of 1840—lighthearted and heavyhearted songs, comical songs, folklike songs, and songs with still other characteristics. But in May, the "wondrously beautiful month of May," when he returned to Leipzig after having spent some days with Clara in Berlin, Schumann created what are arguably his two greatest song cycles: the *Liederkreis*, Op. 39, on poems by Eichendorff, and *Dichterliebe*, Op. 48, on poems by Heine. "My head is still ringing with the happiness of our time together," he wrote to his fiancée, "and such music I have in me that I could sing the whole day through." Which is exactly what he did: sing, with pen and paper.

I want to take a few sentences to say something about the Eichendorff *Liederkreis*, since it immediately precedes the *Dichterliebe* cycle, which is my focus. Joseph von Eichendorff (1788–1857) spent much of his working life as a civil servant, frequently moving from one city to another across Europe's Austro-German–dominated areas, but he also created a substantial quantity of prose works and poetry. To a far greater extent even than Heine, however, his name is known to non-German-speakers mainly for the musical settings of his poems—settings not only by Schumann but also by Mendelssohn, Brahms, Hugo Wolf, Richard Strauss, and many others, including an amateur composer named Friedrich Nietzsche. All twelve of the texts that Schumann chose for his Eichendorff *Liederkreis* are paradigms of German High Romanticism, and most of them are marked by an undercurrent of loneliness and alienation. The first and eighth (both titled "In der Fremde"—Away from Home) are about death and, in the latter, lost love tinged with longing; the second ("Intermezzo") and twelfth ("Frühlingsnacht"— Spring Night) are songs of requited love; the third ("Waldesgespräch"— Conversation in the Woods) and seventh ("Auf einer Burg"—At a Castle) tell mystical, Gothic tales; the fourth ("Die Stille"—Silence), fifth ("Mondnacht"—Moonlit Night), and sixth ("Schöne Fremde"— Lovely Faraway Place) express pleasure in silence and/or wonderment in darkness and nature; and the ninth ("Wehmut"—Melancholy), tenth ("Zwielicht"—Twilight), and eleventh ("Im Walde"—In the Forest) deal, respectively, with sadness and pain, evening and treachery, and fear in the forest. Each poem in the set is darkly lyrical, and in reading all twelve poems in a row one becomes aware of a certain sameness of atmosphere. Schumann, however, endowed each text with a unique musical setting; a glance at the indications he placed at the top of some of them gives an idea of the variety not only of tempi but also of soul-states that he demanded of the songs' potential performers: "always very soft," "tender, secretive," "ardent, turbulent," "quite lively," "passionately." From the long, dark, spun-out legato phrases of the first song, "In der Fremde," to the detached, almost casual, oh-by-the-way articulation of "Die Stille"; from the quiet intensity of "Mondnacht" to the ice-cold remoteness of "Auf einer Burg"; and from the shifting sands of "Im Walde" to the uncontainable joy of "Frühlingsnacht," the expressive range engages, thrills, and moves the listener.

In a sense, *Dichterliebe* may be considered a continuation of the Eichendorff *Liederkreis*, not only chronologically but also because the richness of expression continues unabated, and in some ways even increases. On the other hand, and as its title indicates, *Dichterliebe*, unlike the *Liederkreis*, has a unifying subject: love—in this case, a poet's love. Schumann did compose, in other collections or separately, wonderful settings of some of Heine's "story" poems. There is the cantata-like *Belsatzar*, for instance, which embroiders on the biblical tale of King Belshazzar and the writing on the wall, and the martial "Die beiden Grenadiere," which follows two soldiers from the remnants of Napoleon's Grande Armée as they return from captivity in Russia, and which transmits, as subtext, Heine's despair over the collapse of the principles of the French Revolution. *Dichterliebe*, however, deals entirely with love. Heine filled these poems with gorgeous imagery, and in the original German each poem stands on its own *as verbal music*. Schumann absorbed the texts, made them his own, and presented them in uniquely striking ways.

If we were to be cynically, churlishly reductive, we could summarize each of the *Dichterliebe* texts in one of three ways: (1) a man loves a woman but is not loved in return, which makes him sad; (2) a man loves a woman and is loved in return, which makes him happy; (3) a man loves a woman who used to love but no longer loves him, which makes him sad again. To be fair, however, Heine's love poems are hardly ever entirely happy or entirely sad: there is nearly always a bitter aftertaste to the happy texts and a complicit wink within the sad ones— and Schumann echoes these subtleties, especially in his prismatic piano "accompaniments." I put that last word in quotation marks because the piano parts in Schumann's lieder, as in the lieder of other great song composers, are as important as the vocal lines; indeed, the piano parts in some of Schumann's songs are almost as fascinating by themselves as when they partner a singing voice.

Dichterliebe, in its final, well-known form, consists of settings of sixteen poems drawn from the *Lyrisches Intermezzo* (Lyric Intermezzo) section of Heine's *Buch der Lieder* (Book of Songs), first published in 1827. In its original form, however, the song cycle made use of *twenty* poems from the *Lyrisches Intermezzo* and was not called *Dichterliebe*. Its original title was much longer but much less descriptive: *Poems by Heinrich Heine*.

*Twenty Songs and Airs from Lyrisches Intermezzo in Das Buch der Lieder, for voice and pianoforte, composed by Robert Schumann and dedicated in friendship to Dr. Felix Mendelssohn Bartholdy. Second Song Cycle from Das Buch der Lieder. Op. 29, Volumes 1 and 2.**

Why "Volumes 1 and 2"? Because Schumann first conceived the cycle as two groups of ten songs each, and for three years he tried to sell it in that format to publishers. According to Hansjörg Ewert, who edited *Dichterliebe* for the Bärenreiter company's 2011 edition of the cycle, some scholars have hypothesized that Schumann eliminated four of the songs because he eventually had to accept a lower fee than he had requested in order to have the cycle published at all; others think that he shortened the cycle for artistic reasons, since—they argue—"the abridged version tightens the key scheme, strengthens the dramatic structure in the sequence of moods and forms, and heightens the rigor of the narrative."[10] (Thus writes Ewert.) The eliminated songs had occupied fifth and sixth place in each of the original ten-song groups; Schumann later published the four deleted songs separately.

I have my own theory about the elimination of these songs, and I'll discuss it in conjunction with the fourth song in the cycle. But what is certain is that the cycle that was given the title *Dichterliebe* in 1844, when it was first published, is a group of sixteen—not twenty—songs, and that during the remaining decade of his active life Schumann did not attempt to reinsert the four songs into the cycle.[†] In recent times, some singers have reinserted the four deleted

---

* In German: *Gedichte von Heinrich Heine. 20 Lieder und Gesänge aus dem Lyrischen Intermezzo im Buch der Lieder[,] für eine Singstimme und das Pianoforte[,] componirt und Hrn. Dr. Felix Mendelssohn Bartholdy freundschaftlich zugeeignet von Robert Schumann. 2ter Liederkreis aus dem Buch der Lieder. Op. 29. Heft 1. u. 2.*

† In the order in which they were placed in the original song cycle, the four lieder eventually appeared as Op. 127, No. 2 ("Dein Angesicht"); Op. 142, No. 2 ("Lehn' deine Wang"); Op. 127, No. 3 ("Es leuchtet meine Liebe"); and Op. 142, No. 4 ("Mein Wagen rollet langsam"). In *Dichterliebe*'s final form, its published subtitle was *Liederzyclus aus Heinrich Heines* Buch der Lieder (Song cycle from Heinrich Heine's *Book of Songs*).

songs, whereas others have adhered to the text as Schumann published it—just as some pianists reinsert, in their performances of
Schumann's Symphonic Etudes, the five variations that the composer
removed when he published the work, but others do not. For some
people, the question is a moral one: Shouldn't composers be allowed
to decide the final version in which a work is to be performed? For
others, the matter is of purely historical and musical interest. In any
case, as Ewert points out, the twenty-song version cannot legitimately be called *Dichterliebe*—the title that Schumann attached only
to the sixteen-song version. For our present purposes, we will stay
with Schumann's sixteen-song *Dichterliebe*.

THE FIRST FOUR *Dichterliebe* songs correspond exactly to the first
four poems in Heine's *Lyrisches Intermezzo*, but Schumann chose not
to set to music the *Intermezzo*'s brief Prologue. This lively, six-verse-
long introductory poem tells of a gloomy, solitary knight who spends
his days dreaming vague dreams, but who, at midnight, receives his
beloved, a woman who blooms and glows like a little rose. They fall
into each other's arms, and the knight, filled with desire, becomes
fully alive. They sing and they dance, until all of a sudden the gloom
returns, and the knight is sitting alone—in, of all places, a poet's dark
little den. Thus the Prologue ends, abruptly, and the reader now under-
stands that the solitary "knight" awaiting his "beloved" was actually
a poet waiting for the right images and threads of thought—the right
"songs and dances"—to enter his mind, along with the right words to
express them.

Schumann evidently was not interested in providing performers
or listeners with Heine's sly meta-narrative, or whatever one wishes to
call the forty-two stunning lines through which readers are led into the
sixty-five poems that make up the rest of the *Lyrisches Intermezzo*. In

Dichterliebe, Schumann plunges us right into the heart of the first poem, "Im wunderschönen Monat Mai."*

Im wunderschönen Monat Mai,	*In the wondrously beautiful month of May,*
Als alle Knospen sprangen,	*When all the buds blossomed,*
Da ist in meinem Herzen	*It was then that in my heart*
Die Liebe aufgegangen.	*Love burst forth.*
Im wunderschönen Monat Mai,	*In the wondrously beautiful month of May,*
Als alle Vögel sangen,	*When all the birds sang,*
Da hab' ich ihr gestanden	*It was then that I confessed to her*
Mein Sehnen und Verlangen.	*My yearning and desire.*

Schumann's twenty-six-bar, minute-and-a-half-long song is a masterpiece of ambiguity. The listener is shifted back and forth between F-sharp minor and its relative major key, A, mirroring the poet, who recalls the moment at which he summoned the courage to declare himself to the woman he loved but didn't know how she would react to his confession. Here, as in many other pieces, Schumann hints at the proper tempo—*Langsam, zart* (slow, tender)—rather than providing a clear-cut instruction. The piano moves through the entire piece—including a four-bar introduction and a three-and-a-half-bar conclusion—with quiet, ceaselessly meandering, legato sixteenth notes in 2/4 time, while the vocal line follows the text precisely: eight phrases, each of them two bars long, with a three-bar break (filled by the piano) between the two verses. The only well-defined dynamic mark is *piano*, at the beginning, but there are small hairpin *crescendo* indications over the words that translate as "in my heart," "love burst forth," "confessed to her," and "yearning and

---

* For this and all the subsequent poems, I have made my translations as literal as possible without rendering them unintelligible. I have not attempted to match Heine's marvelous rhymes or rhythmic schemes.

desire." Crowning this apparently simple piece is the piano's final, unresolved dominant seventh chord in the key of F-sharp minor, which leaves the listener hanging in air, waiting to find out whether the harmony will resolve, or dissolve, into the opening of the following song.

It does resolve, but not quite as our ears expect it to do, because instead of landing in F-sharp minor we are taken directly to A major. Here, as in the two following songs, the story of this particular love episode continues:

Aus meinen Tränen spriessen	*From my tears sprout forth*
Viel blühende Blumen hervor,	*Many blossoming flowers,*
Und meine Seufzer werden	*And my sighs become*
Ein Nachtigallenchor.	*A chorus of nightingales.*
Und wenn du mich lieb hast, Kindchen,	*And if you love me, my child,*
Schenk' ich dir die Blumen all',	*I'll give you every flower,*
Und vor deinem Fenster soll klingen	*And at your window will sound*
Das Lied der Nachtigall.	*The song of the nightingale.*

This lied, like its predecessor, is in 2/4 time and is marked *piano* throughout, excepting a single *pianissimo* bar at the end of each pair of phrases and a single *crescendo-diminuendo* sign in the piano part near the end. The whole piece—only sixteen bars long and lasting only about a minute—functions as a brief interlude during which the lover awaits a response from his beloved. An unresolved, long-held B-natural, seconding the lover's still unresolved state, brings the vocal line to a close on the last syllable of the word *Nachtigall* (nightingale), but this time Schumann follows the rules and gives the piano the final chord in A major, leaving us where we expect to be left.

Even shorter, time-wise, is the third song, again in 2/4 time but in the bright key of D major, and marked *Munter* (lively, or cheerful):

Die Rose, die Lilie, die Taube, die Sonne,	*The rose, the lily, the dove, the sun,*
Die liebt' ich einst alle in Liebeswonne.	*I once loved them all in love's delight.*
Ich lieb' sie nicht mehr, ich liebe alleine	*I love them no more, I love only*
Die Kleine, die Feine, die Reine, die Eine;	*The one who is small, fine, pure, unique;*
Sie selber, aller Liebe Bronne,	*She herself, the fount of all loves,*
Ist Rose und Lilie und Taube und Sonne.	*Is rose and lily and dove and sun.**

The song's fleet pace, semi-staccato vocal articulation, and overall excited tone make us understand from the start that the woman has just said yes to the poet: she loves him as he loves her. This is his first, brief outburst of joy. But no shouting! The dynamic mark is a mere *mezzo forte*: in Schumann's interpretation of the text, the poet's joy is internalized, and he isn't ready to share his feelings with anyone. For a calmer view of his soul-state, we need the fourth lied:

Wenn ich in deine Augen seh',	*When I look into your eyes,*
So schwindet all' mein Leid und Weh';	*All my pain and sorrow fade away;*
Doch wenn ich küsse deinen Mund,	*Yet when I kiss your lips,*
So werd' ich ganz und gar gesund.	*I become wholly well.*

Wenn ich mich lehn' an deine Brust,	*When I lie on your breast,*
Kommt's über mich wie Himmelslust;	*Heavenly joy comes over me;*
Doch wenn du sprichst: ich liebe dich!	*Yet when you say: I love you!*
So muss ich weinen bitterlich.	*I must weep bitterly.*

Here we find ourselves in G major and in slow 3/4 time. The tone is calm throughout, except on the words that translate as "I love you,"

---

* In Heine's final version of the poem, the penultimate line reads: "Sie selber, aller Liebe Wonne" (She herself, all love's delight). Schumann evidently used an earlier edition of the text. There are many other differences (which I will not enumerate), in other lieder, between the texts that Schumann adopted and the texts published in Heine's collected works.

for which Schumann indicates a brief slowing down over a strangely melancholy diminished chord in the piano part. Stranger still: Why is the poem's final line about bitter weeping, when the poet has just told us that his beloved has confessed that she loves him?

The answer is not to be found in *Dichterliebe* in its final form but is reasonably clear in the cycle's original twenty-song version, in which the fifth and sixth songs correspond to the fifth and sixth poems in Heine's own cycle. The fifth poem describes a dream in which the "dear and beautiful" face of the poet's beloved appeared to him, but also made him foresee that Death would soon kiss her red lips and extinguish the heavenly light in her eyes. Then, in the sixth poem, the two protagonists weep together while making love passionately—the implication being that the beloved woman will soon be dead. In *Dichterliebe*, Schumann's final version of the cycle, we never learn why the poet has lost his love.

There is a good chance, however, that Schumann did not want us to know how that particular story ended, because after the final version's fifth song, which corresponds to Heine's seventh poem, the composer jumped to later poems in the *Lyrisches Intermezzo*—poems that deal with other love stories, including stories in which the narrator laments love betrayed, rather than love lost to death. So perhaps the answer to the question of why Schumann removed two of the songs in the cycle's first half, and two more (presumably for the sake of balance) in the second, has to do with verbal content: he realized, three years after having completed the original version, that the events recounted in the subsequent poems made no sense if the beloved woman had died.

Whether my hypothesis is right or wrong, *Dichterliebe*'s fifth song lets us know that the love story is over, for reasons that are not revealed:

Ich will meine Seele tauchen	*I want to plunge my soul*
In den Kelch der Lilie hinein;	*Into the lily's chalice;*

Die Lilie soll klingend hauchen	*The lily should resoundingly whisper*
Ein Lied von der Liebsten mein.	*A song of my beloved.*
Das Lied soll schauern und beben,	*The song should quiver and tremble*
Wie der Kuss von ihrem Mund,	*Like the kiss from her lips,*
Den sie mir einst gegeben	*Which once she gave me*
In wunderbar süsser Stund'.	*In a wonderfully sweet hour.*

We are back in 2/4 time here, but in a minor key—B minor—and with a vocal range that extends only a sixth, from the A-sharp above middle C to the F-sharp on the top line of the treble clef. To set the tempo, Schumann merely indicates *Leise* (quiet, or gentle), and he writes only a single *piano* for the volume level. Still, a good singer will know how to appear to push the musical line forward without actually rushing, and the pianist has the even more difficult task of creating a roiling accompanying undercurrent through a nonstop series of thirty-second notes, marked *pianissimo*.

Of all the poems that Schumann chose for *Dichterliebe*, this one contains the most explicitly erotic imagery: the plunge into the chalice, the resounding whisper, the trembling and quivering, the wonderfully sweet hour. The song is beautiful in itself, but Schumann either missed or intentionally avoided the poem's sexual subtext. Nearly twenty years later, another Saxon composer of Schumann's generation would be both bold and skilled enough to set an orgasm to music, in a work called *Tristan und Isolde*.

Entirely different in tone, the sixth song (E minor, 2/2 time, and marked *Ziemlich langsam*—quite slow) begins with a musically ono-matopoetic depiction of the massive, heaving Rhine River.* This open-

---

* Ten years later, Schumann would paint a jollier, purely instrumental description of the Rhine in the second movement of his Third ("Rhenish") Symphony.

ing verse is meant to be sung and played *forte*—the first such indication in the cycle:

Im Rhein, im heiligen Strome,   In the Rhine, in the holy river,

Da spiegelt sich in den Well'n   Mirrored in the waves

Mit seinem grossen Dome,   With its great cathedral,

Das grosse, heilige Köln.   Is great, holy Cologne.

But by the opening of the second verse, the dynamic level has dropped to *piano* for both singer and pianist, and there it remains, right to the end of the song:

Im Dom da steht ein Bildnis,   In the cathedral there is a portrait,

Auf gold'nem Leder gemalt;   Painted on golden leather;

In meines Lebens Wildnis   It has shone in a friendly way

Hat's freundlich hineingestrahlt.   Upon the wilderness of my life.

Es schweben Blumen und Eng'lein   Flowers and little angels hover

Um unsre liebe Frau;   Around our beloved Lady;

Die Augen, die Lippen, die Wäng'lein, Her eyes, her lips, her cheeks

Die gleichen der Liebsten genau.   Are exactly the same as my love's.

Yes: the volume drops as the words of the poem first become more tender and then—in the last line—wistful, even tragic, by implication. Those last five words are sung over a quietly portentous, largely chromatic, harmonically unresolved line; resolution is carried out slowly by the piano in a sort of postlude that occupies more than a quarter of the piece's length.

The whole lied seems connected, in some strange way, to "Auf einer Burg," the mysterious seventh song in Schumann's Eichendorff *Liederkreis*. Although that piece is nominally in A minor, it begins and ends in E, which is also the key of this sixth *Dichterliebe* song; the Rhine appears in both lieder; both contain medieval references—to an old castle in the one, to Cologne's cathedral and a gilded leather painting of the Madonna in the other; both are slow-paced; and both conclude in chilling, resigned sadness.*

The seventh song's tone is bitter, especially in comparison with the sad acceptance of its predecessor.

Ich grolle nicht, und wenn das Herz auch bricht,	I bear no grudge, although my heart is breaking,
Ewig verlor'nes Lieb! ich grolle nicht.	Love forever lost! I bear no grudge.
Wie du auch strahlst in Diamantenpracht,	Although you shine in glory like a diamond,
Es fällt kein Strahl in deines Herzens Nacht.	No glimmer falls upon the night in your heart.
Das weiss ich längst. Ich sah dich ja im Traume,	I've known it for a long time. Indeed, I saw you in a dream,
Und sah die Nacht in deines Herzens Raume,	And saw the night in the chamber of your heart,
Und sah die Schlang', die dir am Herzen frisst,	And saw the serpent that devours your heart;
Ich sah, mein Lieb, wie sehr du elend bist.	I saw, my love, how very wretched you are.

This piece—solidly in C major and 4/4 time but *Nicht zu schnell* (not too fast)—is the most emphatic of the sixteen *Dichterliebe* lieder, and probably the best known. The singer alternates between *mezzo forte* and *forte* (excepting an important soft passage before the song's climax on the

---

* For the text of this sixth song, Schumann jumped to No. 11 in Heine's *Lyrisches Intermezzo*, and for the rest of the *Dichterliebe* cycle he skipped around within the *Intermezzo* as he saw fit for his musical purposes.

phrase about the serpent), and the pianist plays mostly strong half-note octaves in the left hand and relentless eighth-note chords in the right. For the last two lines of text, Schumann provided high-note alternatives for singers capable of performing them; they extend the vocal register to an octave plus a sixth and give further urgency to the entire song.

That sense of urgency continues in the eighth song, although in a wholly different way:

Und wüssten's die Blumen, die kleinen,	*If the little flowers only knew*
Wie tief verwundet mein Herz,	*How deeply my heart is wounded,*
Sie würden mit mir weinen,	*They would weep with me*
Zu heilen meinen Schmerz.	*To heal my pain.*
Und wüssten's die Nachtigallen,	*If the nightingales only knew*
Wie ich so traurig und krank,	*How sad and ill I am,*
Sie liessen fröhlich erschallen	*They would joyfully let*
Erquickenden Gesang.	*A revivifying song resound.*
Und wüssten sie mein Wehe,	*If they only knew my woe,*
Die goldenen Sternelein,	*The little golden stars,*
Sie kämen aus ihrer Höhe,	*They would come down from on high*
Und sprächen Trost mir ein.	*And by speaking bring me comfort.*
Sie alle können's nicht wissen,	*None of them can know,*
Nur eine kennt meinen Schmerz:	*Only one woman knows my pain;*
Sie hat ja selbst zerrissen,	*She herself is the one who has broken,*
Zerrissen mir das Herz.	*Broken my heart.*

Schumann provided no tempo indication at all here, but through most of this song—which is in A minor, in 2/4 time, and marked *piano*—the pianist plays fluttering thirty-second-note figurations with both hands, under a smooth, straightforward vocal line that sets a naturally moderate pace on its own. Through the first three of its four stanzas, the song is what we call "strophic": the words change, but the music repeats, with only minor alterations. The fluttering continues through most of the fourth stanza as well, but Schumann transforms the vocal line; it is mellower at first but, at the third line of the stanza, it becomes more pressing and accusatory. The first iteration of *zerrissen* (broken) is violent, but the last line is meant to be sung more slowly and sadly. In the piano part, the fluttering stops abruptly, and two aggressive chords are struck under the last two syllables of *zer-rissen*; then, after the singer's last phrase ends, the piano plays five bars of tempestuous triplet figurations and brings the piece—and the first half of the cycle—to a dramatic close on two low A-naturals.

———

AN ASIDE FOR MUSICIANS: *Dichterliebe*'s whole first half seems to follow a loose scheme of tonalities, centered on A and with many descending fifths. The first song fluctuates between F-sharp minor and A major; the second is clearly in A major; No. 3 drops down a fifth to D; No. 4 drops down another fifth to G; No. 5 is in B minor, the relative minor of No. 3; No. 6 drops down a fifth to E minor, the relative minor of No. 4. For No. 7, Schumann turns to C major, because he is heading back to its relative, A minor, in No. 8. The second half of the cycle will begin with No. 9 dropping a fifth to D—first D minor, then D major. For No. 10, Schumann drops another fifth, to G minor, but for Nos. 11, 12, and 13 he turns for the first time to flat keys: E-flat major, B-flat major, and E-flat minor, respectively. He then goes back to sharp keys: B major for No. 14, down a fifth to E major for No. 15, and then to C-sharp minor, the relative minor of E major, for No. 16. At the end, however, he converts C-sharp minor enharmonically to D-flat major to conclude No. 16 and the entire cycle.

Schumann wrote *Dichterliebe,* and most of his other lieder as well, for a high voice—soprano or tenor; he even dedicated *Dichterliebe* to Wilhelmine Schröder-Devrient, one of the most famous dramatic sopranos of the day. When these songs are sung by lower voices—mezzo-sopranos, contraltos, baritones, or basses—they usually have to be transposed downward. *Dichterliebe's* verbal texts indicate that a male is speaking/singing, and in modern times this and most of Schumann's other lieder have often been performed by baritones—the great Dietrich Fischer-Dieskau (1925–2012), first and foremost—but there have been many successful interpretations by women as well. For *Dichterliebe,* as for many of Schumann's other lieder, great vocal range is not required: few of the songs stretch the voice more than an octave or a tenth, and three of them—the second, fifth, and twelfth songs—have extensions of only a sixth. I have a terrible singing voice, yet I can sing all the notes in most of these lieder if I transpose them into the bass-baritone register. But to deliver these works as they deserve to be delivered requires extraordinary vocal beauty, technical control, maniacal attention to musical and poetic detail, a clarity of diction that even many native German-speaking singers find hard to achieve, and musical, literary, emotional, and psychological insight.

WITH *DICHTERLIEBE'S* NINTH SONG, the cycle's second half begins as unhappily as the first half ended, but the unhappiness is of a different nature: bitterness, anger, sarcasm, and sorrow replace the self-pity of the previous lied.

Das ist ein Flöten und Geigen,	*There's a lot of fluting and violining,*
Trompeten schmettern darein;	*Trumpets blaring amid it all;*

Da tanzt wohl den Hochzeitsreigen   [And] actually dancing the wedding round-
                                             dance
Die Herzallerliebste mein.   Is she who is dearest to my heart.

Das ist ein Klingen und Dröhnen,   There's a lot of ringing and pounding,
Ein Pauken und ein Schalmei'n;   Of drumming and tooting;
Dazwischen schluchzen und stöhnen   Sobbing and moaning among them
Die lieblichen Engelein.   Are the dear little angels.

The piano sets the tone with a four-bar "vamp"—a quietly but angrily churning waltz tune—so that by the time the voice enters we know what we're in for. The piece, in G minor and 3/8 time, is marked *Nicht zu rasch* (not too quick), but the piano's right-hand, forward-pulsing sixteenth notes run nonstop through it all, accompanied by a stubborn rhythm in the left hand: eighth note, two sixteenth notes, and eighth note in each bar, through most of the song. The piano has solo interludes after the second, fourth, and sixth lines of the poem, and when the vocal line ends there is a substantial postlude in which the piano's *perpetuum mobile* continues, stopping only at the final chord.

The vocal part's opening line is marked *mezzo forte*, but the second line, with its reference to blaring trumpets, is *forte*. The third and fourth are *piano*, and so, at first, is the fifth; but the "ringing and pounding" words of the fifth line are repeated, *forte*, and the *forte* indication continues through the sixth line. All of this seems normal enough; what is unusual is Schumann's indication that all through the last two vocal lines the singer should sing softly, while the pianist must make a crescendo to a *forte* that continues through the singer's last seven bars. The composer evidently wanted the noise of the festivities, represented by the piano, nearly to drown out the pathos of the little angels' sobbing and moaning, represented by the singer. Only during the last eight bars of the postlude is the pianist instructed to make a gradual diminuendo from *forte* to *pianissimo*. Perhaps the jilted lover has moved off, and the sounds of his beloved's wedding are evaporating in the distance.

The poem that serves as the text for the tenth song could conceivably have been given a dramatic musical setting:

Hör' ich das Liedchen klingen,	*When I hear the sound of the little song*
Das einst die Liebste sang,	*That my beloved once sang,*
So will mir die Brust zerspringen	*My heart wants to burst*
Von wildem Schmerzendrang.	*From the wild, painful longing.*
Es treibt mich ein dunkles Sehnen	*A dark yearning drives me*
Hinauf zur Waldeshöh',	*Up to the high woods,*
Dort löst sich auf in Tränen	*There my vast grief*
Mein übergrosses Weh'.	*Releases itself in tears.*

Schumann, however, opted for quiet, almost unutterable depression: a slow tempo (*Langsam*) in G minor, 2/4 time, with the singer never going beyond his or her low-to-middle register or above a *piano* volume level, and with the pianist playing a seemingly endless series of quietly falling teardrops. In the piano's postlude, the teardrops turn into rhythmically jagged, half-stifled sobs, until, in the very last bars, the music dies sadly away.

The eleventh song differs enormously in character from its two immediate predecessors: it's a cheerful (*Allegro*) ditty in E-flat major and 2/4 time.

Ein Jüngling liebt ein Mädchen,	*A boy loves a girl*
Die hat einen andern erwählt;	*Who has chosen another;*
Der andre liebt eine andre,	*That other one loves another,*
Und hat sich mit dieser vermählt.	*And has married her.*
Das Mädchen nimmt aus Ärger	*The girl, out of pique,*
Den ersten besten Mann,	*Takes the first decent man*

| *Der ihr in den Weg gelaufen;* | *Who crosses her path;* |
| *Der Jüngling ist übel dran.* | *The boy takes it badly.* |

Es ist eine alte Geschichte,	*It's an old story,*
Doch bleibt sie immer neu;	*Yet it always remains new;*
Und wem sie just passieret,	*And if it's just happened to someone,*
Dem bricht das Herz entzwei.	*It breaks his heart in two.*

In this, as in many of Heine's other poems, the tone changes in the last line or two. Think, for instance, of the fourth *Dichterliebe* poem, which is all about joy and well-being until the end: "Yet when you say: I love you! / I must weep bitterly." Or the sixth, which is purely descriptive—of the Rhine, Cologne, and a portrait of the Madonna— until, at the end, we learn that the Madonna's eyes, lips, and cheeks "are exactly the same as my love's," which is the point of the whole poem. Or the eighth, in which the poet wishes for sympathy from flowers, nightingales, and stars, if only they could feel his woe, but then, at the end, accuses one woman of being responsible for his pain. And here again, in the eleventh poem, the tone is ironically amused through nine of the first ten lines of verse: A is in love with B, B is in love with C, C marries D, and B marries E to spite C. But the last line of the second verse hints at the ending, and the final two lines of the poem turn serious and deal with the heartbreak of poor A—perhaps the poet himself—who is left out in the cold.

Schumann provides a jaunty setting for the whole text, but he instructs singer and pianist to slow down for the words "crosses her path; / The boy takes it badly," and again for the poem's last two lines. Rightly or wrongly, the very last line, about heartbreak, is often sung with some degree of emphasis on each word—after which the piano returns to its original, carefree tone and tempo, as if to say, "That's the way things are, so get used to it and move on." And so we shall.

THE POEM THAT SCHUMANN chose to set for the twelfth lied in the cycle could be thought of as a continuation of the previous one: the youth whose heart was broken is now shuffling aimlessly and disconsolately out of doors.

Am leuchtenden Sommermorgen	*On a brilliant summer morning*
Geh' ich im Garten herum.	*I walk around in the garden.*
Es flüstern und sprechen die Blumen,	*The flowers whisper and talk,*
Ich aber wandle stumm.	*But I wander, mute.*
Es flüstern und sprechen die Blumen,	*The flowers whisper and talk,*
Und schau'n mitleidig mich an:	*And look at me with pity:*
"Sei unsrer Schwester nicht böse,	*"Do not be angry with our sister,*
Du trauriger, blasser Mann."	*You sad, pale man."*

But the contrast between the music of this song and that of its predecessor is even greater than the considerable contrast between the music of the predecessor and the two songs that preceded it. From the decisive (perhaps also derisive) final chords that followed the breaking of the man's heart, we are suddenly relocated, moved into a place in which resignation reigns—a resignation so intense that it becomes a sensual experience.

Here, for the first time in the cycle, Schumann goes into 6/8 time, with a quite slow (*Ziemlich langsam*) tempo indication, in B-flat major. The piano unveils groups of descending sixteenth notes that lovingly entwine themselves around the vocal line, as if the whispering flowers were gently winding their tendrils around the song's sad, pale protagonist, quietly urging him not to hold onto his anger against their "sister"—his lost beloved. But the music seems to be saying that he *can't* let go of his desire—that he is held in a soft, invisible web of love from which he cannot escape.

To interpret, properly, the music of the poem's last two lines—the lines in which the flowers speak—Schumann instructed the performers to move from a "quite slow" tempo to a "slower" (*langsamer*) one, and from a soft (*piano*) to a very soft (*pianissimo*) volume level. He then insisted that they slow down still more (*ritardando*) on the last three words: "sad, pale man." The piano then continues to meander, alone, with its groups of falling sixteenth notes, for what amounts to more than a third of the song's total length. Under the second-last bar Schumann wrote "dying away" (*morendo*), to make sure that the pianist would end the piece in an absolutely calm and strangely warm repose. The composer seems to have interpreted the poem to mean that even if love is hopeless, it can't die.

Or can it? The thirteenth song is a dirge in 6/8 time, meant to be performed softly (*leise*) in the grim, solemn key of E-flat minor.

Ich hab' im Traum geweinet,	*In a dream I was weeping;*
Mir träumte, du lägest im Grab.	*I dreamt you lay in the grave.*
Ich wachte auf, und die Träne	*I awoke, and my tears*
Floss noch von der Wange herab.	*Still flowed down from my cheeks.*
Ich hab' im Traum geweinet,	*In a dream I was weeping;*
Mir träumt,' du verliessest mich.	*I dreamt you were leaving me.*
Ich wachte auf, und ich weinte	*I awoke, and I wept*
Noch lange bitterlich.	*Still long and bitterly.*
Ich hab' im Traum geweinet,	*In a dream I was weeping;*
Mir träumte, du wär'st mir noch gut.	*I dreamt you were still true to me.*
Ich wachte auf, und noch immer	*I awoke, and on and on*
Strömt meine Tränenflut.	*Poured the flood of my tears.*

A less imaginative composer might have set this lachrymose text with flowing, passionate music, to underline the flow of tears from the poet's eyes, but Schumann opted for brutal starkness. Each phrase of the poem's first two verses is sung with no accompaniment, excepting an occasional, punctuating chord, and is followed by further chords, more or less as follows: Voice alone: "In a dream I was weeping." Piano alone: five chords. Voice alone: "I dreamt you lay in the grave." Piano alone: five chords. Voice alone: "I awoke." Piano alone: one chord. Voice alone: "and my tears." Piano alone: one chord. Voice alone: "Still flowed down from my cheeks." Piano alone: two chords. And so on.

The final verse, however, is entirely supported by chords or octaves in the piano part, and when the words end in despair—followed by two equally desperate chords in the piano part—a bar and a half of silence follows; then there are five very soft chords; then nearly two more silent bars; then two more chords; and then total, empty silence.

Still more tears flow in the fourteenth song, but there is a new twist, verbal and musical:

Allnächtlich im Traume seh' ich dich	*Every night I see you in my dreams*
Und sehe dich freundlich grüssen,	*And see you greeting me amicably,*
Und laut aufweinend stürz' ich mich	*And I throw myself loudly sobbing*
Zu deinen süssen Füssen.	*At your sweet feet.*
Du siehest mich an wehmütiglich	*You look at me with melancholy,*
Und schüttelst das blonde Köpfchen;	*And shake your fair little head;*
Aus deinen Augen schleichen sich	*From your eyes furtively appear*
Die Perlentränentröpfchen.	*Little pearl teardrops.*
Du sagst mir heimlich ein leises Wort	*You secretly say a gentle word to me*
Und gibst mir den Strauss von Zypressen.	*And hand me a cypress bouquet.*
Ich wache auf, und der Strauss ist fort,	*I wake up, and the bouquet is gone,*
Und's Wort hab' ich vergessen.	*And I've forgotten the word.*

This is a gentle, lyrical song, in B major and 2/4 time, with a single 3/4 bar inserted in each of the first two verses. The tempo, once again, is *Ziemlich langsam* (quite slow), which gives a conversational pace to the vocal line; it's as if the poet, via the composer, were chatting unhurriedly with his beloved, who, however, has either rejected him or died—or so the words imply. Like the eighth song, this one is basically strophic: the music of the first and second stanzas is nearly identical, and the third stanza changes only at the end. There are no introductory bars for the piano—singer and pianist begin together—and the last words, about the vanished bouquet and the forgotten word, are tossed off quickly and followed by only two or three seconds'-worth of quiet, concluding chords. We can't help thinking that Heine and, especially, Schumann are telling us that sobbing and tears have their place, but enough is enough.*

And indeed, the second-last and last songs in the cycle are dry-eyed, although not pain-free. They are also, respectively, settings of the longest (eight verses) and second-longest (six verses) poems that Schumann adopted for *Dichterliebe*. I can't help wondering whether, for the second-last song, he at some point considered providing a nostalgic or even sentimental musical setting of the sort that he used for parts of his piano suites *Kinderszenen* (Scenes from Childhood) and *Jugendalbum* (Album for the Young); certainly Heine's text evokes a childlike atmosphere:

Aus alten Märchen winkt es	*A white hand beckons*
Hervor mit weisser Hand,	*From an old fairytale,*
Da singt es und da klingt es	*Where singing and playing*
Von einem Zauberland;	*Come from a magic land;*
Wo bunte Blumen blühen	*Where many-colored flowers bloom*
Im gold'nen Abendlicht,	*In the golden evening light,*
Und lieblich duftend glühen,	*And glow charmingly and fragrantly*
Mit bräutlichem Gesicht;	*With bride-like faces;*

---

* The French adjective *larmoyant* is my favorite descriptor for tear-saturated writing, because it contains a trace of oh-come-off-it-already! sarcasm.

Und grüne Bäume singen	And green trees sing
Uralte Melodei'n,	Ancient melodies,
Die Lüfte heimlich klingen,	The breezes secretly resound,
Und Vögel schmettern drein;	And birds warble along;
Und Nebelbilder steigen	And hazy forms rise
Wohl aus der Erd' hervor,	From the earth itself,
Und tanzen lust'gen Reigen	And dance airy round-dances
Im wunderlichen Chor;	In a wondrous choir;
Und blaue Funken brennen	And blue sparks gleam
An jedem Blatt und Reis,	Upon every leaf and twig,
Und rote Lichter rennen	And red lights race
Im irren, wirren Kreis;	In a mad, tumultuous circle;
Und laute Quellen brechen	And roaring springs pour forth
Aus wildem Marmorstein.	From wild marble.
Und seltsam in den Bächen	And a reflection in the stream
Strahlt fort der Widerschein.	Shines out strangely.
Ach, könnt' ich dorthin kommen,	Ah, if only I could get there,
Und dort mein Herz erfreu'n,	And there gladden my heart,
Und aller Qual entnommen,	And be done with all torment,
Und frei und selig sein!	And be free and blessed!
Ach, jenes Land der Wonne,	Ah, that land of bliss,
Das seh' ich oft im Traum,	I often see it in dreams,
Doch kommt die Morgensonne,	Yet when the morning sun comes up
Zerfliesst's wie eitel Schaum.	It dissolves like mere foam.

In this case, however, Schumann opted for a vigorous approach—a jaunty tune in E major and 6/8 time, marked *Lebendig* (lively), and with a basic rhythmic pattern that vaguely recalls the "tally-ho"-like motifs of the first movement of Mozart's String Quartet in B-flat major, K. 458, nicknamed "The Hunt" by later commentators. But the hunt, here, is not for some poor, frightened fox or hare or deer: it is for the path back to childhood—a path often traveled in German Romantic lieder.* Such wistful backward glances at childhood's presumed innocence seem to hint strongly at a wish to return to the womb, or even to escape life's woes altogether through death.

There can be no doubt that Schumann wanted great expressive variety in this song, because he provided a wider range of dynamic indications for it than for any of the others in the cycle: *mezzo forte, crescendo, piano, forte, sforzando, diminuendo,* and *pianissimo* all occur within the roughly two and a half minutes of the lied's duration. The first six, jolly verses—three-quarters of the text—occupy only about the first half of the song's length, because as soon as the singer reaches the first, rueful *"Ach,"* at the beginning of the penultimate verse, the rhythm slows down to half its previous speed, and the cautionary indication *Mit innigster Empfindung* (with most fervent emotion) appears. Without leaving bright E major, Schumann proceeds straightforwardly, right up to the very last line of the text—at which point, however, he twists the harmony into wrenching wistfulness, and then resolves it quietly, with an *Adagio* tempo mark, as if to say, "Well, what can one do? Once childhood is over, it's over forever." The piano closes the piece with a softer and—at the end—much slower and more subdued version of the jaunty opening.

---

* Another outstanding example is Brahms's second "Heimweh" (Homesickness), Op. 63, No. 8, in which the composer, via the poet, Klaus Groth, longs to find the way back to the land of childhood and wonders why he ever let go of his mother's hand, just to seek happiness elsewhere and, one assumes, fruitlessly.

WHEN THE PIANO REENTERS with the opening bars of *Dichterliebe*'s final song, it doesn't merely play them: it declaims them, with a powerfully solemn chord followed by six successive pairs of stark octaves, all in C-sharp minor. And when the voice enters, the words tell us explicitly that these "old, nasty songs" deserve to be done away with, and right away.

Die alten, bösen Lieder,	*The old, nasty songs,*
Die Träume bös' und arg,	*The dreams, bad and evil,*
Die lasst uns jetzt begraben,	*Let us bury them now,*
Holt einen grossen Sarg.	*Fetch a large coffin.*
Hinein leg' ich gar manches,	*I'll put a lot into it,*
Doch sag' ich noch nicht was;	*Though I won't yet say what;*
Der Sarg muss sein noch grösser,	*The coffin must be even bigger*
Wie's Heidelberger Fass.	*Than a Heidelberg beer keg.*
Und holt eine Totenbahre	*And fetch a bier*
Und Bretter fest und dick;	*And solid, thick boards;*
Auch muss sie sein noch länger,	*They must be even longer*
Als wie zu Mainz die Brück'.	*Than the bridge at Mainz.*
Und holt mir auch zwölf Riesen,	*And fetch me twelve giants, too;*
Die müssen noch stärker sein	*They must be even stronger*
Als wie der starke Christoph	*Than strong Saint Christopher*
Im Dom zu Köln am Rhein.	*In the cathedral at Cologne on the Rhine.*
Die sollen den Sarg forttragen,	*They shall carry the coffin away,*
Und senken ins Meer hinab;	*And sink it into the sea;*
Denn solchem grossen Sarge	*For such a large coffin*
Gebührt ein grosses Grab.	*Deserves a large grave.*

Wisst ihr, warum der Sarg wohl	*Do you know why the coffin*
So gross und schwer mag sein?	*Must be so large and heavy?*
Ich senkt' auch meine Liebe	*I would sink my love in it, too,*
Und meinen Schmerz hinein.	*And my grief.*

Once you've read the poem, you don't need to be told that Heine's mini-saga about his desire to bury forever—at sea, no less!—his love and all the pain that it's caused him is laced with self-irony, and so is Schumann's mock-serious treatment of the text. Through the first four stanzas (in 4/4 time and, yet again, marked *Ziemlich langsam*—quite slow), the emphatic vocal part, seconded by the piano's right-hand line, is accompanied by a forward-driving *oom*-papa, *oom*-papa, in the left hand: quarter note plus two eighth notes, quarter note plus two eighth notes, and so on. And the dominating dynamic indications in these stanzas run from medium-loud to loud, with a couple of soft phrases interjected here and there.

Yet at the start of the fifth stanza, the piano's repetitive *oom*-papa gives way to heavy, quarter-note octaves and chords that function as pillars of support under the vocal line and that then become even heavier half-note chords, climaxing on the word "Grab" (grave). After which, however, the tone immediately softens to a mysterious *piano*, as the poet asks whether we understand why the coffin must be so big and heavy; and the tone changes again, becoming slower (*adagio*) and much more lyrical when he says that he is going to sink his love in it (the word *Liebe*, love, must be sung lovingly); and it changes yet again, becoming darker, for his pain (*Schmerz*).

Then something even more unexpected happens. The singer's last note, an A, is left suspended in air over an unresolved chord in the piano part—a chord that leads to another chord, which feels like it's on the verge of closing the song in C-sharp minor, where it began, but which instead resolves into a dreamy, sensual postlude in D-flat major, 6/4 time, marked *Andante espressivo* (moving along expressively)—an echoing, with many variants, of the postlude to the twelfth song. Was Schumann saying that *he* had no need to sink *his* love and pain in the sea, because now he and the woman he loved would be together, as they had so long desired? The notion is pure conjecture, and yet the substantial, warmly caressing ending to what is not only the last but also by far the longest song in the cycle, makes the conjecture seem not at all far-fetched.

THIRTY-TWO MASTERLY SONGS—the twelve that make up the Eichendorff *Liederkreis* and the twenty that comprised the original version of what would become *Dichterliebe*—were all written in May 1840: an average of just over one a day. The achievement was an extraordinary one, and the flow of lieder from Schumann's pen would continue as the year progressed. Eighteen-forty was significant for him in other ways as well. On June 8, Schumann turned thirty; on August 1, the Saxon court finally decided against Friedrich Wieck and in favor of Clara and Robert; and on September 12, one day before Clara's twenty-first birthday, the couple married.

They lived at first in Leipzig, where both taught for a time at the conservatory. As with the Mozarts, so with the Schumanns: sex played a very important role in the marriage, as evidenced, in this case, not only by the eight children—four girls and four boys—born between 1841 and 1854, but also by the many marks that Robert and Clara put in their diaries after they made love. Robert's income from composing, article-writing, and family money was modest but not insignificant; Clara, whose fame as a virtuoso endured and grew, earned substantial sums from her tours and by giving private piano lessons, and something from her own compositions as well. (Most of Clara Wieck Schumann's music was ignored for generations, but much of it is now in print and has been recorded. Her life and her virtues as a composer, and not only as Robert Schumann's wife, have been widely studied in recent decades; interested readers are referred especially to Nancy Reich's *Clara Schumann: The Artist and the Woman*, a revised version of which was published by Cornell University Press in 2001.) Yet her ability to work was often hampered by pregnancies and maternity—despite the help of servants—and by ceding to Robert's need for silence when he was composing. This last problem was resolved in 1850, when the family moved to a house in Düsseldorf that was large enough to allow both spouses to work at home without disturbing each other. Schumann also held a job as a conductor in Düsseldorf, but he had little talent for the profession and was eventually removed from his position. Still, the family was able to lead a reasonably comfortable, middle-class existence.

Even before their marriage, Clara had begun to urge Robert to expand his musical horizons beyond keyboard music and songs and to experiment with orchestral writing. With her encouragement he composed—among many other pieces—four symphonies and one concerto each for piano and cello; all were written between 1841 and 1851 and all became, and have remained, repertoire staples. Other major compositions of that period include the rarely performed opera *Genoveva*, incidental music to Byron's *Manfred* (of which the overture is often heard), three string quartets, and the justly admired Piano Quartet and Piano Quintet, both in E-flat major.

Beginning in the spring of 1852, Robert began to experience periods of sleeplessness, depression, and general apathy, and later that year he suffered from dizziness and hearing disturbances. He continued to compose well into the fall of 1853, which is also when he and Clara were first visited by the twenty-year-old Johannes Brahms. The young man's compositions so impressed Robert that he wrote a now-celebrated article, "New Paths," for the *Neue Zeitschrift*, in which he more or less declared, with extraordinary generosity, that a successor to Beethoven had appeared on the scene. But the beginning of the rise of this gifted youngster from Hamburg coincided unfortunately with Schumann's dramatic and ultimately fatal decline.

Much has been written about the illnesses that afflicted Schumann in his last years; the symptoms that we know of have been variously described as examples of bipolar disorder, tertiary syphilis, and other diseases. As early as his pre-university years he had been subject to mood swings, to alternations between sociality and withdrawal, to unrealistic self-assurance and paralyzing insecurity, and to panic attacks that led him to contemplate suicide, and these alternating states continued through most of his life.* Whatever the cause or causes may have been, the results were disastrous. In Düsseldorf in February 1854 Schumann began to suffer hallucinations, and on the twenty-seventh of that month he rushed out of his house, ran onto a bridge over the Rhine and jumped into the river; some fishermen saved him and brought him home. A few days later he was taken to a private asylum in the village of Endenich, now part of the city of Bonn, some sixty-five kilometers south of Düsseldorf, and there he stayed for the remaining twenty-nine months of his life, during which periods of lucidity alternated with increasingly long stretches of insanity. Brahms and a few other friends went to see him from time to time, but their visits agitated him, and Clara was not allowed to see him at all until two days before his death, which occurred on July 29, 1856, seven weeks after his forty-sixth birthday.

Clara outlived her husband by four decades and spent much of the rest of her career performing his music and looking after the publication of most of it. Some of her editorial work has been criticized, but her

---

* For summaries of what we now know—and don't know—on the subject of Schumann's pathologies, I recommend the Introduction to Michael Musgrave's *The Life of Schumann* and the chapter entitled "The Mind Stripped Bare" in Judith Chernaik's *Schumann: The Faces and the Masks*; see my bibliography.

dedication to her beloved husband's work and to his memory remains unquestioned.

DURING THE MID-1840S, Schumann had worked, off and on, at a composition for solo voices, chorus, and orchestra that eventually came to be called *Scenes from Goethe's Faust*. The results were mixed: Schumann's *Faust* has some marvelously effective parts, but many of its segments are not up to the level of the composer's finest work.

At the same time, however, a French composer—a man whose earlier work Schumann had examined and praised, and with whom he and Clara had become personally acquainted—was likewise working on a major vocal-orchestral score based on Goethe's dramatic-poetic masterpiece, which fascinated so many nineteenth-century creative artists.

The Frenchman's name was Hector Berlioz.

5

A MONUMENT REIMAGINED

Hector Berlioz : *La Damnation de Faust: Légende dramatique*, Op. 24 (1846)

The very title alone of this work indicates that it is not based upon the main idea of Goethe's *Faust* since, in that famous poem, Faust is *saved*. The composer of *The Damnation of Faust* has merely borrowed from Goethe a certain number of scenes that could become part of the plan that he had laid out, scenes that had irresistibly fascinated his mind. But even if he had remained faithful to Goethe's idea, he would nonetheless have left himself open to the reproach—which several people have already leveled at him (some of them with bitterness)—of having *desecrated a monument*.[1]

HECTOR BERLIOZ WAS AN ANOMALY among nineteenth-century European composers. By the time he wrote *The Damnation of Faust*, in the mid-1840s—his own early forties—he knew that he would be attacked for anything he created that even hinted at innovation. Thus, when he was about to publish this new work, which he scored for four solo singers, four-part chorus, and full orchestra, he felt obliged to defend himself in advance by writing, in the third person, the above-cited foreword. What he had done, he implied, was to use Goethe's revered poetic tragedy as a springboard for his musical imagination.

Two decades earlier, at twenty-four, Berlioz had fallen in love with *Faust*, Part One (Part Two would not be published until a few years later, after Goethe's death), in its then-new French translation by the twenty-year-old Gérard de Nerval. "The marvelous book fascinated me from the start," Berlioz would recall in his *Memoirs*. "I couldn't put it down; I read it endlessly, at the table, at the theater, in the street, everywhere." *Faust*-related musical ideas began to crowd into his imagination: he wrote a setting for Margarete's song, "Autrefois un roi de Thulé" (Once upon a time a king of Thule), and he hoped that he would be chosen to write the music for a planned *Faust* ballet at Paris's Opéra. The ballet project was abandoned, but Berlioz "gave in to the temptation to set [parts of *Faust*] to music," he said; "and no sooner had I got to the end of this task than I was foolish enough to have the score published—at my own expense—without having heard a note of it."[2]

He even had the audacity to send a copy of the score, which he called *Huit scènes de Faust* (Eight Scenes from *Faust*), to the seventy-nine-year-old Goethe, who, impressed with the young composer's accompanying letter, asked Carl Friedrich Zelter, a musician friend, for an opinion of the music. Zelter, a musical conservative who, at the time, was the young Felix Mendelssohn's principal teacher, reacted with horror. Berlioz's music was nothing but "sneezing, croaking, vomiting . . . [the] remains of a miscarriage from a hideous incest," he declared.[3] On the other hand, Giacomo Meyerbeer, who was on the verge of becoming one of the most popular opera composers in Europe, sent Berlioz a congratulatory letter after having seen the score, and, even more remarkably, the highly respected German music theorist Adolf Bernhard Marx praised the work's originality. Marx's comments gave the young composer some "unhoped-for encouragement," Berlioz later recalled, but he soon decided that the work had "numerous and enormous defects." He destroyed all the copies of it that he could find, although he allowed that the basic ideas behind the "Eight Scenes" "still seemed to me to have some value."[4]

Those ideas, accompanied by many others, would come to fruition eighteen years later, when plans for a much grander *Faust* score began to take shape in Berlioz's mind. By then, he was a well-known, although also highly controversial, composer whose mastery of orchestration was almost universally respected, as were his abilities as a conductor. (In this respect, he may be seen as a forerunner of Gustav Mahler, who, during his lifetime, was much better known for his work on the podium than for his largely misunderstood compositions.) In fact, it was during a concert tour in east-central Europe that Berlioz began working on what he referred to, in his *Memoirs*, as his "*Faust* legend, for which I had long been ruminating on a plan." But, distant as he was from France, he "had to resolve to write nearly the whole libretto myself." He had used Nerval's *Faust* translation for the earlier "Eight Scenes," which he "counted on inserting into my new score, while retouching them"[5] (he actually revised them heavily, sometimes almost beyond recognition), and he had already had a writer named Almire Gandonnière provide him with a few other texts. But the rest remained to be done.

> Thus I tried, while ambling along in my old German post chaise, to create the verses intended for my music. . . . I wrote the verses that I needed as the musical ideas came to me, and I composed my score with an ease that I have rarely experienced with my other works. I wrote it when and where I could; in the coach, on the train, on steamboats, and even in cities, despite the various duties required by the concerts that I had to give.

The idea for one piece came to him in a hotel in the Bavarian town of Passau; other mental sparks ignited in Vienna. He jotted down a choral theme by the glow of a shop's gaslight in Pest (this was before the cities of Buda and Pest were united), and still other ideas were conceived in Prague and Breslau (modern-day Wrocław). The rest of the work flowed from his imagination after his return to Paris,

> but always unexpectedly, at home, at a café, in the Tuileries gardens, and even on a milestone marker on the Boulevard du Temple. . . . When the whole draft of the score was at last sketched, I set about reworking everything, polishing the various parts, uniting them, melding them with all the tenacity and all the patience I was capable of, and completing the instrumentation, which had only been hinted at here and there. I regard this work as one of the best I have produced.

The Parisian public, however, wasn't interested. Berlioz recalled that seven years earlier, when he had first presented his "dramatic symphony," *Roméo et Juliette*, at the city's renowned Conservatoire, the demand for seats had outstripped the auditorium's capacity, and he had even made a profit after having covered the considerable expenses that the event had incurred. For his *Faust* he had counted on similar interest, but his hopes proved illusory. On the day of the premiere, December 6, 1846, the weather was bad and the singers he had engaged "were no longer fashionable," he recalled. "The result was that I gave *Faust* twice with a half-empty hall. . . . Nothing in my artistic career wounded me more than that unanticipated indifference."

Berlioz's finances were so badly decimated by the *Faust* enterprise that he agreed to make a long and, at the time, extremely arduous concert tour in Russia, with the main purpose of recouping his losses—and he had to borrow substantial sums from friends and well-wishers just to cover that trip's preliminary expenses. Fortunately, he had long since acquired much useful experience in dealing with adversity.

HECTOR BERLIOZ HAD BEEN DEFENDING his work and his life choices since his early years, and he would continue to combat slews of detractors to the end of his life and, in a sense, beyond. It's true that the protagonists of this book's four preceding chapters also faced myriad difficulties in their careers, but none of them was constantly being told that he had chosen the wrong profession or that his imagination outraced and perhaps even outclassed his abilities—comments that Berlioz often heard. (Mendelssohn, who usually behaved generously toward colleagues, privately but cruelly described Berlioz as a "genius without talent.") Nor must we forget that Mozart, Beethoven, Schubert, and Schumann all came from the German-speaking world—an area in which musical culture, including musical literacy, was spreading through the growing middle class with increasing rapidity during those composer's lifetimes—especially from Beethoven's middle years onward. France, then in the vanguard in literature, the visual arts, philosophy, and the sciences, not to mention the political arena, was not keeping musical pace with its Teutonic neighbors. When, in mid-career, Berlioz became directly acquainted with musical life in Germany and Austria, he exclaimed: "What the devil was the Good Lord thinking of when he had me born in this 'beautiful country of France'?"

Even Berlioz's intelligent, loving father long opposed his son's musical aspirations. Louis-Joseph Berlioz, a liberal-minded, land-owning doctor in the small town of La Côte Saint-André, in the Isère plain, northwest of Grenoble, wanted Hector to follow him into the medical profession; he also hoped that his son, who was born at La Côte on December 11, 1803—a year before the First Consul, General Bonaparte, became Emperor Napoleon I—would continue to increase the family's property holdings in the area, where the Berlioz clan had lived for generations.

Louis-Joseph and his wife, Marie-Antoinette (*née* Marmion), had six children, of whom Hector, the oldest, and two daughters survived to adulthood. Marie-Antoinette was a practicing Catholic, unlike her nonreligious husband, and she made sure that her son attended catechism until his first communion. Berlioz later referred to the religion of his birth as "charming, since it has stopped burning people," and he said that although he and the Church had long since "fallen out," he had "always kept a very tender memory"[6] of Catholic rituals. It was in attending mass, as a child, that he first came to love music—which helps to explain why he later wrote some extraordinarily beautiful liturgical and other religiously inspired music, despite his own lack of faith.* Hector attended school for a short time, but his broad, general education came from his father, who introduced him to great literature; taught him Latin, mathematics, and the sciences; and encouraged the boy's interest in every intellectual sphere.†

Unlike most other composers, Berlioz never learned to play the piano or any other keyboard instrument. He did play the flageolet, a simple woodwind instrument in the flute family, and the guitar, and he taught himself music theory from a century-old treatise by Jean-Philippe Rameau and a more recent one by Charles-Simon Catel. By the age of fourteen he was composing prolifically, although he was still unfamiliar with the works of the most significant composers of either the past or the present. His compositions were immature, but he would later make use of some of the best themes that he had invented for them.

---

* Regarding the birth religions of the ten composers discussed in this book: five were Roman Catholics, three were Lutherans, and two were Russian Orthodox. Eight of the ten composers wrote at least some Christian liturgical or liturgically or biblically inspired music (Sibelius and Prokofiev were the exceptions), but none of them was a regular church-goer, and only the first and last—Mozart and Stravinsky—may be considered true believers in a specific religion.

† Louis-Joseph Berlioz was, among much else, one of the first European medical practitioners to become interested in Chinese acupuncture.

At his father's insistence, Hector went to Paris, at seventeen, to begin his medical studies, but he demonstrated no interest in or aptitude for the subject and was particularly horrified by the experience of watching human corpses being dissected. On the other hand, in Paris he was able to attend performances at the Opéra, where he fell in love with the works of Gluck and heard many of the other operas that were circulating in the early 1820s. At about the time of his nineteenth birthday, he was admitted to Jean-François Le Sueur's composition class at the Paris Conservatoire, although until 1826 he was not officially enrolled at that august institution. Le Sueur was the first major figure to recognize and vouch for Berlioz's talent; under his guidance the young, would-be musician made rapid, often astonishing, progress. Yet despite an encouraging letter that Le Sueur sent to Hector's father, Louis-Joseph Berlioz remained adamant: his son was to be a doctor, not a musician! For years thereafter, Hector's parents alternately reduced or eliminated their financial support, and the young man had a hard time surviving in Paris. Hector's sisters, Nanci and Adèle, whom he adored, tried to influence their parents' attitude toward his endeavors, but to little avail.

During the second half of the 1820s, Berlioz transformed himself from an aspiring student-composer into a full-fledged master and, as well, into a wholly developed artist of wide-ranging and forward-looking interests. His discovery of Goethe early in 1828 has already been noted, but even earlier—in September 1827, two months before his twenty-fourth birthday—he had been overwhelmed by Shakespeare. At Paris's grand, neoclassical Théâtre de l'Odéon, a touring English theater company performed *Hamlet*, *Romeo and Juliet*, and *Othello* before enthusiastic audiences that included the young writers Alfred de Vigny, Alexandre Dumas *père*, and Théophile Gautier, all of whom were or would soon be leading representatives of French Romanticism. These rebels against the formal alexandrine verses of classical French drama saw Shakespeare as a proto-Romantic, in part because he had done away with the ancient Greek dramatic strictures regarding unity of time and place (all action to be set in the same location and within a twenty-four-hour period).

The plays were presented in English, which Berlioz did not understand, but he quickly acquired both the original texts and their French translations and began to study them. Shakespeare's works would remain for him the summit of literary expression, together with Virgil's *Aeneid*, which, as a boy, he had read in Latin with his father. And he was as powerfully smitten with the English company's leading actress, Harriet Smithson, as with the Bard himself. Smithson, a little-known, twenty-seven-year-old Irishwoman, had taken the roles of Ophelia, Juliet, and Desdemona opposite the Hamlet, Romeo, and Othello of the much more famous Charles Kemble, and Berlioz later described the whole episode as "the greatest drama of my life. . . . The effect of [Smithson's] prodigious talent, or rather of her theatrical genius, on my imagination and on my heart can be compared only with the upheaval that I underwent thanks to the poet of whom she was the worthy interpreter."[7]

It was an unusual case of transference: in addition to feeling love and physical desire for the actress, Berlioz longed to possess the states of being of the characters she and her colleagues embodied on the stage—to assimilate Shakespeare's atmosphere and imbibe his poetry by consummating a relationship with one of the poet's interpreters. He pursued Harriet, to her confusion, annoyance, and, at times, fright, for over two years.

VIRGIL, SHAKESPEARE, GOETHE—all made profound impressions on Berlioz. But with respect to direct musical influences on his future trajectory, the strongest influence of all came from a composer whose music was little played in Paris at the time. Berlioz first heard a piece by Beethoven—an overture—at a Conservatoire concert late in 1827, only about eight months after the German composer's death. Two months later, he wrote to his sister Nanci: "it is when one has heard the sublime instrumental compositions of the eagle Beethoven that one sees the rightness of the poet's exclamation: 'O divine music, language, powerless and feeble, retreats before your magic.'"* In January 1829, Berlioz wrote to a friend: "Now that I've heard that frightening giant Beethoven, I know what point the art of music is at, it's a matter of taking it from that point and pushing it further—not further, that's impossible, it has reached the limits of the art, but just as far along another path. Much that is new must be done, I feel this with extreme energy; and I'll do it, I'm sure, if I live." (Although he probably did not know it, in this statement Berlioz came remarkably close to echoing Grillparzer's words, quoted earlier in this book: Beethoven's successors would have to "begin anew," Grillparzer wrote, "for he who went before left off only where art leaves off.") Two months later, after having heard performances of Beethoven's String Quartets Op. 131 and Op. 135, Berlioz wrote to Nanci that that master had "climbed so high that one begins to lose one's breath."[8]

In effect, Beethoven transformed Berlioz's life. Despite France's mistrust of its Teutonic neighbors, especially after those neighbors had helped to defeat Napoleon, Berlioz instinctively grasped Beethoven's importance in the evolution of European music. The overall example of Beethoven's existence confirmed the young man's own life choices and helped him to complete his emancipation from his teachers' musical conservatism. In particular, Beethoven's devastating yet redemptive Ninth Symphony, which Berlioz studied in 1829, was a major influence

---

* I have retranslated into English Berlioz's defective French version of lines from Thomas Moore's poem, "On Music." Moore's original version reads: "Music, oh, how faint, how weak, / Language fades before thy spell!"

on him as he composed the *Symphonie fantastique*—a sort of gigantic set of variations on the theme of his unrequited passion for Harriet Smithson. The work was first performed by the Conservatoire orchestra on December 5, 1830, six days before its composer's twenty-seventh birthday. And just as Beethoven had done in his five-movement Sixth ("Pastoral") Symphony, written more than two decades earlier, Berlioz, in his own five-movement symphony, gave each movement a title: "Reveries—Passions," "A Ball," "Scene in the Country," "March to the Scaffold," and "Dream of a Witches' Sabbath." But he went further than Beethoven by writing descriptive paragraphs that said, among much else:

> A morbidly sensitive and ardently imaginative young musician poisons himself with opium in a fit of lovesick despair. The dose of the narcotic, too weak to kill him, plunges him into a deep sleep accompanied by the strangest visions, during which his sensations, his emotions, and his memories are transformed in his sick brain into musical thoughts and images. The very woman he loves has become a melody for him, like an obsession [*idée fixe*] that he encounters and hears everywhere.[9]

The *Symphonie fantastique*'s success established Berlioz as an original figure on the French musical scene, and it added to the pride he had felt earlier that year on winning the Conservatoire's coveted Prix de Rome, after several failed attempts. These achievements at last persuaded his parents to accept his career choice. At the same time, having given up (temporarily, as things turned out) his plan to win the love of the "ideal" Miss Smithson, he was enjoying an earthier affair with Marie (known as Camille) Moke, a gifted nineteen-year-old pianist whom he was planning to marry. Not surprisingly, he felt that the Prix de Rome, which he had so long desired, had come at exactly the wrong moment: just when he wanted to continue to build his reputation in Paris and to enjoy his relationship with Mademoiselle Moke, he had to depart for

Rome—a cultural backwater, at the time. But he had no choice: off he went. No sooner had he arrived in the papal capital (Italy, as a national political entity, would come into existence only thirty years later) than he learned that his young lover's ambitious mother had arranged for her to marry the forty-two-year-old piano manufacturer Camille Pleyel, a man of substance. Berlioz immediately abandoned Rome and began the arduous return journey to Paris, determined to shoot Pleyel, his bride, the bride's mother, and himself, but by the time he reached Nice his thirst for revenge had dissipated and he turned back toward Rome.*

Berlioz did not love Rome, nor did he produce much music during his time there—although he did revise the *Symphonie fantastique* and write a sequel to it, *Le Retour à la vie* (The Return to Life; later given the primary title of *Lelio*). But his excursions, often on foot, through other parts of central and south-central Italy—Florence, Naples and Pompeii, and the wild Abruzzo region, for instance—made deep impressions on his musical and literary imagination.

Upon returning to Paris, toward the end of 1832, he put on a concert of his own music; it was attended by, of all people, Harriet Smithson. During the following weeks and months, Berlioz courted the flesh-and-blood version of his *idée fixe*, and the couple married in 1833. Their only child, Louis, was born in 1834, but the marriage disintegrated after only a few years. For one thing, Harriet Smithson never became fluent in French, although she lived in Paris for the rest of her life, and her husband's English remained sketchy; communication was difficult. For another, both of them had financial problems—often severe ones. Worst of all, both were quick-tempered and easily offended, and in later

---

* He was probably lucky, in the long run, not to have married Mademoiselle Moke. Even before her affair with Berlioz, the teenage girl had had an "understanding" with the German musician Ferdinand Hiller (likewise in his teens at the time, but from a well-to-do family), and Pleyel, whom she married, would abandon her after four years of marriage, owing, he said, to her many affairs with other men.

years Harriet descended into severe alcoholism. Yet even after they sep-arated, Berlioz continued to treasure his memories of his love for Har-riet, and he supported her financially, often with great difficulty, until her death, in 1854.

BETWEEN HIS THIRTIETH and fortieth birthdays, Berlioz produced several of his finest works: *Harold en Italie* (a symphony with viola solo, commissioned by the great violin virtuoso Niccolò Paganini and inspired by Byron's *Childe Harold* as well as by Berlioz's memories of Italy), the opera *Benvenuto Cellini* (loosely based on parts of the Floren-tine goldsmith's autobiography), the *Grande Messe des morts* (Requiem Mass), the dramatic symphony *Roméo et Juliette* (based, of course, on Shakespeare), and the song cycle *Les Nuits d'été* (Summer Nights, on texts by his friend Théophile Gautier; originally with piano accom-paniment, later orchestrated). Unfortunately, public interest in his music was sporadic and fickle, and even when—as with the Requiem and *Roméo*—his works were applauded at their premieres, they often received few follow-up performances. Not surprisingly, grave eco-nomic difficulties were more the rule than the exception for Berlioz. One bright moment in that bleak story came in 1838, when Paganini made him a gift of 20,000 francs, to show his gratitude and esteem for *Harold en Italie* and its composer.

In order to support himself and his family, Berlioz had to dedicate considerable time to writing music criticism—a profession that he dis-liked but for which he demonstrated dazzling literary talent. *L'Europe Littéraire*, *Le Rénovateur*, the *Gazette Musicale*, and the politically import-ant *Journal des Débats* all published his articles at various times. (The *Journal des Débats'* many other illustrious contributors in Berlioz's day included Chateaubriand, Dumas *père*, and Victor Hugo.) He began to publish books as well: first, the *Grand traité d'instrumentation et d'or-*

chestration moderne (Great Treatise on Instrumentation and on Modern Orchestration, 1843; revised edition 1855); then, the *Voyage musical en Allemagne et en Italie* (Musical Journey in Germany and Italy, 1844); and, in the years following the period in question, *Les soirées de l'orchestre* (Evenings with the Orchestra, 1852); *Le chef d'orchestre: théorie de son art* (*The Conductor: Theory of His Art*; 1856); *Les grotesques de la musique* (1859); and *À travers champs* (Cross-country, 1862). His *Mémoires*, which he arranged to have published after his death, remains the most entertaining autobiography by any major composer; it has been republished many times and in many languages, as have many of his other books. In addition, there have been various posthumously assembled collections of Berlioz's writings—notably a ten-volume compilation of his music criticism* and seven volumes of his *Correspondance générale* plus two supplementary volumes—a tremendous number of words, all in all, from a man who is remembered mainly for his music.

From 1835 on, Berlioz was also active as a conductor, of his own music as often as possible but also of other composers' works. He was a pioneer in the craft of conducting—a craft that was just coming into its own in the mid-nineteenth century. In his *Memoirs*, he named some of the qualities that a conductor had to possess: "precision, flexibility, sensitivity, intensity, presence of mind, combined with an indefinable instinct." His conducting was greatly respected by most of his contemporaries in the field. Sir Charles Hallé, a celebrated pianist and conductor of the day, described Berlioz as "the most perfect conductor that I ever set eyes upon, one who held absolute sway over his troops, and played on them as a pianist upon the keyboard."[10]

Yet despite his great authorial and conductorial talents, Berlioz's true calling was as a composer, and in 1845–46 he overhauled, amplified, and indeed completely transformed the *Faust* music that he had

---

* At time of writing (2020), the tenth volume has yet to appear.

written seventeen years earlier. What emerged was a new, highly original work of extraordinary power and beauty.

A PERFORMANCE OF BERLIOZ'S *La Damnation de Faust* requires substantial forces. There are three major solo vocal parts: Faust, tenor; Mephistopheles, baritone or bass; and Marguerite (Gretchen, in Goethe's text), mezzo-soprano. There is also the small role of Brander, a bass.* A four-part chorus (sopranos, altos, tenors, and basses) must be strong enough to hold its own alongside a powerful orchestra that includes, in addition to traditional winds and strings, a large percussion section and pairs of offstage horns and trumpets. The two-hour-long work is divided into four main parts, each of which is subdivided into contiguous scenes—three in Part One, five in Part Two, and six each in Parts Three and Four.

My aim in the following pages is to focus on certain musical aspects of some of these scenes, and to telescope the rest of the composition's plot into bare-bones comments—especially inasmuch as Berlioz himself was not attempting to present the whole Faust story. In any case, he assumed that his audience would know that the Faust character was a brilliant, elderly scholar who had spent his life seeking all knowledge and who, in despair at not having experienced "real" life, sells his soul to a demon in order to find out, at last, what that life could be.

Berlioz called Part One's first scene an "Introduction," yet it begins straightaway with a tenor aria introduced by only two phrases played by the violas and, at the end, cellos. This spacious, lyrical piece ("Le vieil

---

* Several of the secondary characters who nevertheless have important functions in Part One of Goethe's *Faust* do not appear in Berlioz's work. Most noteworthy among them are Wagner, Faust's famulus, a combination servant and scholarly helper. (According to one Goethe scholar with a sense of humor, today Faust's Wagner would be a college professor's underpaid teaching assistant.) Other characters who do not appear here are Marthe (Gretchen/Marguerite's neighbor) and Valentine (Gretchen/Marguerite's brother).

hiver a fait place au printemps"—Old winter has given way to spring)
plunges listeners immediately into Faust's emotional state, as he rejoices
not only in the springtime but also in his solitude, "far from human
struggle and far from the multitudes."

A gorgeous orchestral postlude leads into the lively second scene—
an exuberant peasant chorus and dance, with frank references to sexual encounters. Faust envies the simple people's easy pleasures, and
his sense of regret continues into the third scene, as he watches troops
massing along the Danube: while everyone else is excited about the battle that is about to take place, he alone "remains cold, insensitive to
glory," he laments.

The Danube? Yes: all of Part One takes place on the "plains of
Hungary"—a setting that does not exist in Goethe's text. Berlioz's
motive behind this choice, as he "sincerely avows" in his foreword to
the published score, was to be able to insert "a piece of instrumental
music, the theme of which is Hungarian," and he added that he would
have placed Faust anywhere had there been "the slightest musical reason
for doing so." The piece in question is the "Hungarian" or "Rákóczy"
March, Berlioz's brilliant expansion and orchestration of a traditional
tune; it had brought the composer great success wherever he had performed it, and he decided to include it in his *Faust* score. "Didn't Goethe
himself, in the second [part] of *Faust*, lead his hero to Menelaus's palace
in Sparta?" he asked, in self-justification. But he need not have bothered
with excuses: the powerful piece usually elicits tremendous enthusiasm,
either as a separate concert item or as part of *La Damnation de Faust*.

Part Two opens with the protagonist, alone in his study, asking himself, in his second aria ("Sans regrets j'ai quitté les riantes campagnes"—
I have left the smiling countryside without regret), what it is that he has
so long been seeking but cannot find, despite his attempt to learn all
that can be learned. He decides to put an end to his life and to discover
a hereafter, if there is one. But as he raises a poison-filled chalice to his

lips he hears a group of worshipers singing an Easter hymn—a hymn to the arisen Christ. Their words and their song revive memories of his childhood, of the sweetness of prayer.

He no sooner sets the potion aside than a huge, startling orchestral chord announces the appearance of none other than Mephistopheles. The demon suggests that Faust forget his melancholy thoughts and worm-eaten books and instead experience life, real life! Faust accepts Mephistopheles's proposal and almost immediately finds himself, together with his demonic guide, in a tavern with a crowd of unruly men who are drinking their lives away. One of them—Brander—sings an absurd song about a rat, to which Mephistopheles adds an equally nonsensical ditty about a flea. Faust, more revolted than amused, asks Mephistopheles to take him away, and they quickly find themselves amid meadows and woods on the banks of the Elbe River.

This new scene—the seventh—is one of the most extraordinary segments of the entire *Faust* score. Beginning with a brief but intense orchestral interlude in B major, in a somewhat deliberate tempo (*Andantino*, 3/4 time); it settles gradually into D major and creates a sunset-like atmosphere that leads into Mephistopheles's warm, caressing, aria (still in D major but marginally slower: *Moderato assai un poco lento*, 4/4 time) that soothingly lulls Faust to sleep: "Here are roses, / Blossoming this very night. / On this perfumed bed / O my beloved Faust, / Repose! / In voluptuous sleep / Where more than one ruby kiss will glide over you, / Where flowers for your bed will open their corollas, / Your ear will hear divine words. / Listen! Listen! / Spirits of the earth and of the air / Are beginning a sweet concert for your dream."*

---

* "Voici des roses, / De cette nuit écloses. / Sur ce lit embaumé / Ô mon Faust bien-aimé, / Repose! / Dans un voluptueux sommeil / Où glissera sur toi plus d'un baiser vermeil, / Où des fleurs pour ta couche ouvriront leurs corolles, / Ton oreille entendra de divines paroles. / Écoute! Écoute! / Les esprits de la terre et de l'air / Commencent pour ton rêve un suave concert."

In that dream, induced by Mephistopheles, Faust sees Marguerite, a beautiful girl, who represents the next stop along his road to perdition. A chorus of gnomes and sylphs, accompanied by gossamer orchestral textures that create a nocturnal fantasy world, whispers details of the girl's virtues into the sleeping Faust's ears. Berlioz creates the atmosphere by combining long, legato melodic lines with silvery, skittish interjections from parts of the chorus and from the orchestra's winds and violas—later also violins, with their mutes in place. (A decade earlier—by the way—Berlioz had created a similarly enchanted atmosphere in the "Queen Mab" Scherzo in his *Roméo et Juliette*.)

The enchantment continues after Mephistopheles commands the sylphs to hover around the sleeping Faust and to "Rock, rock him in his enchanted slumber!"* The melodic line of this lightly orchestrated, purely instrumental waltz (still in D major, *Allegro*, 3/4 time) is played mainly by the muted first violins, accompanied by punctuating figurations in the flutes, piccolos, clarinets, two harps, muted second violins and violas, and, toward the end, timpani. The cellos and double basses hold onto low Ds through the waltz's entire length—one hundred eight bars!—until the piece evaporates into thin air, like the sylphs themselves.

All in all, Scene Seven—much of which was composed during Berlioz's stay in Vienna in December 1845—is among the least overtly dramatic parts of *La Damnation de Faust*, yet it is one of the work's most subtly and brilliantly constructed segments—the one in which Berlioz most fully demonstrates his psychological acumen and his unparalleled skill as an orchestrator. In addition, it allows us to understand why this uncategorizable composition can function, at a practical level, either as a fully staged opera, albeit with parts of the plot missing, or as an oratorio-style concert piece. The score is so strikingly illustrative that,

---

* "Bercez, bercez son sommeil enchanté!"

on the one hand, a musically perceptive and conscientious stage director (a few of them still exist) can discern what sort of setting Berlioz had in mind, yet, on the other, a musically sensitive listener who has read the libretto will know what sort of setting Berlioz had in mind without having to see it represented on a stage.

PART TWO CONCLUDES WITH Mephistopheles and Faust, on their way to Marguerite's house in an unnamed town, making their way through throngs of noisy young soldiers and students, and Part Three opens with horns, trumpets, and timpani playing an evening military retreat. Faust, whom Mephistopheles has brought into Marguerite's empty bedroom, sings an aria, "Merci, doux crépuscule" (Thank you, sweet twilight), in which he expresses his anxious anticipation of what is to come, namely, great happiness after a "long martyrdom"— which, we may assume, refers to his denial of the pleasures of the flesh. Mephistopheles appears after a flashing orchestral chord similar to the one that announced his first appearance; in this brief tenth scene, he orders Faust to hide behind the curtains, because Marguerite is on her way home—and then he vanishes.

Marguerite enters. In a meditative recitative marked by hesitant pauses, she tells of a dream in which she saw her handsome future lover, and she wonders whether the two of them will ever find each other in this life. Her musings lead into a similarly reflective, gently paced aria—"Autrefois un roi de Thulé" (Once upon a time, a king of Thule), in F major, the same key as Faust's previous aria—about a king whose beloved queen died but who remained faithful to her until his own death. This is a reworked version of one of Berlioz's very first *Faust* settings, composed shortly after he had read Goethe's play nearly two decades earlier.

Suddenly, we're on the street in front of Marguerite's house. Mephistopheles, now sounding truly demonic (Berlioz employs a series of aug-mented fourths and diminished fifths—known in pre-modern times as the "devil's interval"), summons a bevy of will-o'-the-wisps to put on a light display. Some observers—this one included—have wondered what the purpose of the following Minuet of the Will-o'-the-Wisps might be within the work's overall plot. At one point, Mephistopheles says that the creatures he has evoked "are going to charm a girl and bring her to us," but in fact Marguerite is already in the same room as Faust. And what can will-o'-the-wisps do that Mephistopheles himself can't accomplish? Never mind: even if the demon's command is merely an excuse for a mini-ballet, we can enjoy the charming music that Ber-lioz inserted here.

The scene ends with Mephistopheles singing a sarcastic serenade, "Devant la maison de celui qui t'adore" (In front of the house of the one who adores you), while imitating the movements of a hurdy-gurdy player. A girl may enter her lover's room as a virgin, he says, but she won't be a virgin when she leaves. Resist—unless he first offers you a wedding ring! But the serenade is meant to entertain us, not Mar-guerite, who is otherwise occupied in her room. Faust steps out from behind the curtain; Marguerite recognizes him as the man she saw and adored in her dream. (Mephistopheles has done his job well.) They sing a love duet, "Ange adoré" (Adored angel), of which one segment, after the indication *un poco animato*, seems, to this listener, somewhat banal and not up to Berlioz's usual standard of originality. In any case, this duet, in E major, strikes terror into most tenors' hearts, because their part rises twice to a high B followed by a high C-sharp—although Ber-lioz mercifully provided alternative G-sharps to the Bs and alternative F-sharps to the C-sharps.

As the duet ends, Marguerite is about to throw herself into Faust's arms when Mephistopheles suddenly appears (Scene Fourteen), warn-ing them that their singing has awakened the neighbors, who are rushing to discover who the man in Marguerite's bedroom may be. They're dragging her mother with them, gleefully warning her that if she doesn't take care she will "see her family grow." Marguerite urges Faust and Mephistopheles to escape through the garden, while Faust, frustrated and desperate, promises to return. Amid tremendous clamor— frenzied music from chorus, orchestra, and the three solo voices—Part Three comes to an end.

Although Part Four opens in Marguerite's room, where Part Three ended, we are meant to understand that a fair amount of time has passed. Marguerite is alone, consumed by memories of Faust's kisses and caresses, and not quite ready to admit to herself that she has been seduced and abandoned. "D'amour l'ardente flamme" (The burning flame of love; F major, 3/4 time) is her most intense aria, although it should really be called a duet: throughout most of it, the mezzo-soprano is paired with an English horn, the mezzo-soprano of the woodwind family. (Berlioz, by the way, was evidently fond of the English horn: he gave it pride of place in the third movements of the *Symphonie fantastique* and *Harold en Italie* as well as in his *Roman Carnival* Overture, among other compositions.) And he was kind to the Marguerites of his day and beyond by making their range a reasonable one: their lowest note is a middle C, and they are allowed to rise gradually to their highest note, the first A-flat above the treble clef. No Rossinian pyrotechnics are required; even harder to achieve, however, is the aria's almost unbearably intense emotional impact. The piece ends with Marguerite peering anxiously from her window, hearing the soldiers and students in the distance singing fragments of the songs that ended Part Two, and awaiting, in vain, Faust's arrival. Her last word is "Hélas!" (Alas!), and it is followed by the strings playing tender pizzicato chords increasingly softly, until the music vanishes altogether.

The violas, alone, play and hold onto a single note, an isolated G-sharp, that Berlioz presumably inserted to prepare listeners to move from F major to C-sharp minor. Faust appears, surrounded by wild forests and caverns. He is no longer thinking about Marguerite; instead, he invokes "Nature immense, impénétrable et fière" (Immense nature, impenetrable and proud) in a verse that was the first part of the *Faust* libretto that Berlioz wrote during his travels in Central Europe in 1845. In this segment, he tried "neither to translate nor to imitate" Goethe's text; he merely let himself "be inspired by it" while letting his imagination create musical impressions. The writing of this piece "gave me the hope of managing to write the rest," he said.

> *Immense, impenetrable, proud Nature!*
> *You alone grant a truce to my endless soul-sickness!*
> *Upon your all-powerful breast I feel my misery diminish,*
> *I regain my strength and I at last want to live.*
> *Yes, blow, ye tempests, shout, ye deep forests,*
> *Crumble, ye boulders, bring forth your waves, ye torrents!*
> *My voice loves to blend with your majestic roar,*
> *I adore you, forests, boulders, torrents!—*
> *Worlds that sparkle,*
> *It is toward you that desire rushes forth*
> *From a heart too vast and from a soul that thirsts*
> *For a happiness that flees from it.**

The aria is not particularly long—well under five minutes, including the introductory and concluding orchestral passages—but it is a sprawling one, sung at a measured pace, wandering through dramatic

---

* "Nature immense, impénétrable et fière, / Toi seule donne trêve à mon ennui sans fin. / Sur ton sein tout puissant je sens moins ma misère, / Je retrouve ma force, et crois vivre enfin. / Oui, soufflez, ouragans! Criez, forêts profondes! / Croulez, rochers! Torrents, précipitez vos ondes! / A vos bruits souverains ma voix aime à s'unir. / Forêts, rochers, torrents, je vous adore! / Mondes, qui scintillez, / Vers vous s'élance le désir / D'un coeur trop vaste et d'une âme altérée / D'un bonheur qui la fuit."

and sometimes startling harmonic modulations, and gradually gathering strength until it climaxes in the last two lines of text—especially with Faust's high A on the word "âme" (soul). Of all the arias and other set-pieces in Berlioz's *Faust*, "Nature immense" is the most original, the most unconventional, and the most powerful.

It is also, in a sense, Faust's last stand. Because no sooner has our protagonist finished what Berlioz called an "invocation to nature"—really as much an evocation of nature as an invocation to it—than Mephistopheles appears, sarcastically asking Faust whether, in gazing up at the sky, he sees the star of faithful love. Faust tells him to be quiet, but the demon nonchalantly goes on to inform him that poor Marguerite is in prison, condemned to death for murder: while waiting in vain every evening for Faust to return, she gave her mother too much of the sleeping potion that Mephistopheles had provided, and the poor woman had died. Faust, horrified, demands that Mephistopheles help him to save Marguerite; Mephistopheles claims to accept the demand, but he insists that, in exchange, Faust sign an "old parchment" and swear an oath to serve Mephistopheles in the future. Faust signs and swears.

Mephistopheles summons Vortex and Giaour, two black horses, presumably to ride off to save Marguerite, but instead, in a scene of tremendous drama—with increasingly weird orchestral effects—he and Faust gallop across the sky, over mountains and valleys, over a group of frightened peasant women and children and a gathering of dancing skeletons, and through a downpour of blood and a flock of night-birds that beat their wings against Faust, until, in the end, they plummet into the abyss of eternal damnation, where Faust cries out in horror—like Don Giovanni at the end of the penultimate scene of Mozart's opera— and Mephistopheles sings of his triumph. Pandemonium—the actual title of the following scene—ensues: the Damned and Demons, singing raucously in a harsh language invented by Berlioz, shout their joy and carry the jubilant Mephistopheles on their shoulders.

But the noise of the Inferno gradually subsides and we find ourselves in an Epilogue that begins on earth and then rises to heaven. A chorus of celestial spirits declares that Marguerite—whom Faust did not manage to save, and who has been put to death—erred purely out of love, has been pardoned, and will now be with her sister seraphs. (In some staged productions, Marguerite is seen again, physically, in this scene, but she does not sing again.) The combination of high violin arpeggios, tremolos in the other strings, and chanting from the chorus's high voices (no basses) plus a children's chorus, makes this ethereal ending something of a dénouement after the high drama that preceded it. But Berlioz's plan is clear: he began *La Damnation de Faust* in D major, with his dissatisfied hero questing for something undefinable, and he ends it in D-flat major, one of the most distant keys possible, with the story completely resolved.

BERLIOZ NEVER FORGAVE the Paris public for the failure of *La Damnation de Faust* at its premiere. He would perform it successfully in Berlin, Dresden, Weimar, and Vienna, but never again in France. In 1859, his countryman Charles Gounod produced a charming *Faust* opera that became tremendously popular around the world and is still frequently performed, and the Italian Arrigo Boito's inventive *Mefistofele*, likewise written within Berlioz's lifetime, also achieved considerable popularity. Not until 1893, when the Romanian-born impresario Raoul Gunsbourg gave *La Damnation de Faust* its first production as an opera, at Monte Carlo, did Berlioz's work begin to receive the attention it deserved, and that production, with modifications, traveled to other major theaters, including the Hamburg Opera and La Scala. Berlioz's *Faust* has since been performed both staged and unstaged all over the world, but, as Hugh Macdonald, one of the composer's biographers, has written, "it is essentially a work for Berlioz's favorite theatre, the imagination." Its brilliant yet subtle instrumentation and masterly vocal writing combine to present a convincing psychological delineation of Faust and Marguerite. (Mephistopheles, a supernatural representation of evil, does not require psychological treatment, although he psychologically manipulates the human *dramatis personae*.)

For those of us who are attracted to Berlioz's unique musical characteristics, *La Damnation de Faust*, despite all the leaps and gaps in its scenario, arouses admiration, fascination, and joy.

IN THE DECADE AND A HALF that followed the completion of his *Faust* score, Berlioz created several other major works—among them a *Te Deum;* the oratorio *L'Enfance du Christ* (The Childhood of Christ), based on the Gospel of St. Matthew; the massive opera *Les Troyens* (The Trojans), based on Virgil's *Aeneid*, which Berlioz had loved since childhood; and the much smaller, lighter opera *Béatrice et Bénédict*, based on Shakespeare's *Much Ado about Nothing*. Among these pieces, only *L'Enfance du Christ* enjoyed immediate public approval, which Berlioz regarded as a mixed blessing: its success was "spontaneous, very great, and yet defamatory toward my prior compositions," he recalled, with a justifiable mixture of pride and resentment.

One doesn't need an exceptionally vivid imagination to hypothesize that the "heart too vast" and the "soul that hungers / For a happiness that flees from it"—Faust's self-characterization in the Invocation to Nature—belonged as much to Berlioz himself as to his work's protagonist. By the mid-1840s, when he was working on this *légende dramatique*, the composer had long since separated from Harriet Smithson Berlioz, and in the meantime he had become involved with a Franco-Spanish mezzo-soprano, Marie Recio, whom he married after Harriet's death. He seems at least to have been less unhappy with Marie than he had been with Harriet; she traveled with him, helped him keep his daily life and household in order (with the assistance of her mother, who lived with the couple), and remained with him until her death, in 1862, at the age of forty-eight.

A year later, the failure to obtain a complete, viable production of his most massive project—*Les Troyens*—made him abandon composition altogether. Shortly thereafter he wrote: "I am in my sixty-first year; I no longer have hopes, illusions, or lofty thoughts; my son is almost always far away from me; I am alone; my contempt for people's imbecility and lack of moral integrity, my hatred of their atrocious ferocity, are at the maximum; and at every hour I say to death, 'Whenever you like!' So why does it wait?"[11]

A late-flowering friendship with a woman on whom he, as a pubescent boy, had had a crush helped to console him in his last years, but in 1867 he was devastated by the death of his son, Louis, who had become a captain in France's merchant marine and had succumbed to yellow fever in Havana. Berlioz had not been an attentive father when Louis was growing up, but father and son had come to love each other deeply. Now, grieving and in ill health, Berlioz nevertheless set out on a pre-planned concert tour in Russia that, despite its artistic success, negatively affected his already poor health. His condition continued to deteriorate after his return to Paris, and he died at home on March 8, 1869, at the age of sixty-five.

Berlioz, rarely of an optimistic turn of mind, would not have been surprised to learn that only one of his major compositions, the *Symphonie fantastique*, would be part of the so-called standard classical repertoire until nearly a century after his death. Nor did he have many imitators or become the head of a "school" of composition: his works were too individualistic, too distant from the principal trends of the day, to attract epigones. But since the 1950s an ever-increasing fascination with his music has led to the revival of almost all of his important works, including the difficult-to-produce opera *Les Troyens*. In his case, as in Schubert's, the recognition came too late to bring him any joy. The joy is all ours.

BERLIOZ HAD NOT MUCH ADMIRED the Italian opera composers—namely, Rossini, Donizetti, and Bellini, creators of the so-called *bel canto* style—who were famous during his first forty years, but he came to hold Giuseppe Verdi, his junior by a decade, in considerable regard. The two musicians got to know each other in the spring of 1855, when Verdi was in Paris for the rehearsals and premiere of his opera *Les Vêpres siciliennes* (The Sicilian Vespers—better known by its Italian name, *I vespri siciliani*) at the Opéra. They saw each other several times, and Berlioz wrote to a friend that he sympathized with Verdi for having to "deal with all the Opéra people. He made a terrible scene yesterday at the dress rehearsal. I feel sorry for the poor man; I put myself in his position. Verdi is a worthy and honorable artist."[12] Five years later, Verdi, in Italy, wrote to his French publisher, Léon Escudier, asking him to "greet Berlioz for me warmly, warmly, I esteem him as a composer and love him as a man."[13]

The two musicians must have met again in 1866 or 1867, when Verdi was once more in Paris, because fifteen or sixteen years later Verdi described Berlioz as "a poor, sick man who raged at everyone," which had not been the case in 1855. "He was greatly and subtly gifted," Verdi wrote. "He had a real feeling for instrumentation, anticipated Wagner in many instrumental effects. (The Wagnerians won't admit it, but it is true.)"

As it happens, Verdi's reason for being in Paris in the mid-1860s was to prepare the premiere of what is now generally considered one of his greatest operas: *Don Carlos*.

6

THE CROWN, THE CROSS, AND THE CRUELTY OF LOVE

Giuseppe Verdi: *Don Carlo* (1867)
(Five-Act Modena Version of 1886)

I don't like the Escorial. . . . It is austere and terrible, like the ferocious sovereign who constructed it.[1]

GIUSEPPE VERDI WAS IN SPAIN in the early spring of 1863 to supervise the Spanish premiere of *La forza del destino*, his latest opera, at Madrid's Teatro Real, and—as the above-cited letter to his friend, Count Opprandino Arrivabene, demonstrates—he took advantage of his visit to do some sightseeing. But he could hardly have imagined, during his side-trip to the sixteenth-century Escorial complex, near the capital, that barely two years later he would begin to write an opera in which Philip II, the "ferocious sovereign" mentioned in his letter, would be the central figure around whom the stories of all the work's other *dramatis personae* would orbit.

The impulse to write that new opera originated with Léon Escudier, Verdi's French publisher, who worked hard to persuade Europe's most popular living and active opera composer* to produce a grandiose work for the Paris Opéra's 1866–67 season. Verdi, who turned fifty-two in 1865, had been reluctant to accept the invitation. He had completed nineteen operas during the first fourteen years of his career (1839–53), when he was trying to establish his reputation (he referred to most of that period as his "galley years"), but in the dozen years since then he had produced only four new works in the genre, in addition to revising some earlier ones. After all, he had already made a small fortune through his labors and had begun to concentrate on expanding and improving Sant'Agata, the farm-*cum*-estate that he had acquired in 1848, near his home town, Busseto, in the Po Valley. He no longer needed to prove his compositional prowess, and his economic survival was reasonably secure. Still, the temptation to reenter the operatic lists, to bring forth another work—one that would demonstrate a further qualitative leap in his development—remained at the back of his mind. If an irresistible subject were to come to his attention, he might rise to the challenge— a particular hope of Giuseppina Strepponi Verdi, the composer's wife, who found extended periods in the country too much of a good thing.

In June 1865, after Escudier had made his proposal for an opera to be based on *King Lear,* or perhaps on the Cleopatra story—or, failing either of those subjects, on Friedrich Schiller's eighty-year-old drama, *Don Carlos, Infant von Spanien* (Prince of Spain)—Giuseppina encouraged the publisher to continue to pursue her husband. "I know him," she wrote. "Once he is caught up the picture will change. He will leave his trees, his building, his hydraulic engines, his guns, et cetera. As always he will give himself up to the fever of creation; he will devote himself wholly to the poem and his music and I hope the whole world will benefit from it."[2]

---

* Giacomo Meyerbeer, whose works were extremely popular at the time, had died the previous year, and Rossini, who was still alive, had not written an opera since 1829. Wagner had already composed all but his last three operas, but none of them had yet found broad international acceptance, and some of them had never been performed at all.

Escudier duly arrived at Sant'Agata in July for consultations. *King Lear*—a text and a subject that had always fascinated Verdi—was rejected as lacking sufficient spectacular display for Parisian tastes, and so was Cleopatra. *Don Carlos*, on the other hand, was "a magnificent drama, . . . a sublime subject and one that I adore,"[3] Verdi wrote to Émile Perrin, the Opéra's director. And Escudier, also writing to Perrin, confirmed that *"Don Carlos* has really thrilled" Verdi, although the composer felt that, in this case, too, some spectacular elements would have to be inserted into the drama. And so, after some further qualms were tranquilized, the complicated process of creating a new opera began.

As Berlioz indicated, Verdi was not at his happiest when he was working with Parisian musicians and theater people. Once, when he had returned to the city for a revival of *Les Vêpres siciliennes* (*I vespri siciliani*—The Sicilian Vespers), which he had composed for the Opéra in 1855, he had fought with the conductor, Louis Dietsch, over a passage that he wanted the orchestra to play at a faster tempo; Dietsch and his musicians had reacted by playing the passage even slower, and Verdi had stormed out of the theater. Nevertheless, Paris offered high fees, not only to composers but to everyone involved in making an opera, which meant that many of the best vocal artists of the day were available, as were the best dancers, choreographers, scene-painters, and costume and wig designers. (There were no stage directors in the modern, creative sense of the term. Singers tended to use stock gestures to indicate specific emotions.) It's true that Stendhal, half a century earlier, had described Paris's opera productions as paltry and crude in comparison with what he was seeing and hearing at La Scala during his stays in Milan, but by the mid-1800s Paris was the hub of the opera world.

The Verdis set out for the French capital in November 1865, so that the composer and his two librettists, Joseph Méry and Camille du Locle, could decide which elements of Schiller's drama to use, which to discard, and which external plot elements to add; they would then weld a satisfactory French text out of the various disparate parts. Three months later, Verdi wrote to Count Arrivabene: "I can't wait till my poets have finished the libretto so that I can go back to Sant'Agata and write [i.e., compose] in peace."[4] And after another month had gone by he informed the count: "The libretto is completely [finished] and I think it's good."[*]

During a four-month stay back in Italy, Verdi composed four of the opera's five acts; then, in July 1866, he and Giuseppina returned to Paris, where the arduous rehearsal process began. On December 10, Verdi wrote to Arrivabene, with typical self-irony:

> I would have written to you earlier if I hadn't had at my fingertips a bunch of notes that were falling onto the orchestra score of D[on] Carlos, and you ran the risk of receiving a letter full of notes that were worth even less than my words. Now . . . I can tell you that the opera is completely finished, excepting the Ballet[,] that the rehearsals are going ahead normally, that the stage rehearsals have begun, and that I hope to be able to give the 1st performance by the second half of January. See what a big heap this opera is! We're never done with it!

Further delays caused the premiere to be postponed until March 11, and the following day Verdi informed Arrivabene: "It wasn't a success!!" But it wasn't a failure, either; it simply didn't elicit great enthusiasm. And in Italy Verdi was accused of cultural treason for having created an opera in France and in the French language—the same criticism that he had received a dozen years earlier, with *Les Vêpres siciliennes*. Such accusations had not been leveled at his immediate predecessors Rossini, Donizetti, and Bellini, who had composed operas for Paris, not to mention such older Italian composers as Niccolò Piccinni and Luigi Cherubini,

---

* Méry died in June 1866, thus all subsequent changes to the libretto were presumably made by du Locle in consultation with Verdi.

who had enjoyed their greatest successes in Paris and had made the city their home. But there was a difference: those composers' Parisian works had been written before Italy's various kingdoms, duchies, papal states, and foreign-held territories had seriously begun to aspire toward unity and nationhood. By the mid-1850s those aspirations were reaching their apogee, and Verdi himself had become, through his music and his outspoken nationalism, one of the symbols of the resurgent Italy that was on the verge of becoming a reality. Some Italians insinuated, at the time of *Les Vêpres*, that Verdi was trying to imitate the style of Meyerbeer, whose grand operas were tremendously popular in Paris; even Francesco Maria Piave, the librettist of seven of Verdi's previous operas, could not resist writing to a friend in terms that were crude, anti-Semitic, and chauvinistic: "I wish [Verdi] were here [in Italy] instead of breaking his balls struggling against that rich Jew Meyerbeer. He renounces the throne offered to him by Italy in order to sit on a bench in France!"[5]

Piave did not specify what sort of throne, if any, Verdi was being offered, or in which of Italy's still disunited parts the coronation would take place. The fact that since the outset of his career Verdi had been forced, all over Italy, to submit his works' plots and libretti to the whims of local censors, and the concomitant fact that he had a more than legitimate right, at the height of his artistic maturity, to the high fees that the Opéra, unlike its Italian counterparts, could afford to pay him, did not sway the opinion of Piave and many others.

Verdi wasn't imitating Meyerbeer, in *Les Vêpres*: he was simply accepting the challenge of picking and choosing those aspects of French-style *grand opéra* that fit his own strong musical personality, just as, earlier, he had adopted the stylistic requirements of Italian opera as they had developed under his predecessors, and then gradually transformed them. Now, however, twelve years after *Les Vêpres*, some Italians accused Verdi of imitating Wagner, in *Don Carlos*, although at the time few Italians were familiar with Wagner's works, not one of which had been performed in Italy. Verdi may have read through some of Wagner's music before 1867, but he did not actually hear any of his German contemporary's operas until *Lohengrin* was presented in Bologna in 1871.

What do we mean—by the way—when we talk about *grand opéra*? In *The New Grove Dictionary of Opera*, the term is defined as "French opera of the Romantic period, . . . generally in five acts, grandiose in conception and impressively staged."[6] The form is often said to have evolved from Daniel Auber's *La Muette de Portici* (The Mute Girl of Portici; 1828) and from Rossini's spectacular, final, French opera, *Guillaume Tell* (William Tell; 1829), passing through the operas of Fromental Halévy (best known for *La Juive*, which had its premiere in 1835), and culminating in those of Meyerbeer. Alex Ross has described grand opera as "a stylistic world unto itself, demanding lavish resources,"[7] and he noted that Meyerbeer "worked on a huge canvas, giving the impression that history itself was invading the stage." Many works in the genre require potentially voice-shattering singing, especially from tenors: Plácido Domingo, who, in his thirties, sang the role of Arrigo in *I vespri siciliani*, called it "probably the most arduous [tenor part] in the Verdi repertoire, although not as nerve-racking as Otello for the simple reason that everyone in the audience knows *Otello* and few know *Vespri*."[8]

Although *Les Vêpres siciliennes/I vespri siciliani* contains much magnificent music, a vast distance separates it from *Don Carlos*. Beyond the fact that Schiller's play stimulated Verdi's creative juices much more effectively than Eugène Scribe and Charles Duveyrier's patchwork quilt of a text for *Les Vêpres* had been able to do, there is the more important factor that Verdi himself had evolved in the interim. During the dozen years that separated the two works, he had produced the darkly powerful *Simon Boccanegra*, the brilliant *Un ballo in maschera* (A Masked Ball), and the vast canvas of *La forza del destino* (The Power of Fate), and his musical mastery and psychological acumen seemed to have developed exponentially. *Don Carlos* embodied yet another milestone in the extraordinary biography of a master whose beginnings had been exceptionally unpromising.

GIUSEPPE FORTUNINO FRANCESCO VERDI was born on October 9 or 10, 1813, in the tiny village of Le Roncole, about five kilometers from the northern Italian town of Busseto in what was then the Kingdom of Italy—a political entity created by Napoleon within his French Empire. By the time the future composer was two years old, however, Napoleon had been defeated and most of northern Italy had been reabsorbed into the Austrian Empire, exactly where it had been before the French conquest. Busseto was now part of the Duchy of Parma, under the rule of Marie Louise (or Maria Luigia, as she became known), who, although she was Napoleon's second wife, also happened to be the oldest child of the Austrian Emperor Francis I. The somewhat morally lax duchess (she had three children with her prime minister—two of them before Napoleon's death allowed her to remarry) was generally beloved in Parma: among other endearing and enduring accomplishments, she commissioned the building of the Teatro Regio —still today the city's magnificent opera house—and created a music conservatory as well as an orchestra that was initially assembled and trained by no less a figure than Paganini. But Le Roncole and Busseto were a full day's carriage ride from Parma, and the duchy's capital was frequented little if at all by humble people like Carlo Verdi and his wife, Luigia, *née* Uttini, Giuseppe Verdi's parents.

The Verdis lived in a small house that functioned as both village inn and general store; it stood near the local church, and when Giuseppe was seven years old the church's organist, recognizing the boy's musicality, persuaded Carlo to buy him a spinet.* At the age of ten Giuseppe

---

* The instrument can be seen in Milan's Museo Teatrale alla Scala.

began to attend school in Busseto, where Antonio Barezzi, a local merchant, gave him room and board and soon had him composing pieces for the local band, which Barezzi—an amateur player of various wind instruments—had founded. When Verdi was eighteen, Barezzi provided him with the wherewithal to go to Milan and audition at the city's conservatory. The auditioners agreed that the young man had talent, but he had passed the age limit for admission and did not meet certain other technical criteria; they suggested that he study privately, which he did, supported by the good Barezzi.

There ensued years of hopes and disappointments for Verdi, who eventually moved back to Busseto and married Barezzi's daughter, Margherita. They had two children during the first two years of their marriage, but both the girl and the boy died before reaching the age of two. In 1839, La Scala's impresario at last commissioned Verdi to write an opera, *Oberto, Conte di San Bonifacio* (Count of Saint Boniface); he enjoyed a modest success with it and was invited to compose a comic opera, *Un giorno di regno* (A One-Day Reign), again for La Scala. While he was working on it, his wife died of an unidentified disease; the distraught, twenty-six-year-old composer managed to complete his opera, but it failed miserably. He went through a period of great distress but finally accepted a commission to write a third opera for La Scala. That work, *Nabucco*, was a tremendous success at and after its premiere, on March 9, 1842: audiences of the day not only loved the music (especially the chorus, "Va, pensiero," which remains tremendously popular in Italy); they also perceived the biblical story of the Hebrew slaves in Babylon as a barely concealed reference to Italy's enslavement to foreign powers. Thus *Nabucco* became the true starting point of a career that would dominate Italian opera for fifty years.*

---

* It is an odd coincidence that Wagner, who would dominate German opera in the second half of the nineteenth century, was born in 1813, like Verdi; had his first major success in 1842, like Verdi; and achieved that success with his third opera (*Rienzi*), like Verdi.

A combination of artistic ambition and desire for financial stability drove Verdi to create one opera after another during the following ten years, for various important opera ensembles, mostly in Italy. *Nabucco* was followed by *I Lombardi alla prima crociata* (The Lombards at the First Crusade), and then, in quick succession, *Ernani*, *I due Foscari* (The Two Foscari), *Giovanna d'Arco* (Joan of Arc), *Alzira*, *Attila*, *Macbeth*, *I masnadieri* (The Robbers, created for Her Majesty's Theatre, London), *Jérusalem* (a reworking, in French, of *I Lombardi*, for Paris), *Il corsaro* (The Corsair), *La battaglia di Legnano* (The Battle of Legnano), *Luisa Miller*, *Stiffelio*, and then the great trio of operas that remain at the core of the world's lyric repertoire: *Rigoletto*, *Il trovatore* (The Troubadour), and *La traviata* (The Lost Woman). Some were successful, others were not, but even among those that did not do well at their premieres, most gradually gained in popularity—*La traviata* being the most outstanding example from the latter category.

In 1847, Verdi, at the age of thirty-four, began to live with the soprano Giuseppina Strepponi, two years his junior. Throughout her twenties, Strepponi had been one of the most acclaimed Italian singers of the day, as well as an early believer in Verdi's talent. But she had destroyed her voice through overwork and repeated pregnancies (she had two children and one stillborn child out of wedlock—none of them fathered by Verdi); by the time her relationship with Verdi began, she had all but retired from the stage and was teaching singing in Paris. When they moved to Busseto, and eventually to Sant'Agata, their cohabitation created a scandal that set local citizens against him—an animosity that endured even beyond the couple's marriage in 1859.

Giuseppina, a highly intelligent woman, spoke, read, and wrote at least three foreign languages (French, English, and Spanish) and was thoroughly familiar with the world of the lyric theater. She was a great support to Verdi throughout the rest of his career, and they remained together for half a century, until her death in 1897, at the age of eighty-two. Among much else, she helped him to discover texts that could be turned into libretti, and her enthusiasm for the Don Carlos story, as told by Schiller, no doubt encouraged Verdi in his choice.

SIMPLIFY. THIS LONE VERB describes the primary task of the poets whose job is to transform an already extant drama into an opera text. With some exceptions, sung words emerge much more slowly than spoken words, and words or even whole lines or verses are often repeated, in solo arias as well as in ensemble and choral scenes. Librettists must be merciless in pruning their sources' subplots and intricate dialogue; in a great opera this doesn't matter, because the emotional nuances that have to be expressed entirely through words in a spoken drama or a novel are conveyed instead through the music.

Although Schiller's play *Don Carlos* and Verdi's opera of the same name are each constructed in five acts, the libretto that Méry and du Locle produced for Verdi contains only about one-seventh the number of words that Schiller wrote for his drama—and a substantial number of the librettists' words were not based even loosely on those of the German dramatist. Act One, in particular, was not connected at all to Schiller's play, which begins more or less where Verdi's second act starts, with Elisabeth already installed as queen of Spain. Schiller used verbal explanations to make audiences or readers understand his plot's background, but Verdi wanted to take advantage of the musical and dramatic possibilities of a direct encounter between Elisabeth and Carlos *before* her betrothal to Carlos's father. To accomplish that, he and his librettists seem to have based their first act on the play *Philippe II, roi d'Espagne* (1846), by the French author Eugène Cormon. It served them well.

Still, the most important question that has to be asked in any discussion of Verdi's *Don Carlos*, also known as *Don Carlo*, is: Which *Don
Carlo(s)*? If you attend a performance of his *Macbeth* (1847), you can
assume—unless other information is provided—that you will be hearing it with the changes that the composer made in 1865; or, in the case
of *Simon Boccanegra* (1857), the performance you observe will include
Verdi's final, 1881 revisions. Likewise, you will hear *La forza del destino*
(1862) as its composer reworked it seven years after its premiere. In all
three cases, the revised versions were the composer's final word on each
work; the original, unrevised versions are occasionally resurrected,
mostly out of legitimate musico-historical curiosity, but the final versions are, precisely, final—at least for those of us who believe that composers ought to be allowed to make up their own minds. *Don Carlo(s)* is
a different case. As we have seen, Verdi originally set a French-language
libretto and called the opera *Don Carlos*, but the opera is more often performed today as *Don Carlo*, without the final *s*, in its Italian version, or,
rather, in one of its Italian versions.

Why the confusion? Here, in brief, is the Saga of *Don Carlo(s)*. Fully
three months before its Paris premiere, Verdi had completed the opera,
including the orchestration (presumably with some lacunae) but without the ballet: we know this from his above-cited letter to Count Arrivabene. By then, fearing that the work was too long, he had already cut
some material from Act Four. But once the ballet had been inserted,
Don Carlos was again deemed too long. Why not cut the ballet? Because
at the Opéra a ballet segment of at least a quarter of an hour was an
absolute requirement, thus Verdi could not avoid making further cuts
elsewhere, of which the main one was the opening scene, before Don
Carlos's entry. (About this scene, more anon.) Immediately after the premiere, an Italian translation was prepared—not, initially, for Italy, but
for London, where operas written in various languages were generally

performed in Italian.* Some butchery was involved in the London production, as Verdi later discovered, and various surgical nips and tucks, mostly unauthorized, continued to be performed upon productions in Italy, where *Don Carlo* (without the s) was given a lukewarm reception and was generally described as too long.

In 1882–83, Verdi, together with du Locle and another librettist, Charles-Louis-Étienne Nuitter, created a four-act French version that eliminated *Don Carlos*'s first act and ballet and comprised various other changes. The fact that Verdi was not altogether happy about performing this operation is clear from a letter to his friend Giuseppe Piroli:

> I'm working, but on something nearly futile. I'm reducing *Don Carlos* to four acts for Vienna. You know that in that city the doorkeepers close the houses' main doors at ten in the evening, and that's when everyone eats and drinks Beer and *Gateaux*. As a result . . . the performance has to be over. Operas that are too long are ferociously amputated as in any old Theater in Italy. Since my legs were going to be cut off, I preferred to sharpen and wield the knife myself.[9]

In the end, Verdi declared himself satisfied with the result, and in this new, shorter form *Don Carlo* was first performed, not in Vienna but in Milan, at La Scala, in Italian, in 1884. How satisfied he could have been is open to grave doubt, however, because only two years later he permitted yet another Italian version—with the first act essentially as it had been performed in Paris, plus the revised four-act version, with further alterations—to be produced in the town of Modena.

The ballet is rarely performed, but an occasional revival of the

---

* Edith Wharton commented wryly on the matter, in the first chapter of *The Age of Innocence*: "An unalterable and unquestioned law of the musical world required that the German text of French operas sung by Swedish artists should be translated into Italian for the clearer understanding of English-speaking audiences."

DON CARLO
Opera in five acts

Principal roles:

Elisabetta (Elisabeth de Valois), Princess of France, later
   Queen-Consort of Filippo (King Philip II of Spain); soprano*

Principessa d'Eboli (Princess of Eboli), Elisabetta's principal
   lady-in-waiting; mezzo-soprano

Don Carlo (Don Carlos), Infante (Prince) of Spain, Filippo's
   son; tenor

Rodrigo, Marchese di Posa (Marquis of Posa); baritone

Filippo (Philip II), King of Spain; bass

Grande Inquisitore (Grand Inquisitor); bass

Secondary roles:

Tebaldo (Thibault), Elisabetta's page, soprano (a "trouser role");
Count di Lerma, tenor; a voice from heaven, soprano; Countess d'Aremberg, a French lady-in-waiting, silent role; royal herald, tenor; the monk, bass; six Flemish representatives, basses;
monks/officers of the Inquisition, basses.

   The chorus represents at various times woodcutters and
their wives, lords and ladies of the French and Spanish courts,
pages, royal guards, soldiers, the populace.

French *Don Carlos* is produced either as it was performed at its premiere
or with the addition of the original opening that had been cut before
the premiere.

   In my opinion, the four-act version eliminates too much important
material with respect to both music and plot; in any case, what follows

---

* Throughout the Italian versions of the opera, Elisabeth de Valois is usually called Elisabetta
but sometimes Isabella, the Italianized version of Isabel, which, in turn, is the Spanish form
of Elizabeth/Elisabeth.

is a commentary on the five-act Modena version, preceded by a glance at the original opening scene. To avoid confusion, I will use only the Italian version of each character's name.* As in my account of Berlioz's *La Damnation de Faust*, my aim is not to provide a complete plot synopsis but rather to focus on some scenes—especially the three major encounters between Elisabetta and Carlo—and to summarize the others as briefly as possible.

The French *Don Carlos*'s original opening scene—about ten minutes in length—functions as a prologue to the rest of the first act and indeed to the rest of the opera. It opens with the orchestra alone, soon joined by the chorus. The tone is somber. We are in France, "around 1560"—as the score indicates—in the royal forest of Fontainebleau in winter. Some half-frozen woodcutters and their wives are lamenting the ongoing war between France and Spain, which is causing terrible hardship. Princess Elisabetta arrives with a hunting party; she witnesses the people's misery, sympathizes with them, and promises them that better times are ahead: she has been betrothed to Carlo, Spain's crown prince, she says, and their marriage will put an end to the war. The people are delighted with the news, and the scene ends joyfully.

The princess, her party, and the commoners depart, and Act One (Modena version) begins with Don Carlo, alone. He has secretly been observing the princess and is much taken with her. In a recitative-soliloquy, he explains that he has come incognito to France, as part of the entourage of Count di Lerma, the Spanish ambassador; he realizes that this act may well arouse his father's "terrible fury," but his desire to set eyes upon the "beautiful fiancée" who will "reign over my heart" was stronger than his fear of King Filippo. This leads directly into his

---

* To musicians and others who are interested in a detailed harmonic and formal analysis of this opera, I highly recommend Julian Budden's *The Operas of Verdi*, vol. 3: *From "Don Carlos" to "Falstaff"* (New York: Oxford University Press, 1981).

romanza (short aria), "Io la vidi": "I saw her, and her smile seemed to make the sun sparkle."

This lovely set-piece has been a source of joy and frustration for generations of tenors: joy, because it fits perfectly the voice of an Italianate lyric tenor—it rises gradually from the tenor's low-to-middle register up to a high A and even a quick B-natural grace note. If sung well, it elicits bravos from the audience. But it is frustrating because it is relatively brief, comes right at the beginning of a long evening, and, worst of all (from a tenor's point of view), is the only solo piece for the title character in the entire, five-act opera. Not that Don Carlo doesn't have plenty more to sing: he does—and most of what lies ahead for him is terrifyingly difficult, technically and emotionally, as well as stunningly beautiful and of the utmost importance within the story's evolution. Still, tenors regret the fact that there are no further arias for Don Carlo.

But back to Fontainebleau. No sooner has the prince's *romanza* ended than the sound of horns from the hunting party is heard in the distance. Suddenly, Elisabetta appears with her page, Tebaldo. They've become separated from the rest of their group, the princess is tired, and fog is setting in. But who is this man standing before them? Don Carlo introduces himself as a member of the Spanish ambassador's entourage. Tebaldo sees the lights of the palace in the distance, and Elisabetta, confident that she can trust an honorable Spaniard, sends the page off to get help. As Carlo begins to build a fire to warm the princess, she reveals her "hidden fear" of leaving her father and her country, and she hopes that Carlo, her betrothed, will love her. Carlo assures her that the prince will "live at your feet." He describes himself as Carlo's messenger and says that he has a gift for the princess: Carlo's portrait. Elisabetta hesitantly looks at it, realizes that she is with Carlo himself, and instantly falls in love with him. And with that, the first of their three great duet scenes becomes a true love scene—a mutual declaration of love.

Up to this point, the drama has unfolded subtly and gradually.

As Carlo begins to build the fire, only the orchestra's strings create the atmosphere—even imitating the fire's first sparks; the tempo
indication is *allegro assai moderato* (very moderately fast). Some wind
instruments—a flute, a bassoon, two horns, then two clarinets, an oboe,
and two trumpets—are quietly introduced into the accompaniment; for
an instant, most of the other winds enter as well, to punctuate Don
Carlo's first utterance of the word "amor." After Elisabetta has asked
this unknown Spaniard whether he believes that a peace treaty will be
signed that evening, the tempo becomes a little livelier, especially as
Carlo confirms that "before a new day" begins the contract for her wedding to "the king's son" must be drawn up. When Elisabetta prepares
to look at the portrait, the tempo changes to *allegro agitato*, and as she
recognizes that the portrait represents the man who stands before her
the whole orchestra explodes in a joyous *fortissimo*.

The two protagonists' duet has thus far been recitative-like: he says
something, then she says something. But now the music becomes fully
lyrical, with both of them singing of their love, sometimes separately,
sometimes together; sometimes with fragments of phrases breathlessly
chasing each other, sometimes with long, ecstatic lines sung simultaneously, an octave apart. It's worth noting, too, that as soon as Elisabetta
has recognized Carlo in the portrait and Carlo has declared his love for
her, both of them switch instantly from the super-formal second person, *voi*, to the informal *tu*. This fact, at a time—Verdi's time—when
even married couples, especially among the upper classes, sometimes
took years to get around to using the *tu* form with each other, signifies
that the composer, as well as the libretto's Italian translators, Achille
de Lauzières and Angelo Zanardini, wanted to indicate that this was
an extreme case of love at first sight. (In the original French version,
however, Carlos goes back and forth between *vous* and *tu* in addressing
Elisabeth, and she continues to use *vous* in speaking to him.)

Throughout the duet, Verdi calls on singers, conductors, and orchestra musicians to vary their delivery constantly, just as the emotional content of the words and the music fluctuates constantly. When Elisabetta, for instance, first realizes that she is in love, the tempo indication is *allegro giusto*—which may be translated as "properly fast, but not too fast"—and Verdi's instruction to the soprano is *cantabile*, lyrical. A few bars further on, Verdi writes *più animato* (more animated), and not more than ten seconds later he incites his forces to move ahead, *stringendo e crescendo* (growing faster and louder)—but then he pulls them back to the earlier tempo, as the two protagonists dwell (*dolcissimo*—very sweetly) on their love.

The duet is briefly interrupted when the sound of a cannon shot is heard in the distance; Elisabetta and Carlo praise heaven for the signal that peace has been concluded between France and Spain, which means that they will soon be united in marriage. The duet then continues, nearly delirious in its intensity, for fully two and a half minutes—until Tebaldo returns, thrilled to be bringing a "happy message" to the princess: "I greet you, my queen, wife of King Filippo."

"No, no!" Elisabetta exclaims, trembling (*tremante*, the score clearly indicates). "My father has engaged me to the crown prince." But Tebaldo tells her the truth, which he thinks will please her: her father, Enrico (Henry II), has "destined" her for the Spanish monarch himself.

Immediately, three ominous chords sound, with unusually detailed dynamic notations from Verdi: the strings are to play their notes *fortissimo*, accented, and with a *tremolo*, embellished with upward-sweeping chromatic scales in the violins; two horns must play a long note in unison, but only *forte*, not *fortissimo*, with an accent followed by a *diminuendo*; and three trombones, ophicleide (generally replaced, these days, by a tuba), and timpani are to play their notes *pianissimo* and with no accent, as a sort of ghostly underpinning to the proceedings. "Alas!" exclaims Elisabetta, before she can stop herself, while Carlo, in an aside, says that his heart has been frozen and that the abyss is opening up before him. Then, addressing a higher power, he imprecates: "And you suffer this to happen, o heaven!"

To a dirgelike accompaniment in C minor, the two of them lament their fate: for a brief moment, happiness seemed to be theirs, but now life will be an endless torment. Almost immediately, however, we hear the commoners gradually approach, to celebrate the peace treaty—and here Verdi, employing essentially the same tempo, but substituting C major for C minor and a jaunty rhythm for the funereal one, combines the masses' joy with the protagonists' sense of doom. Count di Lerma arrives and announces that the king of France wishes to give his daughter to the Spanish monarch, but he adds that Filippo, his own king, wants to know whether Elisabetta wishes to marry him, as he hopes.

It is precisely at this point that we understand why the original beginning of the opera is so important: kind Elisabetta can't help but recall the pleas of the woodsmen and their wives to bring the war's misery to an end. Now, in a few words, the wives beg her to "accept the hand that the king offers you: have pity! We'll have peace at last!"

"How do you answer?" asks the count. Elisabetta is silent for several seconds, as the strings pluck three portentous pizzicato chords, very softly, several seconds apart. Finally, she replies ("in a dying voice" the score indicates), "Yes." The people offer her their grateful blessing, as she, in an aside, reveals her "supreme anguish," and she and Carlo add, also in asides, that they feel they are dying.

The jubilant chorus then resumes, with full orchestral accompaniment, interrupted by dramatic lamentations by both protagonists, until the joy and the horror merge in a huge climax. Elisabetta, escorted by Count di Lerma, is helped onto her sedan chair; she departs, followed by the throng, while Don Carlo "remains alone and desolate," according to the stage instructions. On offbeats, and breaking words into single, strangled syllables, he says: "Such a beautiful dream disappeared! O fatal destiny, o cruel destiny!" The curtain falls.

ALL FOUR HORNS, eventually joined by other winds and timpani, open Act Two with a brief, solemn prelude. The curtain then opens on the cloister of the San Yuste monastery, where Emperor Charles V (Carlo Quinto, in Italian) had spent his last years after having abdicated the throne of Spain in favor of his son, Philip II (Filippo). A monk, prostrate before Charles's tomb, prays silently while a group of monks intones an admonition: "Charles, the greatest emperor, is now nothing but mute dust." The solitary monk (bass) then stands and sings ("grandiosely," Verdi indicates) that God alone is great.

A pallid Don Carlo enters, wandering distractedly under the cloister's vaulted arches. The monk thunderously reproaches him for having brought earthly sorrow to those who seek to remove themselves from the world. Carlo, terrified, is convinced that the monk's voice is really that of Charles V, his grandfather. Rodrigo, Marquis of Posa, Carlo's dear friend, enters and urges the prince to aid the unfortunate people of Flanders by helping to end Spain's oppression of its territories there. Carlo hesitantly confesses his love for Elisabetta, who is now his stepmother. After a moment of shock, Rodrigo again urges the prince to leave his hopeless sorrow behind and go with him to Flanders, to help stop Spain's brutal repression of the Protestants. Carlo agrees to follow Rodrigo, and, in a duet that has become one of the opera's most famous set-pieces ("Dio, che nell'alma infondere"—God, who wanted to instill love and hope in souls), the two friends swear to live and die together in the name of liberty.

They are interrupted by the arrival, in full pomp, of King Filippo (bass) and Queen Elisabetta, who have come to kneel at the emperor's tomb. Don Carlo and Elisabetta tremble upon seeing each other; the king looks "dark and suspicious," according to the stage instructions; and, as the royal couple begins to move away, Carlo exclaims that Filippo "has made her his"—nineteenth-century code language for sexual intercourse—and that he himself has "lost her." But the duet resumes as Rodrigo encourages Carlo to follow the path to freedom. The two men pledge eternal friendship, and the scene ends in a glorious orchestral outburst.

The second act's second scene is set in a "delightful place"—the queen's private garden—outside the previous scene's cloister.* Princess Eboli, Countess d'Aremberg, other women among the queen's ladies-in-waiting, and some pages, including Tebaldo, have gathered by a fountain. To pass the time, Eboli performs a brilliant (and difficult) faux–North African song about a Moorish king and queen. The charming interlude ends with Elisabetta's measured entrance, accompanied by a melancholy oboe passage. Everyone bows to the queen, and Eboli comments to herself that "a mysterious sadness continually weighs on [Elisabetta's] heart." Rodrigo approaches and surreptitiously gives the queen a note from Carlo, who asks Elisabetta to grant a request that Rodrigo will make of her; Elisabetta nervously asks Rodrigo whether she may grant him a favor, and he replies by asking, simply, that she receive Carlo, whose father's heart is closed to him—thus the prince wishes to ask her to speak to his father on his behalf.† As Rodrigo and Elisabetta converse, Eboli, in an aside, wonders whether Carlo is in love with her: she has seen him looking agitated when she is near him in the queen's entourage.

----

* Since the opera's protagonists sometimes appear at or just outside the royal palace in Madrid and at other times at the San Yuste monastery, we are presumably meant to assume that the two buildings are near each other. But the real San Yuste, established by Charles V, lies about two hundred kilometers west of Madrid, in Spain's Extremadura region. During the sixteenth century, a trip from one to the other would have taken many days.

† Those who are unfamiliar with Schiller's play will not know that Carlo has in the meantime asked his father to put Spain's forces in Flanders under his command, and that his father has denied his plea. These facts, had they been included in the opera, would have made Rodrigo's request to the queen more plausible to everyone present in the garden: Carlo would have wanted to ask Elisabetta to intervene with Filippo on his behalf. But they would also have required a separate scene in an opera that was already on the verge of exceeding its maximum allowable length.

Elisabetta agrees to see Carlo, everyone else gradually exits, and the prince enters, thus beginning the second of the opera's three great scenes between the two former fiancés. Carlo's extremely calm, formal, initial words (with the soft, gentle accompaniment of woodwinds alone) reassure Elisabetta, whom he addresses in the formal third person (*lei*), but as soon as all the ladies-in-waiting are out of earshot, the broad tempo (*largo*) of the scene as it has unfolded up to this point gives way to a frantic *allegro agitato*, with gasping syncopations played by the strings. Carlo blurts out that the atmosphere of the court torments him "like the thought of a catastrophe." He must leave, he says: "The King must let me go to Flanders."

Elisabetta, moved, begins to reply: "My son!"—which instantly makes Carlo lose his self-control: "Not that name!"—the strings play a short, gunshot-like dominant seventh chord that remains unresolved— "but the one from a different time!" he exclaims. The queen senses danger and begins to leave, but Carlo stops her, agitatedly begs for mercy, and adds, in despair, "Miserly heaven gave me only one day [of happiness], then stole it from me!"

Elisabetta holds her feelings in abeyance and addresses Carlo with the hyper-formal *voi*: "Prince, if Filippo wishes to hear my request, he can put Flanders in your hands and you can leave tomorrow." The violins provide a steady triplet pulsation to reinforce the steadiness of her response, while a bassoon and the violas and cellos double her melodic line, an octave lower. Elisabetta again indicates that she will leave the garden, but Carlo can't refrain from complaining: "Heavens! Not a single word for the wretch who is abandoning his country! Why can't I hear pity speak from your heart?" His soul is oppressed, his heart is cold, he says—as the orchestra builds in power—and in his delirium he has turned to her for a sign of pity, but she is like a piece of frozen marble from a tomb.

Elisabetta, deeply moved (*molto commossa*), replies in self-defense:

"Why do you accuse my heart of indifference?" she asks as the tempo quickens, like her own pulse. "You ought to understand this noble silence." Then, in long, radiant phrases, she says: "Duty, like a noble ray, shone before my eyes; I shall act as that ray guides me. I place my hope in God, in innocence."

Carlo answers radiance with more radiance, boldly addressing the queen with the familiar *tu*: "My lost love, my only treasure, my life's splendor. At least I can still hear you. At your words, my soul sees heaven revealing itself!" Elisabetta implores God to calm the sorrow of such a beautiful soul, but she adds, dangerously: "O Carlo, farewell, if I could live with you in this world I would think I'm in heaven!"

Verdi now moves abruptly from a very light orchestral accompaniment in B-flat major to a much denser, dreamlike texture in D-flat major, as Carlo begins to lose his bearings. "O wonder!" he says, as his voice moves gradually downward from the middle of the tenor range to its low register; here, Verdi orders the tenor to sing as if speaking (*parlante*): "My heart feels trust, consolation; the memory of sorrow takes flight . . . heaven . . . took pity on such suffering . . . Isabella . . . at your feet . . . I want . . . to die . . . of love!" And he falls to the ground in a faint. Elisabetta, alarmed, prays to heaven to instill courage in Carlo's noble, suffering heart. Verdi now orders his soprano, too, to sing as if speaking: "Sorrow is killing him . . . I'll see him die of grief in my arms, die of love . . . he whom heaven destined for me!"

Carlo begins to revive, and asks "in delirium" (accompanied by English horn, harp, and *tremolo* strings), "Whose voice descends from heaven to speak of love? You, Elisabetta, beautiful, adored one, seated next to me as I saw you one day! [. . .] You are my sweet love!" Elisabetta, desperate, calls on heaven to help her, and Carlo, reviving completely, asks why pitiless heaven didn't let him die. The whole orchestra rises in fury as he demands to be struck by lightning; he shouts his love for Elisabetta, who, horrified (and addressing him at last with the informal *tu*), moves away from him, shouting, in a fury equal to that of the orchestra, but tinged with terrifying irony, "Go, do the job, run, cut your father's veins and then, stained with his blood, you can lead your mother to the altar!" Carlo, stepping back in horror, cries, "I am accursed!" and rushes off in despair. The orchestra subsides, and the scene ends (in E-flat major) with Elisabetta kneeling to thank God for having protected Carlo and herself from transgression.

All in all, the scene is one of Verdi's greatest, musically and dramatically—a series of brilliant fragments seamlessly woven together. It is also one of the few duets in nineteenth-century Italian opera in which two people who love each other hardly ever sing simultaneously. Their encounter begins with jaw-clenching self-control—repression enforced by the fell clutch of circumstance; it moves on through lament, re-crystallization, ecstasy, and rage; and it ends in Carlo's despair and, for Elisabetta, in exhaustion but also relief. The two characters don't so much *express* emotions as *distill* them. Taken by itself, the scene is a linear, Latin *Tristan*, compressed into nine minutes. Of course, two outstanding singing actors are needed to communicate the scene's devastating impact, and so is a conductor capable of grasping Verdi's subtly detailed instructions and of making all the elements fit together convincingly and powerfully—with a first-rate orchestra.*

POOR ELISABETTA HAS TO MOVE immediately from one emotional crisis to another, because no sooner has she thanked the Lord for saving Carlo and herself from sin than the king suddenly enters, followed by everyone who had been in the garden before Carlo's arrival. "Why is the Queen alone?" he peremptorily demands to know. He orders

---

* A stage director who does not transfer the opera's action to a Nazi concentration camp, a lunatic asylum, or a planet in a distant solar system would also be a positive element, but we mustn't be too unrealistic in our desires.

Countess d'Aremberg, who ought to have been attending the queen, to leave the court and return permanently to France. Elisabetta, in a plangent but intense *romanza,* accompanied mainly by the woodwinds, implies that she wishes that she could return to her native land with the countess. She exits, weeping, leaning on Princess Eboli and followed by everyone else—except Rodrigo, whom the king commands to stay.

Up to this point, Filippo has been the barely visible puppeteer whose decisions have wittingly or unwittingly manipulated the story's other characters; now, however, Verdi and his collaborators place the king of Spain at the very center of the story, as the man whose public policies and personal concerns will alter the lives not only of the crown prince and the queen but also of the opera's two other protagonists, Eboli and Rodrigo.

As in the recent Elisabetta-Carlo encounter, so also in this one, between Filippo and Rodrigo, Verdi presents a constantly shifting musical dialogue, with an exceptionally close marriage of words to music. In a scene that lasts not much more than ten minutes there are over fifteen tempo changes, six key signature changes (with many internal modulations), frequent subtle and not so subtle alterations in the orchestral texture, and numerous precise instructions to the singers as to how certain phrases are to be delivered.

The king allows the marquis to speak freely to him; Rodrigo bluntly tells Filippo that the people of Flanders should be allowed their freedom; Filippo replies that Rodrigo doesn't understand human beings, who need to be kept under control by brute force. He tells Rodrigo that he will pretend not to have heard his dangerous statements, but, he warns, "beware of the Grand Inquisitor!" Then, to the marquis's surprise, Filippo begins to reveal his intimate troubles: as a father he is wretched, and as a husband he is even sadder. He suspects Carlo of having stolen Elisabetta's heart, and he asks Rodrigo to observe them and even to oppose the queen's wishes. Rodrigo begins to hope that he will be able to influence the king, and the five action- and emotion-packed

scenes that have made up the second act end in an optimistic, if somewhat abrupt, orchestral *tutti* in F major.

A WARM AND AT TIMES shimmering mini-prelude, in C major—
a sort of fantasy on Don Carlo's first-act *romanza*—introduces the
third act's opening scene, which takes place at night in the queen's
garden. Carlo is reading from a note that he believes to be from Elisabetta, inviting him to meet her in the garden at midnight. He trem-
bles with anticipation as Eboli enters, veiled; when she removes her
veil, he tries unsuccessfully to cover his shock, and she suddenly realizes, and exclaims, that Carlo is in love with the queen. Rodrigo, who
has secretly been watching out for Carlo, suddenly appears, and an
energetic trio ends with Eboli departing in a fury and threatening
revenge. Carlo expresses doubts about Rodrigo's friendship for him,
since the marquis is now part of the king's inner circle, but the doubts
are quickly dispelled, the friends embrace, and the scene ends with the
orchestra playing the theme of their great duet from the previous act.

The third act's final scene, commonly known as the auto-da-fè
scene, is the most spectacular—the most *grand opéra*–like—segment of
the entire work. Not surprisingly, it is also the least remarkable part of
the opera from the point of view of musical invention and character
delineation. And yet it provided Verdi with an opportunity to demonstrate not only his extraordinary ability at organizing and balancing
huge masses of singers and instruments but also his lifelong dislike of
priests and religious dogma.* As the entire orchestra attacks its open-

---

* Verdi may or may not have been an atheist, but his aversion to the Church and its
representatives is well documented. On the other hand, he respected other people's views
on the matter and even had a chapel built at Sant'Agata for Giuseppina, who was a believer,
and for other churchgoers on the estate. And, like Beethoven, Schubert, Berlioz, and many
other lapsed Catholics, Verdi wrote glorious music based on the Latin liturgy.

ing, *fortissimo* bars—nominally in E major but initially in an extremely menacing-sounding, insecure A minor—the curtain opens on crowds gathered in a large square before the Basilica of Our Lady of Atocha, a church that the historical Philip II cherished. The people proclaim their love for and dedication to the monarchy, and they hail Spain's eternal glory, but their triumphalism gives way to a plodding, low-pitched march of priests who are leading a group of chained heretics to be burned at the stake.

An offstage band, punctuated by interjections from the full orchestra, announces the arrival of the court, including Rodrigo and Elisabetta, and the crowd's enthusiasm reaches a peak. Filippo emerges from the church, and the common people prostrate themselves before him. The tempo is *maestoso* (majestic, solemn) as the king "descends the church's steps and goes to take Elisabetta's hand to continue his walk," according to the stage instructions. But there is a sudden change to *allegro mosso*, agitatedly fast, as six Flemish representatives "step forward, led by Don Carlo, and throw themselves at Filippo's feet." The king loudly demands to know who these people are, and, while Carlo is explaining that they are messengers from Brabant and Flanders, the representatives implore the king to have mercy on their people. The king, seconded by the priests, calls them infidels and demands that the guards remove them; this leads into a vast ensemble—soloists plus chorus and orchestra—in which the members of the court and the assembled commoners plead for the Flemish people, while the king and the priests remain adamant. Carlo breaks in precipitately, complaining that he is living an obscure existence at home, and demanding that his father allow him to rule in Flanders, since he is someday to wear the Spanish crown.

The Oedipal side of the story now comes to the fore: Filippo says that he would never give Carlo the sword that would someday be used on himself; he may be speaking symbolically, but Carlo, whose vocal line now rises with nearly insane intensity, shouts that God has read his heart. He draws his sword against his father and announces that he will be the savior of the Flemish people. "The prince is beside himself!" exclaim the other protagonists and the common people. Filippo calls the guards to disarm Carlo, but no one moves to follow his order; the king then draws the sword of the guard nearest him and prepares to fight his own son, until Rodrigo steps forward and orders Carlo to give him his sword. Carlo does as he is told; Filippo instantly raises Rodrigo from marquis to duke, then takes Elisabetta's hand and leads the court and the masses to watch the auto-da-fè. In a gigantic finale, the cries of the priests, the Flemish deputies, and the people meld with a heavenly voice (soprano) that regales the heretics with cold (or perhaps hot) comfort: they will soon be in paradise, enjoying God's peace.*

THE KING IS FRONT AND CENTER through most of the first part of Act Four, which opens in his private study. Dawn is breaking, the candles in two large candelabras are gradually burning out, and Filippo is "deep in meditation" at a table "cluttered with papers," according to the stage instructions. A substantial introduction, dominated by a lightly accompanied solo cello, leads into Filippo's great scene, which combines recitative-like elements within an aria, "Ella giammai m'amò" (She never loved me)—a jewel of the bass repertoire. In it, the king ponders his marriage and his son's disloyalty, and he morosely considers the time when he himself will "sleep alone," in his tomb in the Escorial.

No sooner has Filippo ended his self-pitying solo than the blind,

---

* It's little wonder that Berlioz and Verdi got along well. Readers may recall, from the previous chapter, Berlioz's description of the religion of his birth as "charming, since it has stopped burning people." One can only imagine Verdi's ironic internal laughter as he composed soothing, celestial music for the voice from above, which "consoles" the heretics with promises of heaven through the purification of fire, while their living flesh begins to char.

ninety-year-old Grand Inquisitor enters, guided by two friars. The king
has summoned him for a consultation, the lugubrious first part of which
is accompanied by the lower wind instruments plus cellos and double
basses. The king tells the inquisitor that he is thinking of having rebellious Carlo put to death, and he asks whether the inquisitor will absolve
him. No problem: the peace of the empire is more important than one
rebel's life, says his interlocutor, and, after all, God sacrificed his own
son for the world's sake. (This is Schiller's and Verdi's take on the cyn-
icism of sixteenth-century *Realpolitik*.) Then, however, the inquisitor
rebukes the king, telling him that Rodrigo is a much more dangerous
rebel than Carlo, and demanding the death of the ex-marquis, now
duke. "No, never!" shouts the king: he has found only one true friend
in his life, and he won't sacrifice him. The ancient priest replies that if
he weren't in the king's palace, he would bring Filippo himself before
the Inquisition's tribunal. The inquisitor leaves, and Filippo bitterly
exclaims: "Thus the throne must always concede to the altar!"

It's certainly an eventful morning for the king of Spain, because
Elisabetta, accompanied by the full orchestra, *allegro agitato*, bursts
into his study and throws herself at Filippo's feet, demanding justice.
The chest that contains her jewels and "objects still dearer to me" has
been stolen from her, she exclaims. The king goes to his table, takes the
chest, hands it to his astonished queen, and asks her to open it. When
she refuses, he breaks its lock, opens the chest, and immediately sees a
portrait of Carlo. Elisabetta explains that she has had it since she was
engaged to the prince, but says that she is "as pure as a lily." Filippo
calls her an adulteress; she faints; he calls for help; Eboli rushes in, followed by Rodrigo; and a solemn quartet begins. In it, Filippo curses his
own suspiciousness; Eboli tells herself that she has committed a hellish crime by betraying the queen; Rodrigo meditates that the time for
action has come—although we don't yet know what sort of action he
means; and Elisabetta, as she gradually revives, says that there is no

more hope for her on earth. This is one of those great, Verdian quartets (the most famous one being "Bella figlia dell'amore" in the last act of *Rigoletto*) in which the thoughts and emotions of each character are clearly delineated through the individual vocal lines, yet the musical blend is perfect.

The king and Rodrigo exit, presumably in different directions, leaving Elisabetta alone with Eboli, who, in great agitation (accompanied by the full orchestra, in G minor), prostrates herself before the queen. She was the one, she confesses, who betrayed Elisabetta out of jealousy, because she was in love with Carlo, who scorned her. The queen is about to pardon her when Eboli says that she has another sin to relate. As the tempo abruptly changes from *allegro agitato* to *moderato*, and as the instrumentation is lowered to a few winds and strings playing softly, she says ("in a suffocated voice") that she was seduced by the king—thus she herself committed the "error" that she had unjustly imputed to Elisabetta. At this point, the queen quietly orders Eboli to choose between exile and taking the veil. Elisabetta exits, and Eboli performs her great, three-part aria, "O don fatale" (O fatal gift). In the first, recitative-like segment, she forcefully curses her beauty, which has caused her so much wretchedness; in the second, steadier part, she berates herself for having destroyed the queen and decides to hide herself away in a cloister. But wait: she knows that Carlo is to be killed the following day, and in the aria's passionate, cabaletta-like final section she impetuously vows to save him before she forever shuts herself away from public life. (How she could know about Carlos's impending death is a mystery, since the king has not spoken with her since he made that decision. But this is one of those "opera questions" that is better left unasked.) The aria is primarily in A-flat major/minor, but it is as harmonically bold as it is emotionally varied and gripping. It requires tremendous technical virtuosity and vocal power, but great mezzo-sopranos achieve great success with it.

The rest of Act Four takes place in the dungeon in which Carlo has been imprisoned since he drew his sword on the king at the auto-da-fè. Rodrigo enters, and in a recitative passage Carlos tells him that he has lost all his energy, that his love for his stepmother continues to torment him, and that Rodrigo must look after saving the oppressed people of Flanders. No, says Rodrigo: some inflammatory letters that he had taken from Carlo—letters concerning the Flemish rebellion—were found by the Inquisition, and now he himself will be killed. In a lyrical aria ("Io morrò, ma lieto in core"—I shall die, but happy at heart), he tells Carlo that he will gladly perish in his friend's place, but that Carlo must act now on behalf of the Flemish people. The aria, gentle though it is, is in the "heroic" key of E-flat major, and, after all, Rodrigo is the only heroic, self-sacrificing male figure in the opera—whereas both female leads, Elisabetta and Eboli, demonstrate heroism through self-sacrifice.

A guard employed by the Inquisition enters with a blunderbuss and fires at Rodrigo, who dies in Carlo's arms. When the king arrives to set Carlo free, the horrified prince shouts that Filippo's hands are covered in blood; he reveals that Rodrigo died for him and that he no longer considers himself Filippo's son. Before the father-son encounter can come to a head, a swirling onrush of sound in the orchestra (*velocissimo*, extremely fast, in 6/8 time) announces a popular uprising; the king orders that the doors be opened, and a horde of commoners pours in, demanding that Carlo replace Filippo as king, while Princess Eboli, disguised, slips in and helps Carlo to escape.* Just as the masses seem ready to kill Filippo, the Grand Inquisitor enters and—accompanied by snarling, frightening orchestral outbursts—orders the people to bow down

---

* In the original French version of this scene, the king challenges the masses to strike him, but they hesitate. Also, in that version Eboli reveals to Elisabeth (who is not present in this scene in later versions of the opera) that she herself has stirred up the rebellion in order to save Carlos, and Elisabeth immediately pardons Eboli for her previous transgressions. The original version also contains music that Verdi adapted in 1873–74 for the "Lachrymosa" section of his Requiem setting.

before the king, who is protected by God. The terrified masses obey and beg for mercy, as the scene and the act come to a close.

SINCE HER DRAMATIC DUET with Carlo and her subsequent aria in reaction to the king's dismissal of Countess d'Aremberg, both in Act Two, Elisabetta has not really functioned as a protagonist. She appeared as part of the huge ensemble in the auto-da-fè scene in Act Three, and again in the Elisabetta-Eboli-Rodrigo-Filippo quartet, with some high drama before and after, in Act Four. But she truly dominates the fifth—final—act, in which Verdi gives her one of the greatest scenes that he ever created for any of his soprano heroines and follows it with one of his most beautiful soprano-tenor duets—the third and last of the major encounters between Elisabetta and Don Carlo.

We are back in the cloister of the San Yuste monastery. An orchestral introduction reminds us of the monks' chant in the scene that took place there at the beginning of Act Two. Elisabetta enters "slowly, lost in thought, [and] approaches the tomb of Charles V," the stage directions instruct. Apostrophizing the tomb's occupant, she begins her aria, "Tu che le vanità conoscesti del mondo" (You, who knew the world's vanities), with no lead-in recitative. Nor are there any pyrotechnics in this piece: the highest note—the first A-sharp above the treble clef—lies relatively comfortably within a lyric soprano's range, and there is a dip down to middle C (B-sharp, to be precise; the aria is basically in F-sharp minor) that may make some sopranos a little uneasy. The main difficulty, however, is purely artistic: the scene requires tremendous expressive power and variety. At several points, Verdi inserted specific demands—"broad phrase," "expressive," "very sweet," "emphasized," "grandiose," "dying away"—in addition to normal indications of volume and tempo. The first eight bars of the vocal line, for instance, are meant to be delivered emphatically, in a broad tempo, with only two chords (played softly by bassoons, lower brass, and timpani) briefly punctuating her declamation: "You, who knew the world's vanities and who enjoy profound rest in the tomb. . . ." But the following eight bars (" . . . if there is still weeping in heaven, weep for my pain, and bring it before the Lord's throne") are meant to soar, and are accompanied by flutes and pulsating violins and violas. As Elisabetta asks again to have her weeping brought before God, her supplication is strengthened by the rest of the woodwinds and strings plus the horns. She then interrupts her own plea: Carlo will meet me here, she says, in a recitative; he must leave and forget; I swore to Posa that I would watch over him; he must follow his destiny, blaze his path to glory. As for me, she says—on a sad, repeated note, with pauses interwoven among the words—"my day has already reached evening."

The recitative now turns into a combination recitative and aria. As we hear the main motif from the first act's love duet, the queen's thoughts fly back to her one day of happiness in the forest of Fontainebleau, and she mourns at the thought that she will no longer even be able to set eyes on Carlo, once he has left the country.* Then the aria's main theme returns, along with Elisabetta's plea to the dead Charles V. The vocal line rises to a powerful outpouring of wounded feeling, then dies away in sorrow. Altogether, in the course of an aria that lasts only eight or nine minutes, whoever is representing Elisabetta on stage must communicate commanding power, deep sorrow, wistful tenderness, bitter regret, and despair. Most wise lyric sopranos do not attempt this vocally taxing role before their mid-thirties, but whatever the singer's age may be, she must try to make listeners feel that a very young woman—perhaps a girl in her late teens—has been thrust into a situation so intolerable that her only hope is for the peace that death will, or at least may, bring.

---

* This bit of musical recall makes no sense at all in the four-act version of the opera, since the first duet will not have been heard.

That hope becomes the dominant element of the following duet, which is a brilliantly constructed series of short episodes, each with its own emotional center of gravity. Carlo enters for what is meant to be a brief goodbye. In a quiet, recitative-like passage, Elisabetta says that she wants to ask God to bless Carlo and wants to ask Carlo to forget—and to live. "I wish to be strong," he replies, as the strings provide a backdrop of long, warm notes at a variety of volume levels, "but when love is destroyed, it kills before death." She tells him to think of Rodrigo, who gave his life for him, and Carlo extols his martyred friend, while the flutes play a lyrical motif from the troubled second-act duet between the prince and the queen. The music begins to build in power as Carlo tells Elisabetta that she will either hail his victory or mourn his death, and the tone becomes fully martial (with the accompaniment of cornets, trumpets, timpani, and harp, punctuated by full orchestral chords) as she encourages his "heroic" attitude. Carlo pulls her into an embrace, saying, "Don't you see, Elisabetta? I clasp you to my breast but my virtue doesn't waver, nor will it fail me!"

Now, however, the orchestra becomes both quieter and more sorrowful: the queen weeps, but it is the "healthy weeping of women for heroes!" she says. (Remember: this is a nineteenth-century opera about sixteenth-century characters.) Verdi then moves into a fateful rhythm—deceptively gentle figurations in 4/4 time that announce and accompany a final leave-taking. In a steady, rather slow tempo (*assai sostenuto*), the two protagonists quietly declare that they will see each other "up there, in a better world," where they will finally find the happiness that was denied them on earth. (This presumably means that stepmother and stepson expect to live blissfully together in a hormoneless heaven!) The key is nominally E major, but Verdi provided what I think of as a Schubertian, constant back-and-forth alternation from minor to major, by shifting the third note of the scale from G-natural to G-sharp, back and forth, back and forth; this creates a sense of uncertainty, but the uncertain harmony lies atop a steady rhythmic base—as if Elisabetta and Don Carlo can feel the finality of their goodbyes but can't quite believe in it.

Just as they begin to separate ("Goodbye, my mother!" "Goodbye, my son!" "Forever, goodbye!"), the king bursts in, followed by the Grand Inquistor. Accompanied by the weight of the entire orchestra, Filippo demands a "double sacrifice," and the inquisitor declares that the Holy Office will do its duty. As the guards move to grab Don Carlo, the prince unsheathes his sword in self-defense. Suddenly, a tremendous orchestral *tutti* reveals the presence of the monk who appeared in Act Two. At that time, Don Carlo said that the monk's voice seemed to be that of his grandfather, and now everyone recognizes the monk as none other than Charles V. The former emperor pulls Don Carlo into the cloister with him as the others exclaim in fear and astonishment, and the opera comes to a *fortissimo* close.

WAS THIS REALLY CHARLES V? Or perhaps some sort of spectre? We never learn whether Don Carlo is to stay in the monastery with his still-living grandfather or is being taken directly to heaven by his grandfather's ghost, nor do we know whether Elisabetta will be punished or forgiven. The supernatural element (assuming that it *is* meant to be supernatural) does not exist in Schiller's play, which ends with the king breaking in on Elisabeth and Carlos's last goodbyes, Elisabeth fainting, and Philip calmly ordering the Inquisition to deal with Carlos. But Verdi wanted a more spectacular conclusion, in keeping with the *grand opéra* tradition.

There is a historical pretext, however flimsy, for the opera's ending. According to the stage directions, the story takes place circa 1560; Charles V had died only two years earlier, and six months before his death he had staged his own funeral—or pre-funeral—nominally as a sign of humility before the Lord but surely also to instruct his family and underlings on how he wanted everything done. (Paranoid, megalomaniacal leaders have existed throughout history—and let's not forget that two years before his death Charles had abdicated as Holy Roman Emperor in favor of his brother, Ferdinand, and had passed the monarchy of Spain and its possessions on to his son, Philip, so that he could be sure that the people he trusted would continue his policies.) The idea that the emperor might have staged his own funeral a second time and might still have been wandering around San Yuste, where he had spent his last years, was not entirely far-fetched.

The one thing we know for sure, however, is that despite its odd ending, *Don Carlo* is one of Verdi's masterpieces, thus also one of the greatest works in the lyric repertoire. "I don't know what will happen in the future," Verdi wrote to Count Arrivabene after the tepid reception accorded the work at its world premiere in Paris, but, he added, "don't be surprised if things change."[10] Things did change, but slowly: not until the twentieth century did *Don Carlo* receive its due. For one thing, the work is terribly difficult to perform well—massive, and massively exhausting, for everyone concerned. Enrico Caruso reportedly said that *Il trovatore* is an easy opera to perform—"all you need are the four greatest singers in the world." Well, for *Don Carlo* you need five of them— the soprano (Elisabetta), mezzo-soprano (Eboli), tenor (Carlo), baritone (Rodrigo), and bass (Filippo)—as well as a good, solid second *basso* for the role of the Inquisitor. You also need an orchestra and a chorus capable of both power and subtlety, and an outstanding conductor to unify and give shape and direction to a perilously vast musical structure.

Still, like many or even most of Verdi's other scores, this one can make its intended effect even under unpromising circumstances. After having attended a grossly defective performance of *Don Carlo* at the Vienna State Opera in 1963, Igor Stravinsky was "rapturous" about the work, according to the diary of his assistant, Robert Craft, who quoted the octogenarian composer: "'Verdi could give such grand scale to his people only because his own scope and vitality were unmatched; how I would like to have known him! His was the true spirit of *libertà.*'"[11]

SCHILLER'S *DON CARLOS* AND Verdi's opera of the same name are often described as historical dramas, but they could more accurately be called historical fantasies, because the real-life stories of most of the principal characters bear little resemblance to the ways in which they are depicted in these works. By the time the thirty-two-year-old Philip II (1527–1598; king of Spain from 1556) married the fourteen-year-old Elisabeth de Valois (1545–1568), eldest daughter of Henry II of France and Catherine de' Medici—she of the St. Bartholomew's Day massacre of French Protestants—he had already outlived two previous wives. Elisabeth had several miscarriages but also pre-sented Philip with two daughters who lived to adulthood. She died in childbirth at the age of twenty-three. Two years later, Philip mar-ried Anne of Austria, his twenty-one-year-old niece; one of their chil-dren became King Philip III.

Don Carlos, prince of Asturias (1545–1568), the title character in Schiller's play and Verdi's opera, was Philip's only son from his first marriage and was therefore the crown prince. According to a report by the Venetian Republic's ambassador to the Spanish court, Carlos was "undersized, ugly, physically weak, melancholy, dull in studies as in ath-letics, ill-tempered, vicious, and vindictive; his slow speech consists of interminable questions punctuated by gross insults to all and sundry—even his father."[12] There is no indication whatsoever of any romantic or otherwise illicit relationship between Carlos and Elisabeth. Philip eventually had his son confined to his quarters as a virtual prisoner, because—as the king wrote to Pope Pius V—the prince did not have the intellectual ability or the strength of character to make him a suitable monarch. Carlos, a glutton, was given unlimited access to food, and, if contemporary reports are to be believed, he literally ate himself to death in six months. He was twenty-three when he died.

Doña Ana de Mendoza de la Cerda y de Silva Cifuentes (1540–1592) was married at thirteen to the thirty-seven-year-old court counselor Dom Rui Gómez de Silva, 1st Prince of Éboli, with whom she had ten children. She was reported to have been blind in one eye but strikingly beautiful; there is no record, however, of her having had a romantic or sexual relationship with either Don Carlos or Philip II.

Rodrigo, Marquis of Posa, is a fictional character.

A curiosity: Catherine Michelle, the younger of Philip II and Elisabeth de Valois's two surviving daughters, married Charles Emanuel I, Duke of Savoy. I can't help idly wondering whether Verdi, who was active in the Italian reunification struggle and met Victor Emanuel II of Savoy, the first king of reunited Italy, was aware of the fact that the monarch was a direct descendant of Charles V, Philip II, and Elisabeth de Valois.

VERDI WENT ON TO WRITE more masterpieces after *Don Carlo*: *Aida*, which had its premiere in 1871; the Requiem Mass (1874), *Otello* (1887), *Falstaff* (1893), and the magnificent *Te Deum* and *Stabat Mater* among his Four Sacred Pieces (1895–97, when the composer was in his early to mid-eighties). Although he was born only five months after Wagner and only a few years after Liszt, Schumann, Chopin, and Mendelssohn, he outlived Wagner by nearly eighteen years, Liszt by fifteen, Schumann by forty-five, and Chopin and Mendelssohn by over half a century. When Verdi died, in Milan, on January 27, 1901, at the age of eighty-seven, composers forty and fifty years his junior— Puccini, Mahler, Debussy, and Richard Strauss, among others—were already dominating the European musical scene.

In his time, Verdi was looked down upon by many of his Austro-German contemporaries, especially Wagner and his disciples, who considered his music "commercial" and not sufficiently "profound." Upon reading through the score of Verdi's Requiem, Hans von Bülow, the famed pianist and conductor, dismissed it instantly as "Verdi's latest opera, although in ecclesiastical robes." But a friend of Bülow's—another German musician—had studied the same score and angrily told Bülow that he was wrong. "Only a genius could have written such a work!" he commented.

That musician was Johannes Brahms.

7

ALMOST A TALE OF JOY

Johannes Brahms: String Quintet
No. 2 in G Major, Op. 111 (1890)

NOT LONG AFTER HIS FIFTY-SEVEN BIRTHDAY, in the spring of 1890, Johannes Brahms was on the verge of bringing his career as a composer to a close. "I've been tormenting myself for a long time with all kinds of things, a symphony, chamber music, and other stuff, and nothing will come of it," he told a friend, the musicologist Eusebius Mandyczewski. "Above all I was always used to everything being clear to me. It seems to me that it's not going the way it used to. I'm just not going to do any more. My whole life I've been a hard worker; now for once I'm going to be good and lazy!"[1]

Beethoven, whose gigantic shadow had loomed over Brahms for much of his life, had died at the age of fifty-six; perhaps that knowledge had set up a psychological block. Or perhaps Brahms simply felt that his creative impulses were drying up. Another friend, the famed surgeon Theodor Billroth, visited him at the Austrian resort of Bad Ischl that summer and likewise heard him say that he was not planning to do any further composing. But—as he later told Mandyczewski—his thoughts about retiring from composing made him "so happy, so contented, so delighted, that all at once the writing began to go [well]."[2] In other words, his writer's block disappeared, and when he returned home to Vienna in the fall he brought with him the manuscript of a new quintet for two violins, two violas, and cello—his second work in the genre—which would prove to be one of the most beautiful of all his chamber music compositions and the beginning of a "late period" in his creative life.

I put the term "late period" in quotation marks because in Brahms's case its meaning is mostly chronological, not stylistic. In the artistic development of some composers—Beethoven, Verdi, and Stravinsky, most strikingly, among those included in this book—a few reasonably clear lines of demarcation exist: "early," "middle," and "late" periods for Beethoven and Verdi; "Russian," "neoclassical," and "serial" periods for Stravinsky. Although the personalities of all three artists are as present in their youthful works as in their final masterpieces, their musical languages changed almost beyond recognition during the intervening decades. But some other composers, among whom Brahms is a prime example, seem to have been born with their musical essences fully developed. They mine the same, diamond-laden veins throughout their creative lives, without needing to make new excavations. In Brahms's music, the expressive content varied greatly over the course of his career, but the musical language is as recognizable in his Piano Sonata, Op. 1, composed before he turned twenty, as in the *Four Serious Songs*, Op. 121, written more than forty years later.

The String Quintet No. 2 in G major, Op. 111, is a case in point: a late work that yet is ageless. Early in October 1890, Brahms sent a manuscript copy of the new composition to his friend Elisabet von Herzogenberg (*née* von Stockhausen), wife of the composer Heinrich von Herzogenberg and a highly accomplished musician in her own right. She not only was enthusiastic about the piece but even teased Brahms that she felt she ought to "congratulate you on your thirtieth birthday," so youthful was the new work's atmosphere. It "overflows exquisitely with melodiousness, gentle charm, heavenly delight," she wrote, and she admired its "wonderful clarity and compact conciseness." She had not hesitated to criticize several of Brahms's other works, but she perceived this new composition as "perhaps even more beautiful, pressed from even riper grapes," than his eight-year-old String Quintet No. 1 in F major, Op. 88, although she loved the earlier work, too. After having commented on the new piece's individual movements, Herzogenberg concluded: "In what a happy mood must one have been, to have invented all of this."[3] To which we may add: perhaps.

The first public performance of the G major Quintet was given in Vienna on November 11, 1890 by the Rosé Quartet, named for its twenty-seven-year old first violin, Arnold Rosé, who had been concertmaster of the Vienna Philharmonic and Court Opera (later State Opera) since he was nineteen and would retain that position until the Nazis had him fired in 1938. In December, the Joachim Quartet, led by *its* first violin, Brahms's old friend Joseph Joachim, performed the work in Berlin.* Both performances were successful—a fact that may have helped put an end to the composer's concern over the possible end

---

* The Rosé Quartet's members at the time were Arnold Rosé, first violin; Julius Egghard Jr., second violin; Anton Loh or Hugo von Steiner, viola; and Reinhold Hummer, cello. (Rosé, originally Rosenblum, was Jewish, as was his wife, Justine, Gustav Mahler's sister. Their daughter, the gifted violinist Alma Rosé, would die at Auschwitz at the age of thirty-seven.) The Joachim Quartet's members were Joseph Joachim, first violin, Heinrich de Ahna, second violin; Emmanuel Wirth, viola; and Robert Hausmann, cello. I have not been able to identify the musicians who played second viola in either of these performances.

In both of his string quintets, Brahms followed the instrumentation used by Mozart in *his* string quintets: two violins, two violas, and one cello. Schubert, in his great String Quintet in C major, employed two violins, one viola, and two cellos

of his creative years. It's true that the Double Concerto for violin and cello, written three years earlier, would remain his last composition for orchestra, but he would continue to produce great vocal, piano, and chamber music during the last half-dozen active years of his life.

SCHUMANN, BERLIOZ, AND VERDI, the protagonists of this book's three previous chapters, were born within ten years of each other; Brahms—born in Hamburg on May 7, 1833—was two decades younger than the youngest of them. He was the second of three children of Johann Jakob and Johanna Henrica Christiane Brahms, *née* Nissen. Johanna, a seamstress, was seventeen years older than Johann Jakob, who had migrated from rural Schleswig-Holstein to the Hanseatic port city. Young Johannes's rudimentary musical instruction came from his father, who played various instruments and was eventually engaged as a double-bass player in Hamburg's city orchestra, but by the age of seven the boy was taking piano lessons from Otto Cossel, a respected local teacher. Three years later, Eduard Marxsen, one of the most esteemed musicians in the city, took Johannes on as a piano and theory student, and at fifteen Marxsen's star pupil gave his first solo recitals. Even then, however, the young Brahms's main interest was composition.

In 1853, Eduard Reményi, a well-known Hungarian violin virtuoso, engaged the twenty-year-old Brahms to accompany him on a concert tour, in the course of which the young pianist became acquainted with two other Hungarian-born musicians: Franz Liszt, who was serving, at the time, as music director of the Duchy of Weimar, and Joseph Joachim. Although Joachim was only two years older than Brahms, he was already one of the most famous violinists in Europe—a former protégé of Mendelssohn and a star performer since the age of twelve. Brahms played some of his own compositions for Joachim, who was impressed

by his new friend's command of the keyboard and downright astonished by the depth and originality of his music. He insisted that Brahms,
who was about to go hiking along the Rhine, make a stop in Düsseldorf
to meet Robert and Clara Schumann, with whom Joachim had recently
become friendly.

After some hesitation, Brahms worked up the courage to knock at
the Schumanns' door; they weren't at home, but he knocked again the
following day. Robert invited him in and asked him to play some of his
compositions. After having listened to one piece, he called Clara to join
them; he had Brahms repeat what he had just played and then asked
him to play more of his works. That evening, Clara wrote in her diary
that all of the music the young man had played for them was "rich in
fantasy, depth of feeling and mastery of form. . . . It is truly moving to
behold him at the piano, his interesting young face transfigured by the
music, his fine hands which easily overcome the greatest difficulties (his
things are very difficult), and above all his marvelous works." And Robert wrote laconically, in his own diary: "Visit from Brahms (a genius)."[4]

In the influential *Neue Zeitschrift für Musik* (New Journal for Music),
which he had co-founded, Schumann published an article, "Neue
Bahnen" (New Paths), in which he declared, in typically high-flown
prose, that he had longed for someone "who would bring us his mastery not in the process of development, but springing forth like Min-
erva fully armed from the head of Jupiter. And he has come, a young
blood over whose cradle graces and heroes kept watch. He is called
Johannes Brahms."[5]

This messianic prophecy brought a previously unknown twenty-
year-old to the attention of musicians and music lovers throughout the
German-speaking world and allowed Brahms to find first-rate publishers for those of his early works that he deemed worthy of being issued.
(On that point he was—and would continue to be—extraordinarily self-
critical.) Yet not even Schumann's enthusiasm was sufficient to make

Brahms's professional life easy. The young man certainly would not be able to live even modestly on his earnings as a composer, nor was he the sort of virtuoso pianist who could support himself by traveling from town to town playing flashy repertoire that would dazzle audiences. Ideally, he would find a position as Kapellmeister (music director) in a German city or town, where he would lead local instrumental and choral ensembles and compose new works for them to perform. But, as a shy, socially awkward twenty-year-old, his chances of even obtaining such a job, let alone succeeding at it, were slim.

Brahms returned to his family in Hamburg, where he continued to work on his compositions and to correspond with publishers, but after Schumann's suicide attempt and subsequent confinement in a mental institution—only five months after Brahms's first encounter with him— his protégé hurried back to Düsseldorf to assist Clara, who had numerous children and a major career to look after. He fell deeply in love with her, although she was nearly fourteen years his senior (an age gap similar to the one between Brahms's father and mother). Their fraught, probably platonic, but certainly passionate friendship and mutual musical trust endured until Clara's death, four decades later, despite numerous crises, often caused by Brahms's bluntness and prickliness.

Most people who have any mental image at all of Brahms think of him as the portly, untidy, gray-haired, cigar-smoking man portrayed in photographs taken after he turned forty-five, when he began to sport an enormous, generally unkempt beard. But in his youth and early middle age, Brahms was blond and handsome, short but physically healthy, fond—as Beethoven had been—of taking long, strenuous walks in the woods. In the years that followed his romantic involvement with Clara he was strongly attracted to various other women, but his attitude toward women in general was not straightforward. According to a well-known story, in his early teens he had had to earn money for his family by playing the piano in brothels frequented by sailors in Hamburg's notorious St. Pauli district, and this traumatic experience was said to have contributed to his complicated later relationships with women. But the story has been discredited by most of his biographers. In any case, I don't subscribe to the theory that Brahms saw women as either saintly virgins or whores, since virtually all of his loves and infatuations, which continued into his last years, were with intelligent, gifted, strong-willed women who existed far from either of those extreme categories. His most serious attachment, after Clara, was to Agathe von Siebold, a professor's daughter in Göttingen, when he was twenty-five and she twenty-three; the couple even secretly exchanged rings. But Brahms suddenly broke off their engagement and wrote to Agathe that he loved her but could not be "fettered." She, like most of the other women who later attracted him and/or were attracted to him, gave up on him and married another man, and in all of those cases, so far as is known, Brahms's sense of regret was outweighed by his feelings of relief. He remained a bachelor whose sexual activities were limited to encounters with prostitutes, and he might have echoed a cynical statement made by his younger contemporary, Paul Gauguin: "Like Jesus I say, the flesh is the flesh and the spirit is the spirit. Thanks to this, a small sum of money satisfies my flesh, and my spirit is left in peace."[6]

LIKE MANY OTHER OUTSTANDING artists in all creative fields and at all times, Brahms struggled in his early years to have his works accepted by the public. Especially notorious was the hostile reception that his Piano Concerto No. 1, in D minor, received at its first Leipzig performance in 1859: there was silence after each of the first two movements—at a time when enthusiastic applause between movements was not only tolerated but greatly desired—and open hissing after the finale. Brahms also managed to make enemies of older, progressive or radical musicians like Liszt and Wagner, by maintaining and even proclaiming his allegiance to traditional classical and pre-classical forms. He used those forms for his highly individual, expressively Romantic, and harmonically and rhythmically modern works, but he understood that his gift lay in his capacity to invent within the formal constraints that had been established in the late eighteenth and early nineteenth centuries, rather than in the freer style of a Liszt, let alone the greatly expanded lyric forms of Wagner, whose harmonic genius Brahms nevertheless admired. Wagner spoke contemptuously of Brahms, as he did of most people whose opinions differed from his own, but Brahms studied and attended performances of Wagner's operas. At times he seriously considered writing an opera himself, but whatever ideas he may have had in that area never got beyond the libretto-seeking phase.*

In his twenties and thirties, Brahms published piano sonatas, variations, ballades, and other keyboard pieces; orchestral and choral works; chamber music; and lieder in abundance. But he avoided two forms, the string quartet and the symphony, in which Beethoven's daunting posthumous presence was particularly strong. Or rather: he worked on pieces in those forms but either discarded them or let them gestate for exceptionally long periods. Not until he was forty did he publish two string quartets, after having destroyed as many as twenty others, and his First Symphony did not appear until three years later. By then, however, his fame was secure, thanks especially to the success of what would remain his largest-scale choral-orchestral work, *Ein Deutsches Requiem* (A German Requiem), first performed in its entirety in 1871.

Hamburg had remained Brahms's base until he was nearly thirty, although in his mid-twenties he had spent substantial periods each year as court Kapellmeister in the town of Detmold, the capital of a small

---

* This writer has long dreamt of becoming the artistic director of a well-subsidized festival dedicated to performances of the operas of Bach, Chopin, Bruckner, and Brahms, so that he could draw a handsome salary without having to do anything.

principality. As a young man he had longed for solid recognition—in the form of a steady position—in his home town; when no significant job was offered, he began to gravitate toward Vienna, hoping that once he established his reputation in the musical capital of the German-speaking world his fellow Hamburgers would invite him to return home in glory, so that he could be with his family. But the invitation did not come until his parents were dead and until he was too comfortably ensconced and too greatly admired in Vienna to want to leave. Although he occasionally took up part-time positions elsewhere and toured—generally with Joachim or other concert partners—throughout Germany, Austria, Switzerland, Hungary, Denmark, and the Netherlands, Vienna remained his home from the age of thirty-five to the end of his life.

Brahms greatly admired Otto von Bismarck, the "Iron Chancellor," and favored a united Germany under imperial Prussian leadership, yet, paradoxically, he was a liberal of firmly democratic principles. Many of his closest friends in and away from Vienna were Jewish or part-Jewish—Joachim, first and foremost, but also the composer Karl Goldmark, the conductor Hermann Levi, the composer-pianist Ignaz Brüll, the singer-conductor-pianist-composer George Henschel (who became the Boston Symphony Orchestra's first conductor), the influential music critic Eduard Hanslick, and Brahms's own future biographer Max Kalbeck, among others. At one point in the 1880s or 1890s, when Vienna was in the midst of one of its periodic outbreaks of virulent anti-Semitism, Brahms, out of solidarity with his friends, joked that he was going to have himself circumcised.

Friendship was extremely important to Brahms, who lived alone and in modest quarters even in later years, when his widely performed works had made him well-to-do. He enjoyed emerging in the evening and dining with friends, in their homes or at restaurants, and he liked good food and drink—sometimes too much of both—as well as cigars and cigarettes, which he smoked constantly. At times he could be needlessly and cruelly outspoken (on one occasion, as he left a roomful of friends, he remarked, "If there is someone I have forgotten to insult, I hope he'll forgive me"), but more often he was good company and enjoyed both teasing and being teased.

Of all the celebrated nineteenth-century composers, Brahms was probably the most curious and best informed about the music of the past—not only the works of Bach, Haydn, Mozart, Beethoven, Schubert, and their contemporaries, but also sixteenth- and seventeenth-century music, and this was at a time when relatively few creative musicians cared to extend their studies that far back. Verdi, for instance, was dazzled by the polyphonic writing of Giovanni Pierluigi da Palestrina (c. 1525–1594), whom he placed alongside Bach and Beethoven in his personal pantheon of great composers, but Brahms outshone Verdi and their contemporaries in the breadth and depth of the attention paid to the music of the distant past. The field of musicology—the organized, historico-analytical study of music and its elements—was in its infancy in Brahms's day, and many of the most significant musicologists of the time drew upon his knowledge and advice in their work. He participated, in varying degrees, in the preparation of editions of works by Heinrich Schütz, François Couperin, Domenico Scarlatti, Handel, Haydn, Mozart, Schubert, Chopin, and Schumann, and the process worked both ways: he learned from the older masters' works while helping to make faithful editions of their music available to musicians and music lovers.

Brahms was an enthusiastic Bible-reader but a nonbeliever. And whereas the lapsed Catholics Beethoven, Schubert, Berlioz, and Verdi composed powerful Latin liturgical music, the lapsed Lutheran Brahms, in his *German Requiem*, composed an agnostic's prayer based on a German translation of biblical texts, not in order to beg a possibly nonexistent God to save the possibly nonexistent souls of the dead, but to console the living for the deaths of their loved ones and for the awareness of their own inevitable end. When his friend Carl Reinthaler, organist of the Bremen Cathedral, hesitantly mentioned to Brahms the strange fact that—as Jan Swafford, one of Brahms's biographers, put it— "somehow the piece never gets around to mentioning Jesus Christ,"[7] Brahms replied: "Concerning the text, I confess that I would very gladly have left out even 'German' [in the title] and simply put in 'of Human-kind,' also entirely consciously and willfully I would have done without passages like John 3:16," which refers to everlasting life for believ-ers. "But—I'll stop before I say too much,"[8] he concluded. Years later, Antonín Dvořák, a devout Catholic whose career Brahms had gener-ously helped to advance, remarked about his benefactor: "Such a man, such a fine soul—and he believes in nothing! He believes in nothing!"[9]

MANY YEARS AGO, I began to write a novel in which, at one point, the young protagonist described the approaching departure, possibly forever, of the girl he loved. "That summer," he says, "I couldn't bear to listen to Brahms, one of my favorite composers. His music would make me break down with emotion, and only years later did I under-stand why. Brahms is entirely about loss—anticipating it, feeling it, meditating on it, trying not to feel or meditate on it, glorying in it, dramatizing it, joking about it, fending it off, peacefully or unpeace-fully coexisting with it, accepting it, remembering it. The sense of imminent loss was constantly welling up in me that summer; Brahms invariably made it overflow."

Although, as you see, I have no talent for fiction, the Brahms descrip-tion holds up, in my not unprejudiced opinion, and while I was writing the present chapter I felt vindicated when I came across Nicole Grimes's new (2019) book, with its striking title, *Brahms's Elegies: The Poetics of Loss in Nineteenth-Century German Culture*. There is intense warmth in Brahms's works, but it is the warmth of a man who needs to keep his distance from others, a man who would like to avoid both hurting others and (especially) being hurt by them but can't quite manage either feat. When his music is joyful, the joy is that of someone much more accustomed to *not* having it than to having it—someone who has to fight with himself to experience joy.

Elisabet von Herzogenberg's above-quoted comments to Brahms about the G major String Quintet's "melodiousness, gentle charm, heavenly delight," as well as its seemingly youthful ardor, are correct, but they tell only part of the story. I have called this chapter "Almost a Tale of Joy," but I could just as well have copied the title that the novelist Amos Oz gave to his remarkable memoir of his early years: *A Tale of Love and Darkness*. There is joy and there is love in this quintet—the joy and love of a man who takes pleasure in giving the world everything that he values in himself, especially his ability to absorb and communicate life's unfathomable beauty. Also present in this work, however, and even more unforgivingly than in many of Brahms's other compositions, is the dark awareness of life's brevity. The quintet begins with profound joy and ends in exuberant high spirits, but each of its four movements contains an abyss.

THE G MAJOR STRING QUINTET'S first movement opens in a blaze of pulsating accompanying figures—sixteenth-note groups played by both violins and both violas, with the cello entering almost immediately to introduce the rhapsodic first theme, in G major and 9/8 time. The tempo indication is *Allegro non troppo, ma con brio* (not too fast, but with verve), but in publishing a four-hand piano version of the piece Brahms changed the indication to *Allegro energico*; as Styra Avins suggests, in her valuable book, *Johannes Brahms: Life and Letters*, string players, too, "may want to consider that very suitable designation."[10] As a matter of fact, Brahms tended to be somewhat vague when he was asked for advice about the proper tempi for his compositions, and he provided metronome marks for only a handful of them.*

Another practical consideration: at the time of the work's Vienna and Berlin premieres, the performers complained that the cellist had trouble making his melodic line heard over the four accompanying instruments, since all five parts are marked *forte*. Reinhold Hummer, the Rosé Quartet's cellist, even asked Brahms to write *piano* for the other instruments. "I didn't give in, but the right sound didn't happen either,"[11] Brahms wrote to Joachim. At Joachim's suggestion, Brahms considered rewriting the first few bars of the violin and viola parts, and for a time he added *diminuendo* and *crescendo* signs to them, but he returned to his original plan when he sent the work to be published. The cello part is marked *forte sempre*, the others merely *forte*, and there is no indication except *forte* for any of the instruments throughout the entire first theme. Dynamic marks are always relative—there are degrees of *piano* and *forte*, depending on the context—but there is an additional aspect to this specific detail. Until early in the twentieth century, most cellists used either very short endpins (spikes) or no endpins at all, which meant that instead of keeping the instrument from falling by resting an endpin on the floor, they had to grasp the cello between their knees and calves, which inevitably muffled some of its sound. Contemporary photos demonstrate that Hummer, in the Rosé Quartet, used a very short endpin, and Robert Hausmann, the Joachim Quartet's cellist—and one of the most celebrated cellists in Europe—used none. Today, nearly all cellists, with the exception of those who try to approximate older performance practices, use a long or longish endpin; this eliminates any muffling of sound and certainly helps cellists who perform this quintet

---

* Among the few extant metronome marks, several indicate tempi considerably faster than most performers adopt today. See, for instance, the indications for the first movement (quarter note = 92) and third movement (quarter note = 84) of the Second Piano Concerto, Op. 83. Food for thought!

to project their instruments' voices over the dazzling but dense accompanying texture of the opening bars' accompaniment.

Dazzling, dense, but also radiant: that is how the main theme of this movement emerges, or should emerge—immediately, unhesitatingly, unstintingly. This is Brahms at his most openhearted, joyous, and generous. Max Kalbeck claimed that upon first hearing the theme he had remarked to the composer: "Brahms in the Prater!"—Vienna's public park. To which Brahms had replied, with a smile, "You've got it! And all the pretty girls there, eh?" The opening motif, played first by the cello, then taken up ecstatically by the first violin and elaborated on by the other instruments, must be performed with *Schwung*—the German term for an outgoing momentum that yet comes from deep within. This overflow of good feeling is maintained through the piece's first twenty bars—roughly one minute of music. Each phrase flows uninterruptedly into the next, until Brahms leads us through a brief series of abrupt chords and descending arpeggios into a mellower but still full-throated second theme (D major), in which the instruments playing the melodic line (the two violas at first, then the two violins) are instructed to play *forte espressivo*, while the accompanying instruments are initially brought down to a *mezzo forte*. This passage lasts not much more than half a minute before a third thematic element is introduced—a gentler and more subdued melody (*piano* and *dolce*) than its predecessors. Although it lasts only eight bars, it feels like the most beautiful of slow Viennese waltzes, played initially by the second violin in its middle register and then by the first violin, soaring an octave higher. This is followed in turn by a sort of *codetta*, energetic at first but gradually abating, and leading into a repetition of the entire exposition—everything that we have heard up to this point.

By the time the repeat ends, the movement is five and a half or six minutes old. Brahms begins the development section by taking us abruptly yet gently from D major to B-flat major, as the first viola and

first violin, and then the two violins, play a glowing, slowed-down fragment of the third thematic element, over a shimmering accompaniment. After less than half a minute, however, the glow mutates into
fearful anguish (G minor): four bars of gut-wrenching chords give way
to a series of battling arpeggios in eighth- or sixteenth-note patterns,
some of them proceeding unyieldingly upward while others move defi-
antly downward. When a fragment of the movement's joyous main
theme reappears, played *fortissimo* this time, the battle seems to have
resolved itself, especially since the fragment is followed by a renewed
sense of calm (*piano, dolce*). But the calm is short-lived and illusory,
because Brahms then thrusts us into what may well be the eeriest, most
timorously disoriented half-minute in any of his works.

That segment begins with quietly upward-slithering notes—*pianissimo sempre*—that are followed by hollow, depressed-sounding chords
(violas and cello); these are succeeded in turn by two groups of ghostly,
clashing intervals played by the violins—intervals that set your teeth on
edge, especially if these note groups are played, as I believe they should
be, with a deathly pallid, vibrato-less sound. But the battle reawakens
(*forte, ben marcato*—well emphasized), as the slithering notes combine
with the disturbing intervals and the contrasting elements. The most
apt literary equivalent of this frighteningly mysterious segment may be
the opening lines of Dante's *Inferno*, in which the poet has lost his way in
a dark wood. But Brahms, unlike Dante, has no Virgil to lead him out of
the dense obscurity. He emerges on his own, by force of will—by what
Emerson called self-reliance: he has to "detect and watch that gleam of
light which flashes across his mind from within, more than the lustre of
the firmament of bards and sages."[12]

The instruments strain to sound a series of alarm "bells" (*pesante*—
heavy—is Brahms's instruction here) to pre-announce a final emergence
from confusion into the warm light of the movement's opening theme.
And indeed, the recapitulation—which follows the exposition's pattern

fairly closely, although in a slightly shortened form—brings back all of the uninhibited joy and all of the consolatory mellowness that were present in the opening section. A substantial coda recombines not only all of the movement's thematic elements but also all of its emotional peaks and dips, and it ends in a G major sunburst.

EVER SINCE HIS FIRST VISIT to Italy, in 1878, Brahms had harbored a great love for the country—its people, its art, its natural beauty, and its food and wine—and he returned there seven times during the following fifteen years, usually for about a month in the spring, accompanied by one or more of his friends. These were the only vacations that he ever spent outside the German-speaking countries, and he gradually got to know most of Italy's great cities as well as many less familiar places, from the Alps to Sicily, from the Tyrrhenian to the Adriatic. The second-last of his Italian journeys, in the spring of 1890, shortly before he composed the G major String Quintet, took him from Lake Garda to the towns of Parma, Cremona, Bergamo, Brescia, Vicenza, Padua, and Verona.

Leery though I am of making specific or even quasi-specific connections between occurrences in artists' lives and the works that they create (except, of course, when the artists themselves identify such connections), as a lifelong Italophile I can't help hearing traces of Italy in the sunny exuberance of the opening theme of the quintet's first movement and in the melancholy cantilena that initiates the second movement. Most experts will disagree with me, especially on the latter point, since, as musicologist Margaret Notley has pointed out, the second movement is replete with "short subphrases, dotted rhythms, augmented seconds, [and] tremolos that imitate the cimbalom," all of which would seem to "evoke a gypsy style" that, in Brahms's day, was considered typically Hungarian.[13]

But whether or not my theory has any validity, what's certain is that a convincing performance of the five-and-a-half- or six-minute-long second movement (in 2/4 time, nominally in D minor but really fluctuating between D minor and A minor and between D minor and D major) requires performers to observe Brahms's tempo indication, *Adagio*, according to the literal Italian meaning of the word: "at ease"—in other words, unhurried, comfortable, slowish but not too slow. Otherwise the movement can sound dirgelike. It is a freestyle meditation on three basic, recurring thematic elements: (1) the abovementioned melancholy cantilena, presented by the first viola during the movement's eight opening bars; (2) a hesitant, "questioning," four-bar phrase in which the violins keep interrupting themselves (there are three notes, then a rest; three notes, then a rest; three notes, then a rest); and (3) a two-bar, meandering phrase, played, like the opening, by the first viola. A ten-bar-long variant of the opening element is followed by a four-bar variant of the second element and then by a four-bar variant of the third element—and so on, for about three minutes, through which eighth notes and sixteenth notes carry the discourse forward.

All of a sudden, however, Brahms slows the harmonic motion down to a series of quarter-note chords marked *pianissimo*, then *diminuendo*, and finally *perdendosi*—literally losing themselves, disappearing. These gradually evaporating chords are followed by a dramatic, passionate outburst, with all five instruments jabbing at each other with all sorts of rough-edged rhythms and contrasting upward and downward thrusts. We seem to be in a sort of unorthodox, minute-and-a-half-long development section, complete with a splintering, combining, and transforming of the three thematic elements, until at last the opening element returns and then fades away, ending the movement with four D major chords that leave us somewhere between reassurance and uncertainty, wondering what the next movement holds in store for us.

IN THE LATE NINETEENTH CENTURY, there was a fad among upper-middle-class ladies for collecting autographs on paper fans. A celebrity would be asked to sign his or her name on one of the fan's folds and to add a brief quotation associated with that person's work. Brahms was on the friendliest terms with Johann Strauss II, whose popular waltzes and operettas he enjoyed, and he often visited and dined with Strauss and his third wife, Adèle, who once asked Brahms to sign her autograph fan. The master, in one of his ebullient moods, wrote out the opening bars of Strauss's "Blue Danube" Waltz, followed by the words, "Leider nicht von Johannes Brahms"—unfortunately not by Johannes Brahms.

Yet Brahms did write many beautiful waltzes over the course of his career—not only the sixteen Waltzes, Op. 39, for piano four hands, and the thirty-three *Liebeslieder* (Love Song) and *Neue Liebeslieder* (New Love Song) Waltzes, Opp. 52 and 65, for four voices and piano four hands, but also movements or parts of movements of some of his other works. One example of a "hidden" waltz is the main body of the Third Symphony's third movement; another is this string quintet's third movement, in G minor, 3/4 time, and in typical minuet/scherzo form. It bears the tempo indication *Un poco allegretto* (A little on the quick side), but it is in fact a moderately paced *valse triste* that could easily be danced to, however impractical that might be in a concert setting.

The emotional ambiguity of the second movement's ending continues straight through much of this third movement. There is a sort of Slavic melancholy to the main theme's melodic line, but the syncopated rhythm underpinning that line conveys a typically Brahmsian sense of unease. This unsettled feeling continues even into the movement's middle (trio) section—another waltz—which begins in radiant G major but proceeds with alternating flashes of light and shadow. A reprise of the main section leads into what seems poised to become a repetition of the trio as well, but Brahms cuts the proceedings short with some dark arpeggios capped by three unconvincingly subdued G major chords.

We expect the unsettled nature of the two middle movements to be resolved in the finale (G major, 2/4 time, *Vivace ma non troppo presto*— lively but not too fast), and Brahms doesn't disappoint us. But the resolution comes about only after a great deal of extraordinarily varied, contrasting, and often conflicting material has been packed into a mere five-minute time span.* In fact, as with much of Brahms's other music but to an exceptional degree, the more one delves into this piece the more amazed one becomes by the compositional science that has gone into producing such apparently spontaneous results.

The finale's lead-off instrument is the first viola, as was the case in the second movement. It chugs along quietly with no clear destination in sight, in dark-hued B minor, with the gentle accompaniment of the second viola and the cello. After only about fifteen seconds, however, and after the violins have added their voices to the proceedings, Brahms arrives at the main key, G major, in the form of a carefree peasant dance that is briefly interrupted by an *espressivo* passage. A calmly elegant, extended second theme (D major) leads into the development, the movement's longest and most surprising segment: surprising, because so far the finale's emotional temperature has been on the low side, whereas now it rises precipitately to the level of high drama. A restatement of the viola's ambivalent opening motif is offset by a moment of dead calm followed, in turn, by rebellious fury—complex contrapuntal fury, at that. The darkness that has appeared in each of the previous movements,

---

* A note for musicians: The finale is in a compressed yet complicated sonata-allegro form, with a three-part main theme in B minor and G major, a similarly tripartite second theme in D major (beginning with the upbeat to bar 40), an extended development section (from the upbeat to bar 81), a shortened recapitulation (from the upbeat to bar 171), and a coda (beginning approximately with the upbeat to bar 229).

including the mainly joyous first one, makes itself felt again, more concisely but just as intensely as elsewhere.

When the outburst at last subsides, a long, high trill by the first violin leads into a lyrical but somewhat shortened recapitulation that is almost outbalanced by the following coda—a growing flood-tide of sound that ends in a wild, Hungarian gypsy *czárdás* of the sort that Brahms had first heard forty years earlier, played by his violinist friend and touring partner Eduard Reményi, and that he now often heard played by gypsy bands in the Prater. It was as if he were reassembling his life's accumulated elements as he entered what would prove to be his final creative years.

When Brahms first sent Joachim the score of this quintet, he accompanied it with a letter in which he said: "I very much hope that you may like the piece a little, but don't be embarrassed to tell me the opposite. In that case I'll console myself with the first one" (his String Quintet, Op. 88) "and beyond both of them with Mozart's!"[14] The reference was to Mozart's six magnificent string quintets, which Brahms adored. But he needn't have worried. Joachim loved the new piece, and so have many thousands of listeners who have become familiar with it through the decades since it was created.

"YOU CAN . . . SAY GOODBYE to my notes—because it is really time to stop,"[15] Brahms wrote to Fritz Simrock, one of his publishers, on December 11, 1890, in a letter that accompanied the final page of the composer's four-hand piano arrangement of this quintet. Taken out of context, this oft-quoted statement seems to demonstrate beyond a doubt that Brahms intended to make the quintet his swan song. Yet in the same letter he let Simrock know that he would not allow him to publish any of his other music, because he felt that the publisher was charging potential buyers too much.

Whatever Brahms's own thoughts on the subject of continuing or not continuing may have been, the "time to stop" had not arrived. The quintet was followed fairly quickly by *Four Gypsy Songs* for vocal quartet and piano; Brahms attached them to two other songs that he had written earlier, and he published all six as his Op. 112. He then set about writing Thirteen Canons for female choir, which became his Op. 113. And two compositions of much larger dimensions were about to appear.

In January 1891, not many weeks after the premiere performances of the G major String Quintet, Brahms made one of his many trips to the town of Meiningen, which, at the time, was the capital of the Duchy of Saxe-Meiningen, in Franconia—today part of the state of Bavaria. Duke Georg II and his consort, Helene von Heldburg, were enthusiastic patrons of the performing arts, and Brahms, despite his democratic sympathies, felt such great affection for the couple that he would even, uncharacteristically, don formal wear and some of his medals in order to be able to dine with their highnesses. Fritz Steinbach, who had succeeded the famous Hans von Bülow as music director of Meiningen's excellent court orchestra, had become Brahms's favorite conductor, and, in the course of this particular visit by the composer, Steinbach led such a fine performance of the Fourth Symphony that Brahms asked to have it repeated; the performers complied. But the most important result of the trip was the musical spell cast over Brahms by the beautiful playing of Richard Mühlfeld, the orchestra's principal clarinet; the encounter led to the composition, during the following months, of the Trio in A minor, Op. 114, for clarinet, cello, and piano, and the Quintet in B minor, Op. 115, for clarinet and string quartet. Brahms returned to Meiningen in November 1891 to play the piano in the first, private performance of the trio, together with Mühlfeld and Hausmann; on the same occasion the quintet, one of Brahms's greatest chamber works, and his last one for more than two instruments, was played by Mühlfeld and the Joachim Quartet.

More compositions followed. In 1892 and 1893, just before and just after his sixtieth birthday, Brahms wrote and published twenty short- and medium-length solo piano pieces: Seven Fantasies, Op. 116; Three Intermezzos, Op. 117; Six Piano Pieces, Op. 118; and Four Piano Pieces, Op. 119. Thirteen of these stunning, intimately expressive gems are in minor keys, a fact that gives an idea of the dominant tone of what may be considered one large, contiguous work—the last of his solo compositions for the piano, his own instrument. These pieces, in which Brahms seems almost to be starting out along a new path, bring to mind a poem that Michelangelo wrote in his old age:

> *After many years and many attempts,*
> *the wise man, near to death, seeking,*
> *achieves the right idea for a living image*
> *in hard mountain stone;*
> *for one is late in arriving*
> *at high new things,*
> *and then one lasts but little.*[16]

But Brahms's fascination with the clarinet led him onward once again. In 1894 he created two magnificent sonatas (in F minor and E-flat major, respectively), Op. 120, for clarinet and piano, and he and Mühl-feld played them both for Clara Schumann that November, then gave the public premiere in Vienna in January 1895. With Brahms's permission, they may also be played by viola and piano.

After the two sonatas, no music emerged from Brahms's pen for over a year. But early in May 1896, at the time of his sixty-third birthday, he composed four songs, for bass and piano, that he had been mulling over for some time. The first three, meditations on death, were on texts

---

* "Negli anni molti e nelle molte pruove, / cercando, il saggio al buon concetto arriva / d'un'immagine viva, / vicino a morte, in pietra alpestra e dura; / c'all'alte cose nuove / tardi si viene, / e poco poi si dura."

from Ecclesiastes; the last one, from Ecclesiasticus, is about faith, hope, and, above all, love. Brahms gave them the collective title of *Vier ernste Gesänge* (Four Serious Songs), Op. 121, and in his choice of biblical texts he "consciously avoids any reference to God or to the notion of an afterlife," as Nicole Grimes says.[17] Among friends, Brahms jokingly referred to the songs as "godless *Schnadahüpferln*"[18]—pagan harvest songs. But they clearly reflected his growing preoccupation with death, increased by the fact that a few weeks earlier Clara Schumann had suffered a stroke. And not quite two weeks after he had completed the songs, he received the devastating news that Clara had died, at the age of seventy-six. The longest and most intense relationship of his life had ended.

He attended the first public performance of the *Four Serious Songs* in Vienna in November of that year, but by then Brahms, who had always enjoyed robust good health, was gravely ill with cancer of the liver, although he was never told the exact nature of his disease. When he could, and as best he could, he worked on a series of brilliant, complex chorale preludes for organ; eleven of them—some Baroque in style, others more clearly "Brahmsian," harmonically and rhythmically—were completed and would be published posthumously as his Op. 122. But he became weaker and weaker, and he died in his apartment in Vienna on April 3, 1897, five weeks short of his sixty-fourth birthday. His burial three days later, near the graves of Beethoven and Schubert, was attended by friends, admirers, and representatives of musical ensembles and societies from all over Europe, while in Hamburg, the native city to which he had once longed to return, all the ships in the harbor lowered their flags to half-mast.

BRAHMS SUSPECTED THAT HISTORY would deal with him as it had dealt with Luigi Cherubini, that is, as a highly competent composer, greatly esteemed in his day but relegated by posterity to a minor position in the musical pantheon. He even hung a copy, in his studio, of Ingres's well-known portrait of Cherubini, whose music he admired.

But things turned out differently for Brahms. Throughout the first half of the twentieth century the emotional power of his works continued to increase his worldwide popularity among audiences for Western art music, and today his orchestral, chamber, and piano works, like his lieder and choral pieces, are loved and frequently performed around the globe.

There have been some significant twentieth- and twenty-first-century musicians—Benjamin Britten's name springs immediately to mind—who did not or do not like Brahms's music, but for most people who have had thorough musical training, delving into Brahms's œuvre is an intellectually satisfying experience as well as a profoundly moving one. Of course emotional power is the most immediately striking feature of his work, for musicians and nonprofessional music lovers alike, yet a musician who studies Brahms's scores can hardly help but be overwhelmed by the sheer technical mastery behind each piece. The mastery, however, is not of the razzle-dazzle variety: it is embedded in and gives form to the work without drawing attention to itself. Nonmusicians, or even most musicians, who listen to Brahms's *Variations on a Theme of Haydn* are not constantly thinking: "Wow, in the theme and each variation he does four times five bars, then four times four bars, then three bars extended to . . . ," and so on; or, in the last movement of the Fourth Symphony, they are not counting eight bars plus eight bars plus eight bars plus eight bars. . . . They are too busy experiencing the sheer beauty of the "Haydn" Variations and the terrifying devastation of the symphony's passacaglia-finale.

At the Curtis Institute of Music in Philadelphia I teach a course that I call "The Master Builders: Ibsen, Brahms, and Cézanne." In it, I attempt to show how these three contemporaries, all heirs to the High Romantic traditions in their respective art forms and cultures, were actually classicists in their approaches to technique—especially structure. In Ibsen's last dozen plays, from *Pillars of Society* (1877) through

When We Dead Awaken (1899); in Cézanne's mature works, roughly from the early or mid-1880s until the artist's death, in 1906; and in Brahms's compositions throughout his professional life, the single "cell" is the basis of everything. If you remove even the most apparently casual line of dialogue from one of Ibsen's masterpieces—*A Doll House* or *The Master Builder*, for instance—you risk making the architecture of the entire work collapse, dragging with it the text's cumulative impact. Likewise, Cézanne's tiny brushstrokes create the planes of color that draw the observer into his paintings. With Brahms, two or three notes form the motivic cells out of which phrases, periods, whole movements, and even larger structures are engendered.

James Joyce worshiped Ibsen; Pablo Picasso took Cézanne as a point of departure. And Arnold Schoenberg, notwithstanding his aesthetic-philosophical descent from the more expansive and more radical Wagner-Liszt-Mahler "line," understood—as he explained in his 1933 lecture, "Brahms the Progressive" (later revised and published as an essay)—that Brahms's thoroughly thought-out experiments in motivic development, phrase lengths, and harmonic chromaticism placed the composer squarely among twentieth-century music's immediate precursors.

Were Ibsen, Brahms, and Cézanne concerned with the question of how their works might influence the works of their twentieth-century successors? Perhaps. What is certain, however, is that their main preoccupation was to work and rework the raw materials of each of their creations. They struggled to marshal those materials into something fine and strong, something that might, perhaps, endure beyond their own brief lifetimes. In that, they all succeeded.

In October 1890, just as Brahms was sending copies of the score of his new string quintet to Elisabet von Herzogenberg and a few other friends, a tall, handsome Finn—an aspiring composer, not quite twenty-five years old—arrived in Vienna, where he quickly began to savor the city's cultural and café life. He carried with him a letter of introduction to Brahms from a friend, the even younger (by four months) but already well-known Italian pianist and composer Ferruccio Busoni, who had recently been teaching at the music academy in Helsinki. A few years earlier, Busoni had met Brahms, who had been impressed with the young man's talents. But the young Finn, one Jean Sibelius, would not get that far with Brahms. As he later recalled,

> Brahms stubbornly refused to see me. From a friend, whom I had asked to put in a word for me, I heard that when my "case" was reported Brahms put the well-known quotation of Schubert: *"Kann er was?"* (Can he do anything?) "Yes, he has written a good quartet." This distinction must have seemed scarcely sufficient in the case of an otherwise entirely unknown young man from the north, for the maestro did not relent and I only made his personal acquaintance some months after my arrival, by chance at the Café Leidinger.[19]

After Sibelius had left Vienna, however, the young Finnish soprano Ida Ekman sang some of Brahms's lieder for Brahms himself, at the home of Eduard Hanslick, and she followed them with one of Sibelius's early Swedish songs, "Se'n har jag ej frågat mera" (Since then I have asked no more). Brahms became so fascinated by the Sibelius song that he asked Ekman to sing it again, and he went to the piano to accompany her himself. Afterward, he kissed her on the forehead and told her, "When we next meet you must sing more Sibelius than Brahms."[20]

A handshake at the Café Leidinger and a song sung at Hanslick's home may not establish much of a connection between Brahms and Sibelius, but they will suffice to lead us into this book's next chapter.

PART III

THE AGE OF UNCERTAINTY

The relatively peaceful and prosperous European period known as the "Belle Époque," which had begun circa 1880, in the aftermath of the Franco-Prussian War and the Paris Commune, came to an abrupt close with the outbreak of World War I. Even before 1914, however, European art music had been on the verge of imploding. Mahler, Debussy, and Richard Strauss, among others, were pushing traditional Western tonality in various new directions, and some of their younger contemporaries—Schoenberg, Bartók, and Stravinsky, most notably—were striking even farther into previously uncharted territory, breaking music's already tottering harmonic constraints and challenging its rhythmic and structural formulae as well.

Romanticism in music persisted for a while; in fact, most of the just-named composers had at least one foot and in some cases both feet in the late Romantic zone. But most of the European musicians who lived through the political, social, and cultural watershed of the 1914–18 war, and into the era of the dictators, would find the ground constantly shifting under their feet. Just as the horse and carriage were summarily shoved into obsolescence by automobiles, motorized urban transport systems, and, eventually, air travel, so the slowly evolving musical language of the progressive-minded nineteenth century gave way to a seemingly endless series of upheavals in the frenzied twentieth.

The three chapters that follow focus on three strikingly different paths taken by three strikingly different composers, all born in the nineteenth century but all professionally active primarily or entirely in the twentieth. And whereas all seven of the composers we have observed so far were from Europe's Germanic or Latin countries, the remaining three all hailed from the continent's northern or eastern regions.

8

EUROPE, A PROPHECY?

Jean Sibelius: Symphony No. 4 in A Minor, Op. 63 (1911)

A symphony is not just a composition in the ordinary sense of the word; it is more of an inner confession at a given stage of one's life.[1]

—JEAN SIBELIUS, DIARY ENTRY, NOVEMBER 5, 1910

THE MAN'S THIN-LIPPED MOUTH and massive jaw are set firmly, somewhat forbiddingly, but not quite in a frown. We see three-quarters of his face, as he looks slightly upward and to his right, through narrowed eyes. He is clean-shaven and seems to be completely bald. The brow is creased, the temples veined. A starched white collar, clasped by a dark, properly knotted tie, encircles his thick neck, and—as far as can be determined from a black-and-white photograph cropped more or less at the shoulder—he is wearing a light-colored, three-piece suit. How old is he? Seventy? Seventy-five?

The photo is one of the famous, often reproduced portraits of Jean Sibelius, taken at the composer's home in Finland in 1949 by the well-known Turkish-Canadian photographer Yousuf Karsh; Sibelius was, in fact, eighty-three or eighty-four years old at the time. "The structure of his face reminded me of carved granite, yet with infinite warmth and humanity," Karsh later recalled.

The "carved granite" epithet immediately seems right to many lovers of Sibelius's music. One tends to think of him as "all of a piece," a "man of the north," a person who possessed great determination and an unbending sense of direction—someone unafraid of bucking many of the compositional trends of his day in the quest to express his individuality—and some of this description is correct. But if we poke our noses into Sibelius's diary during the months in which he was at work on the fourth of what would be his seven published symphonies, we glimpse forms of insecurity that border on bipolarity.

[April 27, 1910] Again in the deepest depression. Working hard at the newcomer.

[May 2] Yesterday a wonderful day. . . . New ideas taking form. I have taken on a massive work.

[May 11] Everything stagnant. . . . In the grip of a depression these days.

[August 12] Worked well today on the development of the first movement.

[August 13] Just remember this once and for all: you are a genius!! You know it yourself. Feel it. Forget about trivia. . . .

[August 17] Crossed out the whole of the development. . . .

[August 30] Inspired. The development is ready in my head.

[September 8] Life is difficult again on account of mental lassitude, inability to work and the disdain of others.

[September 15] Have had a sense of my own genius. Worked on III [the third movement].

[September 17] Have doubts about the last movement of the symphony.

[November 24] The miracle I am waiting for will never take place. I cannot work properly.

[November 26] Have been in ecstasy.

[December 13–15] Work and forge on the third movement. But I can't really concentrate properly.[2]

And so on, through the end of 1910 and on into the early months of 1911, until the Fourth Symphony's premiere, which took place in Helsinki, with the composer conducting, on April 3, 1911. Although Sibelius was by then, at forty-five, a national cultural hero in Finland, the new piece was greeted with puzzlement—so much so that Aino, the composer's wife, recalled decades later that after the performance, "People avoided our eyes, shook their heads; their smiles were embarrassed, furtive or ironic. Not many people came backstage to the artists' room to pay their respects."[3]

Nevertheless, Sibelius, after having made some minor revisions, sent the score to his Leipzig-based publishers, Breitkopf & Härtel (the same company whose directors and employees Beethoven had tormented a century earlier). The Fourth Symphony would never become one of the composer's most often-performed works, but for some listeners—this one included—it is his finest masterpiece.

SINCE THE LATTER DECADES OF the twentieth century, Finland has been counted among the most musically advanced countries in the world, thanks to a national educational system that emphasizes musical literacy, not only in itself but also as an aid to proficiency in other areas and to mental development in general. Among many other musicians, the composers Kaija Saariaho and Magnus Lindberg; the conductors Esa-Pekka Salonen, Leif Segerstam, Susanna Mälkki, Jukka-Pekka

Saraste, Santtu-Matias Rouvali, and Okko Kamu; the pianist Olli Mustonen; the singers Jorma Hynninen, Martti Talvela, Matti Salminen, Karita Mattila, and Soile Isokoski; and the Kamus and Meta4 string quartets, are all admired at home and abroad, and it seems safe to say that no other nation of similar size (population: 5.5 million) can boast fifteen professional symphony orchestras, a national opera company, and an important international summer opera festival.

In the mid-nineteenth century, however, Finland—that is, the Grand Duchy of Finland, then part of the Russian Empire—was a musical backwater, physically isolated from the great European musical capitals: Vienna was a seventy-hour train journey from Helsinki, and Paris and London were even harder to reach. Besides, Finland was too sparsely populated to attract many of the itinerant virtuosi of the day, and the frequent outbreaks of anti-Russian political turmoil within its borders, countered by repressive measures imposed by the tsar's government in St. Petersburg, did not enhance its attractiveness to potential visitors. Nevertheless, music-making in the home was as popular among many middle-class Finnish families as it was for their counterparts in Central Europe. This particularly applied to those members of Finland's substantial ethnic Swedish minority who considered themselves culturally superior to the ethnic Finnish majority.

One such Swedish Finn was Christian Gustaf Sibelius, who hailed from the southern coastal town of Loviisa (Lovisa, in Swedish) but ended up as a medical doctor to both the military garrison and the civilian population in the town of Hämeenlinna (Tavastehus), about a hundred kilometers north-northwest of Helsinki (Helsingfors). Dr. Sibelius, a womanizer in his youth, loved music, gambling, cigars, and alcohol, not necessarily in that order of preference, and he was famous for both his generosity and his financial insouciance. In 1862, at the age of forty-one, he married twenty-three-year-old Maria Charlotta Borg, a Lutheran minister's daughter; they had a daughter and two sons, but while Maria Charlotta was pregnant with the third child her husband died of cholera, leaving his widow with an inheritance of twelve marks and numerous debts.

The couple's second child and first son, Johan Julius Sibelius, was born in Hämeenlinna on December 8, 1865. In the family he was known by his nickname, Janne, but later, emulating an admired uncle, he Frenchified his first name to Jean. Raised by his widowed mother and maternal grandmother, Janne/Jean grew up speaking Swedish; Finnish he learned at school, but he did not become truly fluent in the language until he was grown up—an apparent anomaly for a man who, to this day, is probably the best-known representative, globally, of Finland and its culture. Sweden, however, had governed Finland for hundreds of years before the Russians moved in, and in Sibelius's day Swedish was still the official language of most of the country's educational and cultural institutions.

From an early age the boy was fascinated by music. His favorite instrument was the violin, but he did not begin to study it seriously until he was fourteen, too late to develop sufficient skill for becoming a soloist. He also enjoyed writing music but was largely self-taught until, at twenty-one, and after having given up studying law (echoes of Schumann!) at the University of Helsinki, he enrolled in the composition class of Martin Wegelius, the founder of Helsinki's College of Music, now known as the Sibelius Academy. Wegelius had studied in Germany, had become an ardent Wagnerite, and was a leading force in Finland's musical development, contemporaneously with his rival, Robert Kajanus, who founded and conducted the Helsinki Orchestral Society.

At the college, Sibelius met and became friendly with other young students who aspired to give Finland a unique and significant identity within the European musical scene. He also encountered the pianist and composer Ferruccio Busoni, four months his junior but already a celebrity on the international stage. Busoni taught piano at the college for two years and gave many recitals that opened the eyes and ears of Sibelius and his fellow students to some of the important musical developments of the day; he and Sibelius remained friends until Busoni's death, in 1924.

Gradually, Sibelius gave up the idea of becoming a professional violinist and focused his attention on composition. In 1889, at the age of twenty-three, he went to Berlin to continue his studies and to observe high-level performances of classical and contemporary music—operas as well as orchestral and chamber works—and the following year he moved on to Vienna for the same purpose. (In addition to Swedish and Finnish, Sibelius spoke German fluently, got by in French, and had a smidgen of English.) Although, as we have seen, he did not achieve his goal of being taught, or at least counseled, by Brahms, he did manage to receive useful instruction from Karl Goldmark and Robert Fuchs, two composers whom Brahms admired.* In Berlin, but especially in Vienna, Sibelius began to follow in his father's footsteps by running up debts at high-class restaurants and cafés and by becoming overly fond of alcohol and tobacco—addictions that would create severe problems for him during the following decades.

He returned to Finland in the summer of 1891 and set to work on a five-movement, hour-long symphonic suite, *Kullervo*, for mezzo-soprano, baritone, male chorus, and large orchestra, based on Cantos 31 to 36 of the *Kalevala*. For some time, Sibelius, like other Finnish artists of his generation, had been fascinated by this set of mainly pre-Christian Finnish and Karelian† myths, legends, and poems that had been collected and turned into epic poetry in the mid-nineteenth century by Elias Lönnrot. *Kullervo*, the first major work from the *Kalevala* to emerge

---

* Fuchs's other pupils, over the years, included Gustav Mahler, Hugo Wolf, Alexander Zemlinsky, Franz Schreker, George Enescu, and Erich Wolfgang Korngold, among many others.
† Karelia is a region currently divided between Finland and Russia.

from Sibelius's pen, tells of a tormented young man who rapes a young woman, only to discover that she is his long-lost sister; she immediately commits suicide, and he eventually does the same.

Rape, incest, and suicide may seem unlikely themes for a young composer to adopt in introducing himself to his country's music lovers, yet despite the fact that Sibelius had only recently completed his studies of instrumentation the piece was a success at its premiere in Helsinki in April 1892. As Sibelius's British biographer Robert Layton has written, "his position in Finnish musical life was never seriously challenged from that moment onwards."[4] Sibelius himself came to believe that *Kullervo* was immature, and not until his extreme old age did he give permission for it to be published after his death.

Among its other immediate after-effects, *Kullervo*'s success must have helped Sibelius in his pursuit of Aino Järnefelt, daughter of General Alexander Järnefelt, the head of one of the most important families in Finland's liberal-nationalist movement. Both the Russian authorities and portions of Finland's large Swedish community viewed that movement with suspicion, but Sibelius wholeheartedly embraced it. The couple married two months after *Kullervo*'s premiere and eventually had six daughters, of whom the third died in childhood. During the first decade of the twentieth century Sibelius had a villa built on a piece of land that he had bought at Järvenpää, forty kilometers north of central Helsinki. He named the home Ainola, after his wife, and he and Aino raised their daughters there and lived there themselves for the rest of their long lives.

Throughout the 1890s, the *Kalevala* continued to supply Sibelius with ideas for new orchestral works: first, the tone poem *En Saga* (A Saga), and then four more tone poems that he eventually grouped together as the *Lemminkäinen* Suite. Two of these pieces—the mysterious *Swan of Tuonela* and the exuberant *Lemminkäinen's Return* (also known in English as *Lemminkäinen's Homecoming*)—remain part of the international symphonic repertoire, as does *En Saga*, which Sibelius heavily revised in 1902. Even better known is *Finlandia* (1899–1900), the main theme of which has become one of Finland's national hymns.

Permeating these pieces, and indeed nearly all of Sibelius's orchestral works, and many non-orchestral works as well, is his strong feeling for the natural surroundings of his native country—its lakes and forests, its dark autumns and winters, and its brief but welcome, life-giving springs and summers. In the opinion of the pianist and conductor Vladimir Ashkenazy, a devoted interpreter of Sibelius's music, "the most important element in Sibelius is his identification with nature. It's not superficial—it's not a depiction of nature. It is what we are and what surrounds us; it is our existence, it's in our hearts and minds. His identification is lyrical and it is dramatic—it is everything."[5]

This feeling of identification with and immersion in nature abounds in most of Sibelius's seven symphonies, which he considered his most important compositions. The Symphony No. 1 in E minor, Op. 39, written in 1898–99 and revised in 1900, owes much to Tchaikovsky's symphonies with respect to structure, instrumentation, and at times even harmonic progressions, yet a strong individuality can immediately be felt, especially in the alternately brooding and bracing first movement. With the Second Symphony, in D major, Op. 43 (1901–2), Sibelius truly came into his own as a symphonist: the self-dramatizing, heart-on-sleeve atmosphere of the First had been replaced by an enfolding warmth and—especially in parts of the second movement—by a sort of subtropical lushness that may have been conceived during the weeks that the composer and his family spent in Rapallo, on Italy's Ligurian coast, thanks to the generosity of a group of his supporters. Not that the Second Symphony lacks conflict: it, too, contains plenty of high drama and negativity, but those qualities have become more internalized than they were in the First. The Second remains the most often performed of all of Sibelius's symphonies, a staple of orchestras everywhere even during the two or three decades after the composer's death, when his musical reputation sank to its lowest point.

Closely following the Second Symphony came the almost equally popular Violin Concerto in D minor, Op. 47 (1903–4, revised in 1905), a piece that requires such great virtuosity on the soloist's part that some violinists have jokingly described it as Sibelius's revenge for not having had a solo career of his own. Not until four years after he had completed the Second Symphony, however, did Sibelius set to work on the Symphony No. 3 in C major, Op. 52 (1906–7), with which he set off in a new direction. The most immediately noticeable difference is the new piece's concision: the First and Second symphonies generally last forty to forty-five minutes each, whereas the Third should clock in at just under half an hour, and its four successors range from twenty to thirty-five minutes in length. Also, after the Second, Sibelius lightened his symphonic palette by eliminating the tuba and deploying the other wind instruments more subtly than before. Even more important is the fact that his approach to form became increasingly unorthodox: he did not ignore classical norms, but he bent them to his purposes in more original ways than he had previously dared to do. This is particularly noticeable in the Third Symphony's third movement: it begins with a wild scherzo, in which the ground constantly shifts under our feet, and it ends with a savage, repetitive, chest-thumping finale.

But then came trouble.

OVER THE YEARS, SEVERAL FINNISH MUSICIANS have told me various versions of a story about Sibelius, the gist of which is simple: The composer and a friend meet in a Helsinki tavern and begin slowly and silently knocking back shots of aquavit. After an hour or so, the friend hesitantly (probably also somewhat hazily) asks Sibelius, "How's your family?" To which Sibelius replies, "Are we here to drink or to talk?"

Whether or not the story is true, Sibelius certainly did develop a serious drinking problem. Crisis followed crisis, in his marriage and in his work, although from time to time he would manage to free himself of the habit. The months during which he did most of the work on the Third Symphony constituted one such "clean" period in his life, although by the time he completed the composition he was again indulging in alcohol as well as going ever deeper into debt, wining and dining at Helsinki's most expensive hotels and restaurants. Aino suffered exhaustion—perhaps a form of nervous breakdown—as a result of her husband's behavior, and had to spend time in a sanatorium.

In May 1908, a doctor discovered that Sibelius had a throat tumor. A biopsy performed in Helsinki showed that the tumor was benign, but Sibelius was sent to a specialist in Berlin, who more or less confirmed the prognosis but warned the composer that the condition could worsen and that he had to avoid alcohol and tobacco. He obeyed, but, as he wrote to his brother, Christian, "Life is something totally different without these stimulants." For several years, through his early and mid-forties, Sibelius lived in fear of developing a life-threatening malignancy, and sometimes he seemed glad to have given up the bottle. "It was so pleasant to be sober for once when I conducted," he wrote to Aino after having led much-applauded performances of *En Saga* and *Finlandia* in London in 1909.* And a few days later, after a reception at a noblewoman's home, he boasted: "We left her Ladyship at three in the morning in the highest good spirits, and all this without my having had any alcohol or smoked."[6] At other times, however, he felt that the restrictions hampered his creativity.

---

* I once asked a talented conductor who was known to have a drinking problem what, in his opinion, was the most difficult aspect of conducting. His answer: "For me, walking from the wings to the podium. Once I'm on the podium, it's easy."

In the winter and spring of 1909 Sibelius composed a string quartet, "Voces Intimae" (Intimate, or Inner, Voices), in D minor, Op. 56—his only mature work in the genre—and in the fall he and his brother-in-law, the painter Eero Järnefelt, traveled to Koli, an isolated area (now a national park) in the mountains of northern Karelia, five hundred kilometers northeast of Helsinki. Järnefelt spent his days painting while Sibelius took long hikes in the forest and mulled over his existence. All in all, the stay was "one of my life's greatest experiences," he later wrote in his diary, and some of the ideas for what would become his Fourth Symphony likely began to form in his mind during or shortly after the Koli trip. And yet, that symphony is not a "nature" tone poem like Debussy's *La Mer* or Strauss's *Alpine Symphony*. Sibelius even took the unusual step, after the work's premiere, of sending a protest to a newspaper that had published a program note in which some of the symphony's specific elements were linked to Koli and its woods, lakes, fields, and plant and animal life.

In reality, the biological life referenced in the Fourth Symphony is the internal life of human beings in general and of Jean Sibelius in particular. As he said in the diary entry quoted at the beginning of this chapter, "A symphony is not just a composition in the ordinary sense of the word; it is more of an inner confession at a given stage of one's life." And, regarding the tone of *this* symphony, he wrote to his friend and admirer Rosa Newmarch, an English music commentator: "My new symphony is a complete protest against the composition of today. Nothing—absolutely nothing of the circus."[*]

Circus? To whose works was Sibelius referring? His most likely targets were Mahler and Richard Strauss, his close contemporaries, both of whom he had met, and whom he regarded with a mixture of admiration,

---

[*] In the original German: "Meine neue Sinfonie ist eine vollständige Protest gegen die Composition heutige Tage. Nichts—absolut nichts von Cirkus."

diffidence, and, in Strauss's case, envy. (At the time, Mahler's works were not much better known internationally than those of Sibelius, whereas Strauss's music was probably performed more than that of any other living composer.) When Sibelius wrote the just-quoted letter to Newmarch, early in May 1911, just a few days before Mahler's death, that composer's *Das Lied von der Erde* and Ninth Symphony had not yet been performed, but the vast proportions of the Eighth Symphony were known to Sibelius. As for Strauss, the overheated emotions and orchestral gigantism of his recent operas, *Salome* and *Elektra*, would have fascinated but probably also appalled Sibelius, whereas the musical and theatrical nostalgia of *Der Rosenkavalier*, which had its premiere while Sibelius was completing the Fourth Symphony, must have appeared to him as a retreat. (How striking it is to think that the premiere of *Petrushka* by the as yet barely known Stravinsky, Sibelius's junior by nearly seventeen years, would receive its first performance only two months after the premiere of Sibelius's new symphony, and that a circus-like, or in any case carnivalesque, atmosphere was part of the scenario of that groundbreaking ballet score!) But whichever unnamed culprit or culprits Sibelius was castigating with the term "circus," there is no denying that it's not a word that his Fourth Symphony readily brings to mind.

Work on that piece coincided with several private and public crises in Sibelius's life. Not only was the withdrawal from alcohol and tobacco weighing heavily on him at the time: heavier still, and increasingly so, were his financial problems. Since the 1890s, the Finnish authorities, who were allowed independence from Russia in many internal matters, had been granting him a small annual stipend, but it was insufficient for even the basic needs of the composer and his family, and his earnings from his works could not fill the gap, let alone cover his extravagances. A friend and supporter, Baron Axel Carpelan, kindly undertook some partially successful fundraising campaigns among his wealthy acquaintances; Sibelius felt simultaneously grateful for and humiliated by these efforts, which reduced but did not eliminate the gap in his domestic economy.

The public crisis was political. In 1910, the year in which Sibelius did most of the work on the Fourth Symphony, Finnish nationalists, divided though they were between conservatives and socialists, became increasingly vocal in their demands for independence from Russia. In retaliation, the Russian duma enacted regulations to subordinate Finnish economic, cultural, and political life to Russia's pan-Slavic policies. Sibelius strongly favored Finnish independence, but he also admired Russian music and musicians and wanted his own music to continue to be performed in Russia. "All empty talk on political questions, all amateurish politicizing I have always hated," he wrote. "I have tried to make my contribution in another way." And, in a different letter: "I cannot help in any other way than by laboring 'for king and country.' I am working on my new symphony."[8] He tried to focus on his musical work, which included writing some commissioned short pieces that drew his attention away from the symphony but were meant to bring in much-needed money.

Sibelius continued to compose both at home and during concert tours that took him to Oslo, Berlin, and Leipzig in October 1910 and to Sweden, Latvia, Estonia, and, again, Berlin the following February. The score was completed in March, at home in Finland, and, as we have seen, Sibelius conducted its uncomprehendingly received premiere in Helsinki on April 3, 1911. He dedicated the work to Eero Järnefelt, the brother-in-law who had accompanied him on his trip to Koli, but the symphony's opening is not reminiscent of Koli or of any of the cities and countries that Sibelius had visited while he was working on the piece, or of his home at Järvenpää, or of any other precise geographic location. It begins, proceeds, and ends in a dark recess of the mind.

WHERE ARE WE? THE SYMPHONY'S TITLE tells us that we are in A minor, but its first movement begins, *fortissimo* ("as harsh as fate," Sibelius said),[9] with the bassoons and some of the muted cellos and basses playing C and D, the first two notes of the C major scale, while the other cellos and basses hold onto a low C. And the third note that we hear is an F-sharp, which belongs to neither A minor nor C major: juxtaposed against the low C, it forms what is called a "tritone." In earlier times this interval of three whole-tones was considered a diabolical dissonance, *diabolus in musica*, and this particular F-sharp jars our senses: it doesn't "belong" here, it's a foreign substance, a troublemaker, and it occurs only two or three seconds into the piece, creating a feeling of anxiety. The F-sharp quickly falls back onto a neutral E-natural, but then it recurs.

Not only is the opening's tonality (key) uncertain: its rhythm is jagged, too, and this increases the overall atmosphere of precariousness. Those F-sharps and E-naturals rock back and forth, first as quarter notes, then, more slowly, as dotted quarter notes, and at last settling down as half notes. The volume level also shifts: beginning in the second bar a gradual *diminuendo* pulls us away from the opening *fortissimo*, and by the end of the fourth bar the bassoons and half of the cellos have temporarily dropped out of the soundscape. When the piece is about twenty-five or thirty seconds old, a solo cello enters, *piano* (accompanied by the remaining cellos and the basses, *pianissimo*), with a fragmented theme that feels as if it were being intoned by a low-voiced tribal elder crouching before a fire and trying to recount an age-old saga of which not even he, let alone his listeners, can grasp the meaning. For a while, we feel anchored in A minor, but then the timpanist sounds the tritone note (as a G-flat instead of an F-sharp); the muted violas enter on a D-flat; and the muted second violins, followed by the bassoons and muted first violins, begin to crescendo toward a powerful C major resolution, with all four horns and both clarinets joining in.*

Many composers have used the opening passages of some of their works for playing aural tricks on listeners. As I mentioned in the second chapter, Beethoven, at the start of his First Symphony, makes our ears tell us that we are in F major, then, a few seconds later, possibly in A minor, and then, clearly, in G major—or so we believe until he gradually positions us where he wants us, squarely in C major. Sibelius, however, isn't joking. He is shoving us into a no-man's-land between comprehension and incomprehension; he pulls tonal centers out from under our feet, hints at new ones, brings back the old ones, then makes them disappear again.

Up to this point, his initial tempo indication has held, although the words *Allegro molto moderato, quasi adagio* (very moderately fast, almost slow)† make Brahms's often ambiguous tempo descriptions look crystal clear by comparison. In the last bar and a half of this initial climax, however, we read the words *poco larg.*; my guess is that Sibelius wrote *poco largo*, or broadening out a little, but a typesetter mistook his final o for a dot. In any case, that indication is followed immediately by *Adagio*, with the horns, trumpets, trombones, and timpani packing a tremendous wallop, and the violins and violas responding by removing their mutes and rising to their high D-sharps, as we make a drastic change of key, to F-sharp major.

---

* In this symphony, Sibelius deploys the instruments that had become more or less standard in mid-nineteenth-century symphonies: among the woodwinds, two each of flutes, oboes, clarinets, and bassoons; in the brass section, four horns, two trumpets, and three trombones; for percussion, timpani, plus (unusually) glockenspiel in the finale; and standard strings (first and second violins, violas, cellos, and basses, although he often divides each section into two separate parts). The gigantic, post-Wagnerian orchestra required in many of the works of Mahler, Strauss, and several other prominent contemporaries of Sibelius, and even in some of his own works, is avoided here.
† As mentioned earlier in the previous chapter, *adagio* means, literally, "at ease"—in other words, slow-ish but not really slow—but Sibelius, like many other non-Italian-speaking musicians before and since, employed it to mean, simply, slow.

Like the first movements of the works by Mozart, Beethoven, Schubert, and Brahms described in previous chapters, this first movement, too, is in sonata form (exposition-development-recapitulation), but Sibelius has twisted that form into an odd shape. Instead of a first theme and a second theme, the exposition is made up of a series of thematic fragments: the shocking introductory bars; the saga-like motif, which grows and transforms itself into something briefly exhilarating; an interruption by snarling brass chords; a brief, upward sweep by the violins and violas;* another blood-chilling snarl; another upward sweep, this time by the violins alone, reaching even higher than before; some peaceful horn calls, as if from the Beyond; a more peremptory call to order from the trumpets and trombones; and, to bring the exposition to a close, echoes of the saga-like theme, but more tranquil in tone, under a descant by the first clarinet alternating with the first oboe.

Tranquility evaporates in the development section, which begins with four introductory bars (we are back in A minor) followed by an extended, syncopated riff on the saga-like thematic element, played first by the solo cello, then by the second violins and violas, then by the first violins, then with both violin sections reaching a *fortissimo* climax and gradually giving way to waves of tense, shimmering tremolos—soft, at first—tossed from one string section to another, with stark, mysterious comments interjected by woodwinds and timpani. This trembling, nervous, lost-in-the-middle-of-nowhere passage continues for a full minute, building to another *fortissimo* climax but then abruptly giving way to the snarling brass motif, which announces the recapitulation, much shorter than the exposition. We do not hear a reprise of the

---

* I respectfully disagree with the musicologist Marc Vignal, who considers this upward-sweeping motif—from the A in the treble clef to the first D-sharp above the staff—the onset of a real second theme. In my opinion, it is simply a more dramatic version of the tritone "shocker" that opens the movement, and one of the many thematic fragments that make up the entire exposition. See Marc Vignal, *Jean Sibelius* (Paris: Editions Seghers, 1965), p. 106.

saga-like thematic element from the beginning of the movement, but only the various transformations that it underwent. Its final incarnation occurs during an enigmatic mini-coda, only four bars long, played by the strings and ending on one note—a long-held A that fades from *piano* to *pianissimo* to nothing.

A BRIEF ASIDE: In one of Sibelius's diary entries from the period during which he was working on the Fourth Symphony, he reminds himself of the limitations of the professional orchestras of his day— limitations that we, today, read about with near disbelief, accustomed as we are to outstanding technical prowess even from players in second-rank orchestras. He mentions, for instance, that "the oboe, usually badly played, has to be treated with the same caution as the trumpet"; that "the bassoon in its middle and high register cannot play *piano*"; that "the lower register of the flute is almost only usable in *forte*"; and that "usually both in the wind and brass, the initial entry can be tentative and leaves much to be desired in terms of intonation and ensemble." Also, regarding the "routine, which is all too often found in some of the Continental orchestras of note," he describes musicians' "unwillingness to concern themselves with the refinements of tempo and rhythm, which are central to the nervous system of music."[10] Bear in mind that by this time Sibelius had heard, and in some cases conducted, the best orchestras that Berlin, Vienna, St. Petersburg, and other major musical centers could offer.

And yet, when it came to putting his musical ideas down on paper, Sibelius disregarded his own warnings and wrote as if in anticipation of the virtuoso orchestras of the mid twentieth century and beyond. For instance, in the course of the Fourth Symphony's first movement, which is only nine or ten minutes long, there are twelve changes of time signature—frequent shifts between 4/4 and 3/2 time, with occasional forays into 3/4—and this would have been enough to make many orchestra musicians of the day balk and complain. (Little could they have imagined the Stravinsky phenomenon that was about to hit them!) Sibelius, however, proceeded to write what he needed to write, presumably hoping for the best but expecting the worst.

SOME RESPITE IS NEEDED in the wake of the emotional bleakness and musical unsettledness of the symphony's first movement, and Sibelius gives us such a break in the second movement—briefly, at least. This scherzo in all but name is in F major and 3/4 time, with a tempo indication of *Allegro molto vivace*. Whirring violas accompany a long, lyrical melodic line played by the first oboe; the line is then taken over by the first violins (with questioning incursions from the oboe) accompanied by the rest of the string section. This quietly exuberant, half-minute-long segment gives way to a portion of roughly equal length in 2/4 time that begins lightly, staccato, with the violins and violas, but becomes more menacing with the entrance of the timpani and basses, followed by the cellos and finally the bassoons. Then, again in 3/4 time, the strings plunge downward and disappear, ceding the stage to the brass, timpani, and woodwinds, who initiate and quickly ramp up a sense of anxiety. The strings reenter, at first with a succession of tritones but gradually resuming the lightheartedness of the opening; there are even two brief, lovely *tranquillo* passages for the flutes, accompanied by violas and cellos, who strum a pizzicato accompaniment.

The lyrical segment continues; at one point it recalls the passage that sets off the growing (and glowing) transition from scherzo to finale in Sibelius's Second Symphony. In this case, however, the transition fades gradually into what, in a normal scherzo, would be called a "trio" section. Sibelius marks this new part *doppio più lento* (twice as slow), and, suddenly, the lighthearted theme played at the beginning of the movement by the oboe and first violins becomes a lugubrious, descending line for the oboes and clarinets, accompanied by trembling strings and punctuated by tritone flashes from the first violins. Long, mostly understated timpani rolls sound like distant thunder.

There will be no further relief: the scherzo proper does not return at all, as well-behaved Classical and Romantic-era scherzos are supposed to do. Instead, the trio section continues, with varied instrumentation but following along an unchanging path; altogether, the trio occupies almost two of the movement's nearly five minutes. The notes F-natural and C-sharp clash with each other until the movement simply wears itself out and dissolves into three timpani strokes on Fs an octave apart, leaving us, as at the end of the first movement, in a void.

How can the Fourth Symphony's third movement properly be characterized? From a technical point of view, it is in 4/4 time; it bears the indication *Il tempo largo* (broad tempo); and it is even more harmonically adventurous than its predecessors: nominally, it's in C-sharp minor, but, for instance, the first half of the first bar is in A minor (a motif that begins on A and ends on D-sharp—the famous tritone, again), the second half of the first bar seems to be in G-sharp minor, and the first half of the second bar is in C minor. These are important matters for musicians and music theorists to ponder, but what is most significant for all listeners is Sibelius's accomplishment in establishing, from the movement's outset, an atmosphere of quiet, meandering melancholy. At first, he achieves this through ascending melodic fragments played by the flutes and first clarinet hovering over notes held at length by the cellos and basses. After forty-five or fifty seconds, the horns enter, *piano, dolce*, with a consolatory, chorale-like motif (also ascending), but after only two bars the cellos intervene, repeating the melancholy flute-clarinet motif but in a different rhythmic pattern. The other strings join in, and then there is a quietly heartfelt outburst by most of the orchestra.

This fragmented yet somehow cohesive procedure continues through roughly the first three and a half minutes of the ten-minute-long movement, until the motifs that have so far been ascending begin to turn downward, first via the woodwinds, then with the violas and violins. All of a sudden, the violins begin to play ice-cold, nightmarish tremolos, mainly in what are called open fifths—C-sharp falling to F-sharp, G-sharp falling to C-sharp, and so on—as the cellos initiate a rising motif, perhaps attempting to cut through and emerge from the nightmare.

The nightmare does end, but nothing has been resolved. The meandering melancholy of the opening resumes under various guises until, a minute and a half or so before the movement's end, the whole orchestra raises a protest, an outcry that leads to a life-affirming A major chord. But that chord is immediately squelched and the protest suffocated by a C-sharp played over and over, *mezzo forte* and in syncopation, by the violas, while the horns simply hold the same note through many, many bars. There are quiet interjections, to no avail, from (in succession) a flute, a clarinet, first violins, second violins, cellos, and, finally, basses playing five desolate pizzicato notes. Together, horns and strings hold the very last C-sharp until the movement vanishes, just as the first movement vanished on an A and the second on an F. There are no "happy" major or "sad" minor chords or even hollow open fifths to hang onto: just one single, subdued, lonely, enigmatic note.

DESPITE THE ATMOSPHERE OF DARKNESS and uncertainty that fills so much of Sibelius's Fourth Symphony, a tensile strength runs through the whole work and prevents it from becoming maudlin or depressing. The composer's mind seems always to be grappling with internal turmoil but never surrendering to it. And just as the symphony's second movement manages at times to soar, to gain a bit of perspective from above the fray, the fourth movement does likewise—not always or even primarily, but enough to provide some light here and there. On the other hand, in this movement Sibelius made use of some thematic material that he had composed for *The Raven*, an abandoned work for soprano and orchestra, based on a translation of Poe's celebrated poem; this fact provides some advance insight into the finale's overall tone.

This fleet *Allegro* in 2/2 time, initially in A major, begins almost jauntily, with the strings playing a warm theme, although the reappearance of that devilish tritone (A–D-sharp) as early as the second bar makes one wonder how long the pleasant atmosphere can last. Arousing further suspicion are the brief, much too forced-cheerful calls from the clarinets, flutes, and even a glockenspiel, about twenty seconds into the piece.* These interjections are like the exclamation points that you might insert into a communication with a parent or a partner, to emphasize how well things are going when they are in fact on the verge of disaster.

Sure enough, a few seconds later the clarinets and horns produce a quietly threatening minor chord; this is followed by quick scale passages played first by one cello, then by one violin, then gradually by most of the rest of the strings. Sibelius marks these passages *affettuoso*, by which he presumably means "with emotion" or even "warmly," but there is also a frantic dimension to them. They lead into a brief, joy-

---

* Some conductors have chosen to use tubular bells instead of the glockenspiel, although we now know that this was never Sibelius's intention. The bells have the advantage of being better able than the glockenspiel to cut through a somewhat heavy orchestral texture later in the movement, but their tone is too proclamatory. Sibelius wanted the cheerful, tinkling lightness of the glockenspiel to tell us, untruthfully, that all is well as we face the devastating, oceanic forces that surround us in the rest of the orchestra.

ful, full orchestral outburst—another unconvincing exclamation point. The strings then go into a sort of tribal dance, *pianissimo* yet sharply rhythmic, in A major but intermittently pierced by dissonant E-flats and G-naturals from the flutes and first oboe.

I'll refrain from burdening readers with the details of musicological debates over the extent to which this movement is in sonata form as opposed to rondo form (it combines both) and over the point at which the exposition ends and the development begins (Sibelius specialists are of two minds on the subject). Instead, I'll limit myself to mentioning that much of what has been heard up to now is repeated with substantial variants until, after a sort of jagged mini-climax a little over two minutes into the movement, the strings begin playing a series of hollow-sounding chords over which the woodwinds and then the horns offer alternatingly meandering and chorale-like passages. The violins then begin to play a long, syncopated line over ongoing chords from the rest of the strings; the syncopated line is transformed into a more direct, ascending melodic line that echoes the third movement's melancholy; and suddenly, all the winds and the timpani reenter, playing quiet chords over swirling bundles of *pianissimo* sixteenth notes—literally hundreds of sixteenth notes—in the strings. This whirlwind continues for nineteen bars, with, at one point, the trumpets and timpani intervening, triple *forte*, alongside the glockenspiel's desperate good cheer.

A charming pizzicato section has the charm knocked out of it when the two oboes start playing worrisome, syncopated lines overhead. Eventually, the ascending, melancholy line returns, and the various thematic elements recombine into a sort of unorthodox recapitulation: unorthodox, because instead of beginning in A major, where it "should" be, it's in the tritone key of E-flat major. We gradually sneak into A major through a harmonic back door, but the proceedings begin to break down thanks to a seemingly chaotic but really brilliantly conceived combination of dissonances and cross-rhythms. After a climactic collision that lands everyone firmly in A minor, the strings try to pick themselves up from the heap, but the woodwinds scold and the horns snarl until the subdued strings resign themselves to defeat. Interjections from the solo flute and solo oboe only add to the feeling of hopelessness, and the symphony ends not with a bang *or* a whimper, but solemnly, severely, on an A minor chord played—*mezzo forte* and *dolce*—by the strings alone.

The emotional bleakness may remind us of two other nineteenth-century-born Scandinavian artists: Sibelius's close Norwegian contemporary, Edvard Munch, and his older Swedish contemporary, August Strindberg. In fact, when asked about the Fourth Symphony, Sibelius would quote Strindberg: "Det är synd om människorna"—It's a pity to be human.

SIBELIUS COULD NOT, OR AT LEAST should not, have been surprised by the blank stares and barely polite applause that his new symphony elicited at its premiere in Helsinki. The audience, including his supporters, must have wondered what had happened to the man who had created the blood-and-thunder drama of the First Symphony, the life-embracing warmth of the Second, and the sheer exuberance of the Third. To most of those first listeners, this new work must have seemed largely incomprehensible, and the parts that were somewhat easier to follow may have been perceived as the self-lacerations of a lost soul. Worse, when Sibelius subsequently conducted the symphony in Gothenburg, Sweden, it "was actually received with hoots," he later recalled.[11]

Not until he performed the Fourth in England (Birmingham, Liverpool, Manchester, Bournemouth, and Cheltenham) in October 1912, a year and a half after its premiere, did it begin to garner a modicum of respect and understanding. After having attended the dress rehearsal, the composer Frederick Delius wrote to his wife, the German painter Jelka Rosen, that Sibelius "is trying to do something new & had a fine feeling for nature & he is also unconventional—Sometimes a bit sketchy & ragged. But I should like to hear the work again."[12] Of greater interest, however, is a review of the Birmingham performance that the well-known music historian, Wagner biographer, and critic Ernest Newman published in *The Nation*. "The work confuses, at a first hearing, by its drastic simplification of both idea and expression," Newman wrote.

> Sibelius has no need of the grossly swollen orchestral apparatus of the average modern composer. His scores are as simple in appearance as those of Beethoven. With his clean strength of thought he has no need to be dressing platitudes in sumptuous raiment. In this fourth symphony he has carried his normal simplicity and directness of speech to extraordinary lengths. . . . [T]he soul of the man has now obviously retired further into itself, and is brooding at a depth to which it is not easy to follow him without a guide. But even the Philistine, one imagines, must feel at once that here is a powerful brain seizing upon life in its own way.[13]

At home in Järvenpää a month later, Sibelius wrote to Rosa Newmarch: "Many artists—including Busoni—have spoken enthusiastically about my Symphony IV. . . . Inwardly I grow stronger and my ideas clearer day by day. I begin—like Beethoven (mais sans comparaison)—to believe that strength is really human morality. I mean of course strength in its highest and widest sense."[14]

Not in its military sense, of course. Sometimes, however, in considering the spiritual devastation that the Fourth Symphony conveys, I can't help but reflect on the cataclysm of the First World War, which would overtake Europe, and Western civilization in general, barely three years after Sibelius had completed this work. In particular, the whirling strings and the chaotic climactic section of the symphony's finale bring to mind the line about the "shrill, demented choirs of wailing shells" from Wilfred Owens's poem, "Anthem for Doomed Youth," written during the war (in which Owens was killed).[15] And then there is the warning in William Blake's *Europe a Prophecy*, written more than a century earlier: "Shadows of men in fleeting bands upon the winds / Divide the heavens of Europe. . . ." Sibelius was no prophet, but a sense of the coming implosion of a Europe that had somehow held itself together for a century, since the end of the Napoleonic Wars, may have been in the air. The recent discoveries of Freud and Einstein, and the older but still, at the time, not entirely digested writings of Darwin and Marx, were turning old ways of thinking on their heads and reverberating with seismic force in artists' psyches as well as in the world at large.

In the spring of 1914, shortly before the war broke out, Sibelius visited the United States, to conduct some of his own compositions at the Norfolk Music Festival in Connecticut and to receive an honorary doctorate from Yale University. He enjoyed his stay, but, despite the offer of a professorship at the Eastman School of Music in Rochester, New York, he never returned to America. During the war, he wrote his Fifth Symphony in E-flat major, Op. 82, which the Finnish government had commissioned to mark the composer's fiftieth birthday; he conducted its premiere in Helsinki on that date, December 8, 1915, which was declared a national holiday—an honor never, so far as I know, accorded to any other composer, living or dead. Although its character feels vastly more positive than that of its immediate predecessor, the Fifth in its original form carried forward some of the harmonic adventures that Sibelius had embarked upon in the Fourth, whereas in its final, revised version (1919) most of the radical elements were erased. It was around this time that Sibelius wrote about "this life that I love so infinitely, a feeling that must stamp everything I compose," and, in effect, the concluding section of the Fifth Symphony's first movement is one of the most exhilarating orchestral passages ever written. Not surprisingly, the Fifth is much more popular than the Fourth, but the Fourth's bold, restless, questing nature is absent in its successor. "I see how my innermost self has changed since the days of the Fourth Symphony," Sibelius wrote in 1918. "And these symphonies of mine are more in the nature of professions of faith than my other works."[16]

The Symphony No. 6 in D minor, Op. 104, and the Symphony No. 7 in C major, Op. 105, were completed in 1923 and 1924, respectively, but initial ideas for both of them had emerged as early as 1914, around the same time that the Fifth Symphony was taking shape. There is a vast distance, however, between the Fifth on the one hand and the Sixth and Seventh on the other. The Sixth is an intimate, poetic work—"cold spring water," Sibelius called it, as opposed to the "cocktails" that he claimed were being offered by the more attention-grabbing works of the day (which, however, he did not identify). And in discussing the Sixth he restated his concept of a symphony as "an expression of a spiritual creed, a phase in one's inner life."[17]

The Seventh Symphony, composed as a single-movement, roughly twenty-two-minute piece, is an even more intense composition than the Sixth. Probably by pure coincidence, its premiere took place only weeks before the one hundredth anniversary of the premiere of Beethoven's Ninth Symphony, but Schiller's words, "Be embraced, you millions! / By this kiss for the whole world!"* which Beethoven used in his last symphony's choral finale, could have served as a motto for Sibelius's final published work in the symphonic genre. From beginning to end, the Seventh seems to observe life on earth from a point somewhere in the ionosphere, while it urges us to accept and embrace human existence, despite all its horrors. (I don't wish to sound cynical, but the fact that Sibelius was drinking heavily during the most important phases of his

---

* "Seid umschlungen, Millionen! / Diesen Kuss der ganzen Welt!"

work on this composition may have helped him to feel relatively good about humankind.)

In 1926, on a commission from the conductor Walter Damrosch and his New York Symphony, the sixty-year-old Sibelius wrote *Tapiola*, a mysterious, harmonically bold tone poem; its name refers to the forest god Tapio, from the *Kalevala*'s legends. Along with some substantial incidental music for Shakespeare's *The Tempest*, *Tapiola* would remain Sibelius's last major composition, as far as is known. He spoke often, during the 1930s, about an Eighth Symphony, even claiming from time to time that it was near completion. This may have been true—he may even have finished it—but in the end he destroyed, for reasons unknown, whatever work he had done on the symphony, with the exception of a few largely unenlightening sketches. It's true that by the time he reached his early sixties, Sibelius had already lived longer than any of the composers featured in this book's first four chapters and almost as long as those in the fifth and seventh. Still, if we compare him with his near contemporary Richard Strauss or with Verdi, both of whom composed extraordinary music in their eighties, Sibelius appears to have spent the last thirty years of his life in unproductive retirement.

He and Aino lived on at Ainola, often visited not only by their daughters, grandchildren, friends, and colleagues, but also by musicians who came from all over the world to pay tribute to the composer. During the 1930s, Karl Ekman, a musician friend of Sibelius (and son of the soprano Ida Ekman, who had sung a Sibelius song to Brahms— see the end of the previous chapter), interviewed Sibelius at length and wrote a brief, affectionate biography that shines light on Sibelius's character. Around the same time, the composer engaged a young clerk and amateur musician, Santeri Levas, to help him with correspondence and other nonmusical duties; Levas, too, made notes of the composer's conversations and later published another charming account of the man's warm nature. Most important, during the last decade of his life, Sibelius became friendly with the musicologist Erik Tawaststjerna, who, after the composer's death, was given virtually unrestricted access to his papers and produced a five-volume biography (abridged into three volumes, in English) that also provides analyses of and commentary on all of the major compositions and many of the minor ones as well. Tawaststjerna's work, first published in the 1960s and 1970s, is the essential source for anyone involved in Sibelius studies.[*]

On every birthday in his last years Sibelius received so many consignments of cigars from admirers, famous and otherwise, all over the globe, that he had to request a halt to the gifts. Having outlived by decades the doctors who had raised dire warnings about his health when he was in his forties, he had long since resumed his consumption of tobacco and alcohol, despite which—or perhaps because of which—he continued to enjoy his excursions in the woods around Järvenpää until he was well into his eighties.[†] Sibelius died at home on September 20, 1957, in his ninety-second year.

FROM THE 1930S ONWARD, the mysterious Fourth Symphony began to come into its own, up to a point, as famous conductors brought it into their repertoires. Arturo Toscanini performed it with the New York Philharmonic in 1931 and later with the NBC Symphony Orchestra, and in 1932 Leopold Stokowski made the first recording of it, with the Philadelphia Orchestra. Sir Thomas Beecham recorded it with the London Philharmonic in 1937, and after the Second World War,

---

[*] As I do not speak Swedish or Finnish, the original languages of these books, I have relied on their English translations; see my bibliography.

[†] Currently (2020) one can find on YouTube a six-minute film of the Sibelius couple at home in 1945, at the time of the composer's eightieth birthday, along with clips of him and two of his daughters, shot at home in 1927. The link is https://www.youtube.com/watch?v=EDqn3Z1ktpk.

despite a serious dip in Sibelius's reputation within large swaths of the musical community, the Fourth was performed and recorded by such renowned conductors as Ernest Ansermet, Herbert von Karajan, and Sir John Barbirolli. The Fourth is too austere a work to become vastly popular among lovers of classical music, but it will continue to attract the attention of many serious listeners.

The dip in Sibelius's reputation, roughly from the 1950s through the 1970s, had little or nothing to do with the quality or content of his music; it was based on the fact that Sibelius had not followed either the Wagner-Mahler-Schoenberg "line" or the Debussy "line" (although he was influenced by Wagner and was fascinated by the other three) or joined hands with such younger modernists as Bartók and Stravinsky. The new orthodoxy espoused after the Second World War by the young Pierre Boulez and others, who seemed to view the history of art music as an ongoing avant-garde that had continually to murder its progenitors, rode roughshod over the likes of Sibelius, who had simply followed his own musical instincts and inclinations. Today, fortunately, the perspective that time offers has allowed us to love, like, or at least be interested in the works of all of the above, including Boulez himself and dozens of others, without having to exclude those who, a few decades ago, were deemed insufficiently radical.

Among the many composers much younger than Sibelius whose works the post–World War II radicals treated with contempt, there was a Russian who, during his student days, had gotten into trouble precisely because of Sibelius. As a sixteen-year-old, this highly talented boy had attended the St. Petersburg premiere, in 1907, of Sibelius's Third Symphony (conducted by the composer), and the following day he had submitted an exercise in orchestration to his teacher—no less a figure than Rimsky-Korsakov—who reprimanded the youngster for having inserted a solo cello part into his exercise. When had he ever heard such a passage? Rimsky demanded to know.

"Yesterday, in the Sibelius symphony," came the answer.

"God in heaven! Sibelius!" Rimsky shouted. "Why listen to Sibelius? Isn't the second subject of [Glinka's] *Ruslan [and Ludmilla]* overture good enough for you?"[18]

Like Sibelius and so many other creative artists, this youngster, whose name was Sergei Prokofiev, would face attacks from conservatives early in his career and from radicals later on. But he would also have to face more serious political-existential problems than had ever befallen Sibelius: Prokofiev lived his last seventeen years under the terror regime of Joseph Stalin.

9

CREATIVE SUFFERING

Sergei Prokofiev: Piano Sonata No. 8
in B-flat Major, Op. 84 (1944)

A writer . . . cannot put himself today at the service of those who make
history: he is at the service of those who are subjected to it.

—ALBERT CAMUS, NOBEL PRIZE SPEECH, STOCKHOLM, DECEMBER 10, 1957[1]

ISLOVODSK IS A SPA TOWN about fourteen hundred kilometers south of Moscow, near the Georgian border on the broad
isthmus that separates the Black Sea from the Caspian Sea. Its name
means "sour waters," and for over two centuries the resort has been
frequented by privileged Russians in search of warm and presumably
curative mineral waters. Tsars before the Bolshevik Revolution and
Communist Party officials in the following decades vacationed in Kislovodsk, and so did the writers Alexander Pushkin, Mikhail Lermontov,
Lev Tolstoy, Anton Chekhov, and Maxim Gorky. Alexander Solzhenit-
syn lived there during his childhood. Among Russian musicians, the
composers Mikhail Glinka, Nikolai Rimsky-Korsakov, and Alexander
Scriabin all enjoyed the town's relatively mild, sunny climate, and the
world-famous basso Fyodor Chaliapin acquired a villa there in 1917.

Sergei Prokofiev visited Kislovodsk many times, beginning in the summer of 1909, when, at eighteen, he accompanied his mother there. He was there, too, when the Revolution began, in October 1917, and as the area was cut off from Moscow and Petrograd by the anti-Bolshevik forces of General Alexei Kaledin, he ended up spending eight months in the town, until Kaledin's troops surrendered and the general committed suicide. But it was in the summer of 1939—the summer during which the Soviet Union signed a shocking non-aggression pact with Nazi Germany and the Germans invaded Poland, thus plunging Europe into war—that a vacation period in Kislovodsk most strongly impacted Prokofiev's professional and private life.

His reading material that summer included Romain Rolland's popular biography of Beethoven; Rolland's description of the "Appassionata" Sonata as a union of "unrestrained passion and rigid logic" seems to have motivated Prokofiev to return to the piano sonata form, which had not attracted his full attention for sixteen years. It's true that he had in the meantime made some sketches for another work in the genre, but Rolland's book must have jolted him into expanding and developing his ideas.

Another jolt that summer came from his burgeoning relationship with Maria (known as Mira) Mendelson, a twenty-four-year-old student of literature and aspiring poet whom he had met at Kislovodsk a year earlier. Prokofiev, twice Mira's age, was enchanted by the young woman, who in turn was overwhelmed by the attentions of one of the two most internationally established composers in the Soviet Union. (The other was Dmitri Shostakovich, Prokofiev's junior by fifteen years.) Prokofiev, however, was married and the father of two young sons; three years earlier, his wife, who was not Russian, had accepted his decision to move the whole family from Western Europe to Joseph Stalin's USSR. A life-changing collision loomed just as clearly for the Prokofievs and Ms. Mendelson as a global collision loomed on the geopolitical scene.

To what degree the threat of a second world war affected Prokofiev at the time is difficult to assess, because he tended to isolate himself as much as possible from external realities. Since childhood he had been obsessively dedicated to and possessed by his talent, and the more his work absorbed him, the better he was able to ignore the outside world. Yet the combination of international and internal tensions may well have set off a creative explosion in him. During that Kislovodsk summer of 1939, he put a few already formulated ideas together with many new ones and set to work on ten different movements that would eventually coalesce into his Sixth, Seventh, and Eighth piano sonatas. These works, completed between 1940 and 1944, are often lumped together as Prokofiev's "War Sonatas," but they are not onomatopoetic depictions of battle scenes: they contain reflections on and moments of respite from wars that were taking place inside as well as outside the man who composed them.

I MENTIONED IN AN EARLIER CHAPTER that although necessity is often the mother of invention—as the adage tells us—invention is not always a child of necessity. Among the composers discussed here, Beethoven, Schubert, Verdi, and Brahms were born into families that lived below or barely above the poverty line; by the time those four budding musicians reached their mid-teens, they were seeking to use their talents for survival. The other six, however, had parents who, at the very least, did not have to worry about where the next meal would come from, and some were from solidly bourgeois families.

Sergei Sergeievich Prokofiev was among this last group. Both his father, Sergei Alexeievich Prokofiev, an agronomist, and his mother, Maria Grigorevna Zhitkova Prokofiev, the daughter of a serf who had been emancipated in 1861, were well educated and highly cultivated. Sergei Alexeievich ran a friend's estate at Sontsovka (now called Sontsivka) in a rural part of Ukraine, where Sergei Sergeievich was born, on April 23, 1891. The senior Prokofievs had married in 1877, when Sergei Alexeievich was thirty-one and Maria Grigorevna was twenty; they had had two daughters before their son was born, but the girls had died in infancy. Although both parents took a strong interest in their son's upbringing, Maria Grigorevna particularly doted on him. She played the piano reasonably well, and Seryozhenka (diminutive of Sergei) was attracted to music from an early age. Composing, which he began to try at the age of five, was a game for him, like chess, which also fascinated him and at which he eventually became more than proficient. Composition, too, would remain a strategic challenge as well as an artistic calling for him, and after all, music-making has always had a ludic side to it.* As the overwhelmingly self-referential character of late Romantic art music began to transmute into something different, the seriously playful–playfully serious aspect of Prokofiev's artistic personality would attract growing attention.

When Seryozhenka was eleven, his parents engaged the twenty-seven-year-old composer Reinhold Glière—Kiev-born, but of German-Polish parentage—to spend his summers at Sontsovka and guide the boy's musical studies. Two years later, on the advice of another composer, Alexander Glazunov, Prokofiev tried out for and was admitted to the St. Petersburg Conservatory. Accustomed as he was to being the center of attention and the object of admiration on a remote Ukrainian estate, he suddenly found himself, unhappily, among much older students, most of whom paid him little attention amid all the distractions of a great metropolis. He studied harmony and counterpoint with the well-known composer Anatoly Lyadov and orchestration with the even better-known Nikolai Rimsky-Korsakov, but the greatest influences

---

* In English, as in many other languages, the verb *to play* is the same for musical instruments, sports, board games, and card games. In French, it's *jouer*; in German, *spielen*; in Russian, играть (igrat'), and so on.

on his musical development grew out of the friendships he eventually developed with the young composers Boris Asafyev, seven years his senior, and Nikolai Myaskovsky, three years older still. Under their enthusiastic mentorship, he began to attend performances of music by some of the avant-garde composers of the day, including not only Russia's own Alexander Scriabin and, a little later, Igor Stravinsky, but also foreigners like Strauss, Debussy, and Schoenberg. Equally important, at least from a practical point of view, were Prokofiev's advanced piano studies with Anna Esipova, a former star pupil (and one of the ex-wives) of the famed pedagogue Theodor Leschetizky, who had also taught Ignacy Paderewski, Artur Schnabel, and many other celebrated keyboard artists. Prokofiev, now in his late teens, bridled at Esipova's strict discipline, but her instruction provided him with an ironclad technique that eventually allowed him to develop a satisfying and lucrative international career as a performer of his own and others' works.

When Prokofiev was nineteen, his father died and the estate at Sontsovka had to be abandoned. He and his mother continued to live in middle-class comfort in the St. Petersburg apartment that she had rented for both of them when he had entered the conservatory, but he understood that he would eventually have to earn a living through music—the only career for which his training had prepared him. He began to publish a few compositions (his Piano Sonata No. 1 became his official first opus), and little by little a distinct musical personality began to emerge—nowhere more clearly than in his First Piano Concerto, written mainly when he was twenty. This episodic, fourteen-minute-long work displays the percussive, mechanistic characteristics as well as the lyrical, post-Romantic elements that would continue to converge in so much of Prokofiev's subsequent output and that would become his musical fingerprint.

And speaking of fingers: the concerto requires a high level of technical prowess, which Prokofiev had acquired by 1912, when he gave the piece's premiere in Moscow. He was the soloist in most of the concerto's other early performances, too, and his playing of it won him the Anton Rubinstein competition in St. Petersburg in 1914; that performance aroused tremendous enthusiasm from avant-gardists and equally vehement opposition from conservatives. Even before he won the Rubinstein prize, however, Prokofiev had produced the technically difficult Toccata, Op. 11, for solo piano, and the even thornier Second Piano Concerto. Clearly, he was glorying in his virtuosity and eager to show it off while metaphorically sticking his tongue out at conservative audiences.

As a gift for her son's victory at the Rubinstein competition and his graduation from the conservatory, Maria Grigorevna paid for his first trip outside the Russian Empire—to London, where he was introduced to Sergei Diaghilev, the forty-two-year-old creator and impresario of the culturally groundbreaking Ballets Russes. After a number of meetings, Diaghilev, then at the height of his fame and influence, engaged his young interlocutor to write the score for a ballet, *Ala and Lolly*, which would be choreographed by no less a figure than Vaslav Nijinsky. At a personal level, however, the twenty-three-year-old Prokofiev did not make a positive impression. His manners were "abrupt and sometimes crude," according to Harlow Robinson, one of his biographers, and he demonstrated "remarkable selfishness" and "insensitivity toward other artists."[2] Fortunately, Diaghilev was able to sense the powerful talent behind the callow, child-prodigy-like behavior, and Prokofiev began to feel that he was on the brink of an international career. Then came the First World War.

AFTER THE COLLAPSE, IN 1989, of the Berlin Wall, and the subsequent disintegration of the Warsaw Pact bloc and then of the Union of Soviet Socialist Republics, a well-known musician of my acquaintance laughed—in private—about some of his equally famous colleagues who had jumped at the chance to use those historical events for self-promotion by performing at the Wall or at other symbolic sites. "History as a backdrop to my career" was his ironic take on his fellow performers' attitudes.

The young Prokofiev did not see historical events as a backdrop to his career; he seemed, rather, to consider them annoyances that prevented his career from moving forward as quickly as possible. To be fair, however, any young musician who was on the brink or even in the midst of a career in 2020–21, when the Covid-19 pandemic shut down concert venues and opera houses all over the world, will understand the young Prokofiev's frustration at finding himself blocked at home. Diaghilev did manage to arrange a concert for him in Rome in March 1915, shortly before Italy entered the war, but thereafter the young composer was confined for three long years within his native country.

He worked on the *Ala and Lolly* ballet with the poet Sergei Gorodetsky, who provided him with a scenario, but the project fell apart when Diaghilev rejected the score; Prokofiev later used the music in his orchestral "Scythian" Suite, much of which strikes many listeners—this one included—as an imitation of Stravinsky's *The Rite of Spring*, which had premiered in 1913. Although Prokofiev completed a second ballet, *The Tale of the Buffoon* (also called *Chout*), for Diaghilev in 1915, external circumstances prevented it from being performed until 1921. Other works composed during the war years included the opera *The Gambler* (revised before its premiere in 1929), the Violin Concerto No. 1, the Symphony No. 1 ("Classical"—which remains one of his most popular works), a number of songs set to poems by Konstantin Balmont and Anna Akhmatova, *Visions fugitives* (twenty short pieces for piano solo), and the Second and Third piano sonatas. In 1917 he began to compose his Third Piano Concerto, which he did not complete until 1921; it became and is still today his most often-performed work in the genre.

The Bolshevik Revolution of October 1917, like the war that had spawned it, interested Prokofiev mainly because it prolonged the disruption of Russia's musical life. In the spring of 1918 he asked Anatoly Lunacharsky, newly appointed People's Commissar for Education in the nascent Soviet government, for permission to travel to the United States. Lunacharsky, a multilingual cosmopolite of broad cultural interests, replied: "You are a revolutionary in music, as we are in life. We should work together. But if you want to go to America I will not stand in your way."³ Prokofiev was duly provided with the necessary documents for going abroad; he took only a few of his scores and other basic possessions with him, thinking that he would return home after a few months.

Western Europe was still at war when Prokofiev left Petrograd; in order to reach New York he had to travel by train across Siberia to Vladivostok, then by ship to Japan and across the Pacific, and finally by rail from San Francisco to his destination. But the four-month-long trek proved worth the effort: his debut recital at New York's Aeolian Hall* in November 1918 was a great success, and it was followed by further American engagements—most fruitfully in Chicago, where the acclaim he received for a performance with the Chicago Symphony Orchestra persuaded Cleofonte Campanini, director and conductor of the Chicago Opera Company, to commission him to write an opera. Prokofiev quickly completed *The Love for Three Oranges*, based on a fairy-tale-like *commedia dell'arte* play by Carlo Gozzi, but complications arising from Campanini's death, in 1919, forced the postponement of its premiere until 1921. Prokofiev would continue to appear many times in the United States until the late 1930s, but beginning in the spring of

---

* The Aeolian Hall existed from 1912 to 1926 on the third floor of the building on West 42nd Street that now houses the State University of New York's College of Optometry. Many famous musicians, including the pianists Paderewski, Rachmaninoff, Busoni, and Josef Hofmann, performed there, but the most celebrated event to have taken place at the Aeolian Hall was the 1924 world premiere of George Gershwin's *Rhapsody in Blue*, with the composer as soloist with Paul Whiteman's orchestra.

1920 he made his home in Western Europe—mainly in Paris but with substantial periods spent in Brittany, Bavaria, and elsewhere.

In 1923, at the age of thirty-two, he married twenty-six-year-old Carolina (Lina) Codina, a part-Spanish, part-Polish soprano known by her stage name, Lina Llubera, whom he had first met in New York in 1918, and with whom he occasionally undertook concert tours. During the first year of their marriage they lived with Prokofiev's mother, who, having suffered severe deprivations in the fledgling Soviet Union, had immigrated to France, where she died in 1924. Lina and Sergei had two sons, Svyatoslav and Oleg, both born in Paris; the couple's married life was not always easy, since both partners were egotistical, but together they became attracted to Christian Science, found consolation in it, and established a satisfactory *modus vivendi*.

Throughout the 1920s and the first half of the 1930s, the catalogue of Prokofiev's works continued to grow, although many of his compositions were either received unenthusiastically or not performed until long after they were written. He composed another opera, *The Fiery Angel*; several more ballets, the best known of which are *Le Pas d'acier* (The Steel Step) and *L'Enfant prodigue* (The Prodigal Son); the Second and Third symphonies and a first version of the Fourth; the Fourth and Fifth piano concerti (the Fourth, for the left hand, was commissioned by the pianist Paul Wittgenstein, who had lost his right arm during the war, but who disliked the piece and never played it); the Second Violin Concerto; and the Fifth Piano Sonata.

As early as 1923, Prokofiev had begun to receive invitations to give concerts in the USSR, but, no doubt influenced by accounts from his mother and other émigrés of what they had witnessed there, he had always demurred. Eventually, however, his curiosity about Russia's latest musical developments, combined with a strong desire to reconnect with old friends and to make his works known in his native country—not to mention assurances from the Soviet authorities that he would be allowed to return to the West—made him decide to try his luck. Thus, in January 1927 he traveled by train to the city that he had known as St. Petersburg and then Petrograd and that was now Leningrad. Over a three-month period he gave thirty-one concerts there and in Moscow and other major cities, and he observed and enjoyed a production of *The Love for Three Oranges*. The idea of a permanent return began to seem reasonable.

Paris, however, was an exciting place of residence for artists in all fields during the 1920s. Lina Prokofiev, in conversations that I had with her in 1982,* recalled encounters there with Rachmaninoff, Stravinsky, Paul Hindemith, Francis Poulenc, Darius Milhaud, Aaron Copland, George Gershwin, Nadia Boulanger, Pierre Monteux, Georges Rouault, Henri Matisse, André Derain, Pablo Picasso, Salvador Dalí, Mikhail Larionov, Natalia Goncharova, and Charlie Chaplin. Prokofiev, although anything but a social butterfly, was at least acquainted with, and in some cases a friend and/or collaborator of, these and other important figures in contemporary culture.

He followed a second visit (1929) to the Soviet Union with tours in the United States, Canada, Cuba, and Western Europe, including Fascist Italy, but from 1932 on Prokofiev returned to Russia almost every year. He was receiving interesting and important commissions from Soviet musical organizations, and many of his friends, including the famed theater director Vsevolod Meyerhold, were urging him to resettle in his native land. And so in the spring of 1936, Sergei, Lina, and their two young sons moved from Paris to Moscow.†

---

* At the suggestion of Vladimir Ashkenazy, I was trying to help Lina Prokofiev prepare a memoir, but the plan was never realized.

† In 1918, when Sergei had left what was then known as the Russian Soviet Republic, he had traveled on a passport issued by the new government. But since, in those years, many Western countries did not recognize the legitimacy of that government or its successor, the Union of Soviet Socialist Republics, he had often faced bureaucratic hassles upon crossing foreign borders. After the Norwegian explorer, diplomat, and humanitarian

One person who must have wondered what in the world could have induced Prokofiev to leave the West for the USSR was the nearly thirty-year-old Dmitri Shostakovich, whose story is often mentioned in the same breath as Prokofiev's but was in fact vastly different. At the time of the Revolution, Shostakovich was only eleven years old. He lived more than half of his adult life under Stalin's regime, rarely left the Soviet Union—and only under surveillance—and was profoundly affected by the shifts and bumps in governmental policies, artistic and otherwise. In January 1936, not many weeks before the Prokofiev family moved to Moscow, Stalin and other high-ranking officials had attended a performance of Shostakovich's opera, *Lady Macbeth of the Mtsensk District*; Stalin's dislike of the lurid, overtly sexual work was evident to all present, and days later the composer was castigated in *Pravda*, the all-important newspaper of the Soviet Communist Party. Shostakovich promised to mend his ways by writing music that would respond to the party's precepts (although those precepts fluctuated with the whims of Stalin and his subordinates) and thereby avoided arrest or worse, but he would continue to live in fear of offending the people in power.

By contrast, Prokofiev, twenty-six when the Revolution took place, was by then already a multilingual man of the world with a positive and growing reputation in his field, and by the time he moved back to Russia he had lived outside the country for eighteen years. As we have already seen, he was accustomed to paying as little attention as possible to political events, at home and abroad, and yet, once he was a full-time resident of Stalin's USSR he could not entirely avoid noticing what was

---

Fridtjof Nansen devised an internationally recognized document for Russian émigrés and other stateless people, Prokofiev availed himself of a "Nansen passport," which greatly facilitated his travels. During his 1927 visit to the Soviet Union, however, he exchanged his Nansen document for a Soviet passport, after which he remained a Soviet citizen for the rest of his life. Lina, who was a Spanish citizen by birth but had traveled on a Nansen passport after her marriage to Sergei, became a Soviet citizen upon moving to Russia with her husband, and so did the couple's two sons.

going on around him. In August 1936, not long after he and his family had moved into their flat in the Soviet capital, the first of what came to be known as the "Moscow show trials" got underway, and Stalin's already dictatorial regime blossomed into an out-and-out reign of terror. Like tens of millions of other Soviet citizens, Prokofiev and his family would be profoundly affected and permanently scarred by the events of the following years.

THIS CHAPTER BEGAN WITH a quotation from the speech that Albert Camus gave in Stockholm in 1957, upon accepting the Nobel Prize in Literature, and in which he declared that a writer "cannot put himself today at the service of those who make history: he is at the service of those who are subjected to it." But the question of how a writer or any other artist can perform such a service, especially when some of the world's cruelest history-makers are in power, defies straightforward answers. Artists who live under dictatorial regimes and who openly resist the edicts of the people in power are silenced by imprisonment, exile, or death. Perhaps the only service that an artist can offer under such conditions, to "those who are subjected" to history, is a degree of consolation—consolation for the human condition in general and for human-created horrors in particular. Music, given its nonverbal nature, can console more openly than literature, at least in theory. Camus's novel *La Peste* (The Plague), for instance, was published two years after the end of the Second World War and is often described as an allegory of the rise, dominance, and demise, or at least abeyance, of fascism. Had Camus completed and tried to publish it three or four years earlier, in either the German-occupied portions of France or the areas governed by the Germans' French collaborators in the so-called Vichy Republic, he would certainly have failed and probably have died in the attempt. Musicians, on the other hand, could declare their thoughts and feelings through wordless sounds.

The story of Sergei Prokofiev's last seventeen years, which he lived entirely as a citizen and resident of Stalin's USSR,* is in part a story of creating consolations—for himself, of course, but also for those who listened to his music. At this point, however, we have to examine, briefly, a once-sensitive issue. Throughout the nearly half-century-long Cold War that divided the Soviet Union and its bloc from the United States and *its* bloc, analysts of Prokofiev's music on both sides of the political barrier tended to split his output into two main periods. For cold warriors in the West, Prokofiev's work before his permanent return to Russia was bold, forward-looking, yet also often witty and entertaining, whereas the music that he wrote under Stalin's regime was pallid stuff that had to conform to Communist Party dictates. For Prokofiev's Soviet commentators, on the contrary, his pre-homecoming works tended to be emotionally superficial and aimed at an intellectually sterile elite; only after his return to Russia—according to these observers—did he fully realize his potential as a composer whose music went directly to the hearts of the Soviet people and, by extension, to the hearts of "good" people everywhere.

No one should be surprised to learn that neither of these ideological hypotheses holds up under scrutiny, although there are fragments of truth in both. In his twenties, thirties, and early forties, Prokofiev sometimes used his formidable talents to thumb his nose at musical conservatives and to experiment by pushing and pulling tonality and formal conventions in extreme directions, although never to the breaking point.

---

* Prokofiev was allowed to make brief tours in Western Europe and America in 1936 and 1938; another tour was planned for 1940, but World War II intervened. After the war, his health was so poor that he probably would not have been able to travel even in the unlikely case that Stalin's increasingly paranoid regime had allowed him to leave.

(The music of Schoenberg and his disciples interested Prokofiev, but he was not tempted to follow their path.) On the other hand, some of his most enduringly popular pieces—the "Classical" Symphony, the Third Piano Concerto, and both violin concerti, among other works—date from the pre-Soviet period and can in no way be described as catering to an intellectually sterile elite or to any other specific class of people. Likewise, during the years following his repatriation he sometimes felt constrained to write party-line pablum that would satisfy the shifting demands of Stalin's regime, but he also wrote most of his deepest and most thoroughly satisfying masterpieces during his Soviet period—not to mention a piece that he probably considered a trifle but that is the most frequently performed of all his works: *Peter and the Wolf.* (This "symphonic fairy tale" and guide to the instruments of the orchestra was commissioned for the Central Children's Theater in Moscow by its director, Natalya Sats, whose life story reads in part like an exaggeratedly horrifying novel.)

I don't believe that suffering purifies people or makes them better human beings, but it can push some people toward taking a broader and more sympathetic view of the human condition. All of the other nine composers evoked in this book went through periods of acute suffering, for various reasons, whereas Prokofiev, during his youth and his years abroad, had faced only minimal obstacles along his path. There had been some setbacks—delayed premieres and other technical glitches in his career, relatively minor economic difficulties, and personal issues that had had to be resolved—but, all in all, his progress had been fairly smooth. Yet once he was firmly under the control of Stalin's minions, his problems became more serious, indeed potentially life-threatening. The manufactured emotion that I, at least, hear in some, although by no means all, of his earlier works began to fall away as he faced the realization that he had brought himself and his family into a hellish situation from which they could not escape, and that they would be lucky merely to survive.* In the finest of the works from his Soviet period, Prokofiev mined his suffering, turned it to account, and produced some truly outstanding music, including the piece that, in my opinion, is the greatest of his works for solo piano: the Sonata No. 8, in B-flat major.

THE EIGHTH SONATA IS THE LAST of the three so-called "War Sonatas" for piano that Prokofiev composed between 1939 and 1944; the fact that he considered them a group is confirmed by the consecutive opus numbers (82, 83, and 84) that he gave them, although the Sixth Sonata was completed two years before the Seventh and four years before the Eighth. These works were preceded by several other milestones in Prokofiev's Soviet career—among them, the popular Romeo and Juliet ballet, which he had begun before his move back to the USSR but which was not completed and performed until 1938; the score for Sergei Eisenstein's film Alexander Nevsky, which likewise opened in 1938; and the opera Semyon Kotko, completed in 1939 but first presented in 1940. (Kotko was to have been staged by Meyerhold at Moscow's Stanislavsky Theater, but before it could be performed Meyerhold disappeared, and agents of Stalin's NKVD—People's Commissariat for Internal Affairs, a precursor of the KGB—posing as thieves, burst into his apartment, took his papers, and stabbed and killed his wife, the actress Zinaida Reich. Kotko was performed anyway at the Stanislavsky, but it aroused little enthusiasm. Only after Stalin's death did the world learn that Meyerhold had been forced under torture to confess to crimes he had not committed, and had then been shot.)

---

* In-depth analyses of Prokofiev's life in the Soviet Union and his relationships with his wife Lina and their sons would far exceed this chapter's scope. To readers interested in learning more about these absorbing subjects I recommend two books by Simon Morrison: The People's Artist: Prokofiev's Soviet Years (Oxford and New York: Oxford University Press, 2009) and The Love and Wars of Lina Prokofiev (London: Harvill Secker, 2013).

The distance between Prokofiev's first five piano sonatas and the three "War Sonatas" was spiritual as well as temporal. His First Sonata (F major, 1907–9), composed when he was sixteen to eighteen years old, was necessarily derivative—it could have been subtitled "Rachmaninoff Meets Scriabin"—but it was followed by the severe, hard-edged Second (D minor, 1912). The Third (A minor, completed in 1917) makes some Romantic gestures but is nevertheless as iconoclastic as its predecessor; the Fourth (C minor, also completed in 1917) pushes tonality to extremes, its lyrical moments notwithstanding; and the Fifth (C major, 1923) feels even more experimental and somewhat self-consciously avant-garde. (Late in life Prokofiev made some noteworthy but not transformative changes to the Fifth Sonata and republished it as his Op. 135.)

The four-movement Sonata No. 6, in A major, is a different creature altogether. From the opening movement's very first bar, a tremendous rhythmic and dynamic power commands the listener's attention. The first theme is an onslaught, an assault; although it is tonal, it seems to convey a "liquidation of pitch itself for sheer sonic effect," as Simon Morrison, the preeminent expert on Prokofiev's Soviet years, has written.[4] On the other hand, the slow third movement is a glowingly erotic waltz (*Tempo di valzer lentissimo*), and one doesn't have to go too far out on a biographical limb to imagine that in this piece a composer in his late forties was writing to or about his adoring lover, Mira Mendelson, then in her mid-twenties. Mira later recalled that as early as 1939, when their affair was just beginning, Sergei had told her that the Sixth and Seventh sonatas would be "restless and storm-like" and the Eighth "tender and dreamlike,"[5] but in the end both descriptions would apply to all three of the sonatas: restlessness and storminess exist side by side with tenderness and dreaminess.

At a private, preview performance of the Sixth Sonata that Prokofiev gave on March 8, 1940—a month to the day before its public premiere—a twenty-five-year-old pianist, Sviatoslav Richter, turned pages for the composer and made up his mind to learn the work him-self. "The remarkable clarity of style and the structural perfection of the music amazed me," Richter later wrote. "I hadn't heard anything like it before. The composer, with barbaric audacity, breaks with the ide-als of the Romantics and includes the shattering pulse of the twentieth century in his music."[6] In fact, Prokofiev had done those things in some of his earlier works, too, but never with as much apparent emotional involvement as in this piece.

In March 1941 Prokofiev left Lina and their sons and moved in with Mira, and most of the Seventh Sonata, in B-flat major, was composed during the first year that he and Mira spent together; it is a more theatrical work than the Sixth but no less agitated. Prokofiev dedicated it to Richter, who gave its first performance, in Moscow, on January 18, 1943, and who immediately had to repeat the entire work for the extraordinarily enthu-siastic audience. Myaskovsky described the sonata as "superbly wild,"[7] and Richter wrote that its first movement thrusts listeners "into the anx-iously threatening atmosphere of a world that has lost its balance. . . . In the tremendous struggle that this involves, we find the strength to affirm the irrepressible life-force."[8] The Seventh is sometimes called the "Stalin-grad" Sonata because it reached the public at a decisive moment in the horrendous, six-month-long Battle of Stalingrad, by the end of which Soviet fighters had turned the tide against Nazi Germany on the Eastern Front; that may be one of the reasons for which the work was awarded a fifty-thousand-ruble Stalin Prize (second class). Its American premiere was given by Vladimir Horowitz in January 1944 at the Soviet consul-ate in New York City, despite the fact that Horowitz had emigrated from the USSR twenty years earlier. His subsequent performances of this vir-tuosic piece contributed enormously to the early growth of its popular-ity in the West. With its alternately anxious and violent first movement (*Allegro inquieto*—restless), tender second movement (*Andante caloroso*—warm), and jagged, energetic, and ultimately triumphant finale (*Pre-*

cipitato, entirely in 7/8 time), the Seventh remains the most frequently performed of all of Prokofiev's piano sonatas and one of the most popular of all twentieth-century works in the genre.

The Eighth, however, exists on a different plane. Here, war has become at least as much an internal conflict as a physical one; the battlefield is located within the composer's psyche, and within the listener's as well. Richter said that "of all Prokofiev's sonatas, this is the richest. It has a complex inner life, profound and full of contrasts. At times it seems to grow numb, as if abandoning itself to the relentless march of time. If it sometimes seems inaccessible, this is because of its richness, like a tree that is heavy with fruit."[9]

Prokofiev was able to complete the sonata on June 29, 1944, while the Soviet army was pushing the last German troops beyond the USSR's borders, and the other Allied forces, three weeks after the D-Day invasion, were beginning to crush Hitler's hordes on the Western front. Sergei was staying with Mira, the sonata's dedicatee, at a retreat for members of the Union of Soviet Composers outside the town of Ivanovo, about three hundred kilometers northeast of Moscow; he jokingly referred to the rural outpost as the State Chicken Farm or State Pig Farm, but he enjoyed taking walks in the nearby woods and simply being away from the hardships of life in wartime Moscow, where he was also in uncomfortable proximity to Lina. He even managed, that summer, to come close to completing his *Cinderella* ballet score and his Fifth Symphony; the latter would become the most frequently performed of all of his symphonies, with the exception of the brief, atypical First ("Classical") Symphony.

The honor of the Eighth Sonata's first performance—on December 30, 1944, in the Great Hall of the Moscow Conservatory—fell to twenty-eight-year-old Emil Gilels, who had studied the work with Prokofiev and possessed a magisterial command of the keyboard—a prerequisite for dealing with this piece. Richter, who was present at the premiere, described Gilels's performance as "quite simply phenomenal," played "with sovereign skill."[10] Gilels later wrote that the work "demands the greatest emotional effort" from its performers, and he added that it "captivates through its symphonic-style development, its tension and breadth, and the charm of its lyrical episodes."[11] He could have mentioned that it demands great emotional effort from listeners as well as performers, because its impact can be shattering, and many of the work's charming lyrical episodes contain undercurrents of disquiet and sadness.

The sonata's first movement, longer than its two other movements combined, is also the most emotionally, spiritually, and intellectually intense part of the work. Vladimir Ashkenazy, one of the work's finest interpreters, has described the whole composition as Prokofiev's greatest masterpiece for the piano, and its first movement as "the most personal of the revelations that can be found in Prokofiev's music."[12] Marked *Andante dolce*, the movement opens quietly in B-flat major and 4/4 time, and the feeling that something arising from deep inside a complex mind emerges from the piece's very first bars. The atmosphere is subdued yet charged— but charged with what? Is it nostalgia, perhaps, or a simple longing, a search to capture or recapture something intangible?

I sometimes think of this opening as a sort of lullaby, not for a baby but for an exhausted adult who can fall asleep only by drawing upon a previously untapped internal wellspring. We do not find, here, the acute angst and the sense of disorder and uncertainty that open the Seventh Sonata's first movement, with its fast-moving, monodic parallel octaves, its uneven phrases, and its elimination of chords, except for some brutal, punctuating "special effects." Instead, the first movement of the Eighth begins with a series of well-behaved four-bar phrases (although the first phrase is extended by a meditative fifth bar) and four-part harmonies, albeit modern ones, not to mention contrapuntal voice leadings (separate melodic lines for what musicians call the soprano, alto, tenor, and bass parts) reminiscent of Bach. Here, as in many of Prokofiev's other works, the main melodic line often jumps from one octave to another, but whereas he often made use, elsewhere, of abrupt upward and downward motion to delight or disconcert listeners, in this case he turned to them for atmospheric changes, for darkening or lightening the musical discourse, often for only a few seconds at a time.

Through the whole exposition (approximately the first five and a half or six minutes of the piece), the dynamic level ranges mainly from *pianissimo* to *mezzo forte*, with an occasional crescendo to a brief *forte*. Rather than thinking in terms of "first theme," "second theme," and so on, I hear the exposition as interconnected groups of thematic materials: the first of these groups lasts about two or two and a half minutes; the darker second group (which begins at the indication *Poco più animato*—a little livelier—and ends by returning to the opening *andante* tempo) occupies another minute or minute and a half; and the third, which takes roughly two minutes, has an eerie quality that grows out of an extreme contrast between high and low notes and ends with a repeated figuration that sounds like, and may represent, distant bells.

The development section, roughly four and a half minutes long, is a sort of commentary, in nightmarish, even catastrophic, sound-images, on everything that was so calmly laid out in the exposition. It's true that most developments are more dramatic than the preceding expositions, but the contrast here is extreme, as if a person who had been quietly, soberly meditating on life's ups and downs were suddenly overwhelmed with infernal visions of a fast-approaching, horrific destiny. Or perhaps the terrifying visions have nothing to do with the future but are simply describing present reality. Demonic sixteenth notes hurtle over a bass line that alternately quotes and mocks the exposition's themes. Occasional breaks in the sixteenth-note onslaught provide no respite for player or listener, because they are filled with devastating, dissonant octaves and chords. Toward the end of the development, one of the exposition's quieter thematic elements is transformed into brain-rattling assaults, until a series of terrifying, upward-sweeping scales and arpeggios—and some bass notes that should be played "almost like timpani," according to Prokofiev's instruction—lead back to the calming, tolling bells with which the exposition also ended.

The recapitulation begins with a nearly verbatim reprise of the exposition's thematic material, but it is shorter by approximately two minutes and lacks the bell-tolling ending. Instead, Prokofiev plunges us into an agitated, two-minute-long coda that sounds at first like an echo of the development but that goes on to present a different panorama of the development's horrors: it lacks the earlier section's cataclysmic effects and instead races headlong toward what could be a devastating conclusion. Shortly before the end, however, a series of fast, brusquely interrupted downward scales brings us up against an insurmountable brick wall. Two violent, upward-sweeping scale passages (mini-protests?) seem to dissolve into quiet defeat, but the movement ends on a high, gentle B-flat major chord. Perhaps this final, pallid, difficult-to-achieve smile was as close as Prokofiev could come to expressing optimism in Europe in 1944, and particularly in Stalin's wartime USSR.

IN EARLIER CHAPTERS, I mostly avoided discussing specific interpretations of the works under consideration. In this case, however, we have recordings made by Gilels, who studied Prokofiev's Eighth Sonata with the composer and gave its premiere, as well as recorded versions by other first-, second-, and third-generation Russian interpreters of the work. Gilels's two different recordings of this sonata—a live concert performance (1967) and a studio recording (1974)—inadvertently provide a cautionary lesson about "authentic" performances: the tempi of the first movement's exposition and recapitulation are so much slower in the later version that the whole movement clocks in at just under seventeen minutes, as opposed to just over fifteen in the earlier version. In listening to the two versions one after the other, I sometimes felt that I was hearing two different pieces. (The main divergences in all of the performances mentioned in this paragraph and the following one occur in the movement's exposition and recapitulation; in both of these, some pianists prefer simplicity, whereas others do more underlining. Everyone takes the development section—*Allegro moderato*—at a quick tempo.)

Even more interesting than Gilels's two recordings—both made long after Prokofiev's death—is Richter's 1946 recording, which, one may reasonably assume, was made at least in consultation with the composer himself, and possibly under his direct supervision, since the pianist had learned the work under Prokofiev's tutelage. The piano sounds a bit clunky, and in the last movement Richter has a number of minor "road accidents," but the performance overall is well worth hearing. The timing of the first movement in this recording is just under fourteen minutes—the second-fastest of any version familiar to me. I have also heard four other Richter recordings of the piece. A live performance and a studio recording, both made in London in 1961, have identical timings for the first movement—15:45 each. Another live performance (1974) by Richter clocks in at 14:33, and a third studio recording at 15:21. Ashkenazy made two studio recordings of the sonata, one in 1968 (16:20) and the other in 1993 (15:12). A version of the movement played by Grigory Sokolov lasts 14:39. Yefim Bronfman's 1988 studio recording runs to 14:34, and his 2015 live performance (13:25) is even faster than Richter's earliest recording. Boris Giltburg's 2005 studio recording and 2013 live performance differ by only nine seconds (14:25 as opposed to 14:16); and, at 16:45, a live performance by Yevgeny Kissin is nearly as long as Gilels's later recording.

These performances are all worth hearing, but I am particularly attracted to Richter's 1974 live performance, Ashkenazy's 1993 studio recording, and Bronfman's 1988 studio recording, all of which seem to me to plumb the work's depths without ever resorting to exaggeration or, on the other hand, risking superficiality by underscoring the movement's virtuosic aspects. One point that I found particularly interesting: no matter which tempi any of these pianists chose, all of them avoided dawdling for effect on individual notes in the melodic line, which does not work at all in this overwhelming first movement.

THE SECOND MOVEMENT, in complete contrast to the first, is a warm, lovely, moderately slow waltz that lasts only about four minutes and that Prokofiev marked *Andante sognando* (dreaming) and *dolce*. Its gently erotic tone has led some commentators to hypothesize that it was meant to be a sort of love song for Mira Mendelson, but most of its thematic material was drawn from incidental music that Prokofiev had composed in 1936— two years before he met Mira— for a stage production of Pushkin's *Eugene Onegin*. The *Onegin* project was abandoned and Prokofiev never completed its score, but he was fond enough of this number to transform it into a sonata movement. The deceptively simple piece is in D-flat major, 3/4 time, and what musicians call three-part song form, but it passes through various key changes, has an engagingly mysterious middle section, and ends as delicately as it began, unobtrusively fading away on the sole note of D-flat. The movement as a whole makes me think of lines from the first scene of Shakespeare's *Troilus and Cressida*: "But sorrow that is couched in seeming gladness / Is like that mirth fate turns to sudden sadness."

IN AN ESSAY TITLED "Is Music Unspeakable?" the renowned cultural historian Jacques Barzun described a composer sitting down at a piano and playing, for some guests, a piece that he has just written.

Afterward, one of the guests asks him what the piece means; by way of response, the composer returns to the piano and plays the piece a second time. "The composer's answer was entirely right," Barzun wrote. "The meaning is inside any work of art and it cannot be decanted into a proposition."[13] Of course, if a piece of music accompanies a verbal text, its meaning becomes clear—or so we think. But I am certain that if a person unfamiliar with Verdi's *Aida*, for instance, were to hear the tenor line in the aria "Celeste Aida" played by a clarinet or a viola instead of being sung, that listener would not necessarily be able to guess that it is a song about love and female beauty and male devotion, as opposed to, simply, an exceptionally beautiful, melodious piece in B-flat major.

And yet, there are works of "pure" instrumental music that invite extramusical interpretations, sometimes for plausible reasons. In the case of this Eighth Piano Sonata, we know that when it was being composed, much of the world's population (including an individual human being named Sergei Prokofiev) was living through the extreme terror and anguish of World War II, and that the people of Russia were being oppressed not only by the doings of foreign dictators but also by their own homegrown paranoid megalomaniac and his enablers and henchmen. Thus, the temptation to "psych out" this work can become irresistible, as the present author can testify. Yet whereas the internal conflict contained within the sonata's first movement, and the warmth of the interlude created by the second, seemed to me relatively clear, the tensions present in much of the finale are more resistant to extramusical analysis. Still, into the fray we go!

The final movement is nominally in B-flat major, and, sure enough, it begins and ends on multiple-octave B-flats. But during the intervening nine or ten minutes, the movement's key centers jump all over the diatonic map. If played at the *vivace* (lively, very fast) tempo that Prokofiev indicated, our initial sense of being in B-flat major lasts less than one second, although it will return from time to time. We're immediately off and running, with galloping triplet figurations forming all sorts of triads (major, minor, augmented, diminished, and others) that intentionally leave us in a harmonic quandary. Not only that: after barely ten seconds in the original 12/8 time signature, we're thrust into 4/4 time, with sinister staccato eighth notes replacing the galloping triplets. A few seconds later, the 12/8 triplets whirl us onward again—and this 12/8–4/4 alternation continues through the movement's first two minutes: fly away; no, keep your head down; fly away; no, keep your head down—over and over, until the reins are tugged and the headlong rush ends on a series of longer notes and we're confronted with a lumbering bear.

Instrumental music usually suggests no visual images to me, but in this case I'm convinced that Prokofiev is depicting a bear—not the growling, tormented, tightly chained bear at the Shrovetide Fair in Stravinsky's *Petrushka*, but a grinning bear that looms before us, waltzing clumsily in D-flat major, the same key as the second movement's dreamy waltz, but with a menacing undercurrent: the dream has been transformed into a nightmare. For nearly three whole minutes we can't take our eyes off the sight, although we know that we could be mauled or even devoured at any time. Then, as the waltz rhythm continues, the eerie, mysterious third thematic segment from the sonata's first movement makes a surprise entrance in the form of a clear-voiced descant over the bass line's ongoing threatening, ursine waltz-beat. This goes on for about a minute, until the bear wanders off and a drastically slowed down fragment of this finale's galloping theme materializes. At this point, Prokofiev not only indicates a new tempo (*andantino*) and a return to 4/4 time, but also provides a most unusual word—*irresolute*—to tell pianists to give this segment a feeling of uncertainty that eventually subsides into what feels like hopelessness.

A sudden return to the movement's opening *vivace* tempo brings us back to the land of the fully alive, but instead of beginning, as before, with the gallop in 12/8 time, Prokofiev restarts this quasi-recapitulation with the menacing motif in 4/4 time and only gradually returns to the gallop. This time around, however, the ambiguity, the mix of death-defying high jinks with cries of despair, reaches even higher levels of intensity than it had achieved earlier in the movement. And at the very end, a cyclonic, four-bar, four-second-long codetta brings the whole structure down with a tremendous thud.

AT ITS PREMIERE, THE SONATA NO. 8 was received reasonably well, but not as enthusiastically as the more easily grasped Sonata No. 7 had been from the very start. Nevertheless, the piece brought Proko-fiev a First Class Stalin Prize in 1945, and this fact, as Simon Morri-son has written, demonstrated above all the ever-growing esteem in which the composer was held by his colleagues. Barely two weeks after the sonata's first performance, Prokofiev conducted the premiere of his freshly completed Fifth Symphony—an immediate success—but that event would remain his last public performance. He was suf-fering from high blood pressure, and at home, just a week after the symphony's premiere, he blacked out, fell, and suffered a concussion. Recovery took months, and for the rest of his life he would experience alternating periods of relative well-being and bouts of ill health that would confine him to his bed. Whenever he felt even moderately well, he returned to his writing desk, and between that first collapse, early in 1945, and the end of 1947, he completed, among other works, the mysterious, profoundly moving Sonata No. 1 in F minor for violin and piano, Op. 80, which he had worked at off and on since 1938; the often subtly effective score for Eisenstein's film *Ivan the Terrible* (although Eisenstein died of a heart attack before the epic film could be com-pleted); and the devastating Symphony No. 6 in E-flat minor, Op. 111—which I hear as a violently, sarcastically bitter denunciation of Stalin's regime. Revisions of the massive opera *War and Peace*, much of which he had written during the war years, also date from that period, and so does the Piano Sonata No. 9 (C major, Op. 103), which many pianists admire but which some listeners, this one included, find weaker than its predecessors.

Early in 1948, Prokofiev, Shostakovich, Aram Khatchaturian, and several other Soviet composers were censured in a resolution by the Central Committee of the Communist Party of the USSR, headed by its second secretary, Andrei Zhdanov. (The first secretary was Stalin himself, and Zhdanov was seen as a possible successor to the dictator, who turned seventy that year.) Stalin had put Zhdanov in charge of Soviet cultural policy, and it was in that role that the second secretary decided that too many Soviet artists in various cultural fields were creating "hermetic," "formalist," art-for-art's-sake works instead of making use of folk and popular sources to produce art for that eternally indefinable, indeed ephemeral entity known as The People. The great poet Anna Akhmatova was also censured, and so were Russian literary historians who had dared to suggest that some of the country's most celebrated nineteenth-century writers had been influenced in any way by foreign literature. Zhdanov, who knew little if anything about music, decided that Prokofiev and company were foisting hard-to-grasp—therefore anti-communist—compositions upon the Soviet people. Eight of Prokofiev's works, including the Stalin Prize–winning Eighth Piano Sonata, were suddenly banned from public performance.

Prokofiev, like his colleagues, duly ate crow—in his case, by sending the chairmen of the Composers' Union and the Committee on Arts Affairs a letter that was part breast-beating and part self-exoneration. These chairmen, like their counterparts in other dictatorial bureaucracies, hesitated to risk their necks by deciding whether to accept or reject such submissions without receiving a nod from their bosses; thus Prokofiev's letter was given to Stalin and other Politburo members, "who offered it their tacit sanction," according to Morrison.[14] But the ailing composer, not yet fifty-seven years old but frail beyond his years, began to experience fear. (By a stroke of poetic justice, or injustice, depending on which of the players one happened to be, Zhdanov died suddenly, at the age of fifty-two, only six months after his attack on Prokofiev, Shostakovich, and the other composers. He was an alcoholic and was said to have died of a heart attack, but his death may have been "encouraged" by Stalin, who had recently removed him from his position as number two man in the USSR.)

In January 1948, just before the Zhdanov censure, Prokofiev had married Mira Mendelson. Lina had never agreed to a divorce, but a Soviet court had declared that since her marriage with Sergei had taken place abroad and had never been properly registered in the USSR, it was null and void. A month later, Lina, fifty years old at the time, was arrested on trumped-up charges of espionage and betrayal of the fatherland—which was not even her fatherland! She was imprisoned and interrogated for the better part of a year, then condemned to twenty years in the gulag. Prokofiev was shocked, but he was powerless to help.

When his health permitted, he continued to compose, but not much music of significance emerged from his pen after the Zhdanov censure. Sergei and Mira generally spent winters in their Moscow apartment and the rest of the year in a dacha in the village of Nikolina Gora, about thirty kilometers west of the city. On March 5, 1953, a month and a half before his sixty-second birthday, Prokofiev died in his Moscow apartment, of a cerebral hemorrhage. The Soviet press paid little attention to his death because, by an extraordinarily strange coincidence, Joseph Stalin died on the same day, possibly even at the same hour.

With the so-called "Khrushchev Thaw" that followed Stalin's death, Svyatoslav and Oleg Prokofiev were able to petition for their mother's release from the camps; Lina returned to Moscow in 1956, after eight years of punishment for crimes that she had not committed, and she and her sons eventually left the Soviet Union, although at different times. Lina lived in Paris and later in London, on royalties from her husband's compositions (in the West, Prokofiev's Soviet divorce from Lina and marriage to Mira had no legal standing), and she was happy to resume, albeit in a toned-down manner, the cosmopolitan life that she had led during the interwar years.* Not surprisingly, given what she had been through, she was a suspicious person—"more Russian than the Russians," as Ashkenazy described her to me. She died in London in 1989, at the age of ninety-one. Oleg, an artist, was married three times, had seven children (including the composer Gabriel Prokofiev), and died on the Isle of Guernsey in 1998, at sixty-nine. Svyatoslav, an architect, married once and had one son; he died in Paris, the city of his birth, in 2010, at eighty-six. Lina, Svyatoslav, and Oleg all dedicated a great deal of their time to promoting Sergei Prokofiev's artistic legacy.

So did Mira Mendelson, but she outlived the composer by only fifteen years and died at the age of fifty-three.

IGOR STRAVINSKY, THE PROTAGONIST of this book's next, final chapter, was nine years older than his compatriot Prokofiev. His early masterpieces had impressed and influenced his younger colleague, and the two men had often met, especially in Paris during the interwar years. At a personal level, however, they often seemed to be at loggerheads. "I could not feel any warm feelings of friendship toward him," Prokofiev wrote of Stravinsky, "for he did not allow anyone

---

* In 1982, when I worked with Lina in Paris, she told me that she spoke (as I recall) English, Russian, French, Spanish, Catalan, Polish, Italian, and German, although not all of them well. She hadn't lived in the United States for sixty years, yet her English was absolutely fluent, with a sort of old-fashioned, upper-class New York accent. She occasionally enjoyed speaking French with me because her French was better than mine and she could correct my mistakes, but when she discovered that my Italian was better than hers she avoided speaking it with me.

to develop sentimental feelings about him. I was never confident of relying on his friendship throughout life."[15] And Stravinsky characterized his younger colleague as a blank slate: "one could see Prokofiev a thousand times without establishing any profound connection with him."[16] Both men were easily offended, and especially prickly when their works were under discussion. And yet, Stravinsky once managed to pay a half-compliment to Prokofiev by describing him as "the greatest Russian composer of today—*après moi*."[17] Coming from that particularly acerbic observer, a half-compliment may be considered a remarkable tribute.

10

AN ICE-COLD QUESTION MARK

Igor Stravinsky: *Requiem Canticles* for Contralto
and Bass Soli, Chorus, and Orchestra (1966)

IN THE FALL OF 1964, Igor Stravinsky, who was living in Los
Angeles, received a cablegram from an old friend in France. Nadia
Boulanger, the esteemed composer, conductor, and mentor of musicians from Aaron Copland and Elliott Carter to Dinu Lipatti and Daniel Barenboim, informed him that he had been offered ten thousand
dollars to compose a piece to mark the centenary of the birth of the
Princesse de Polignac, née Winnaretta Singer, who had been one of his
most generous patrons during the First World War and beyond.

"Regret infinitely," Stravinsky cabled back to Boulanger, "but
charge 10,000 to conduct in a concert today and no less than 25,000 commission for a short piece."[1]

Life, for Stravinsky, was an increasingly difficult proposition. At
eighty-two, he was suffering from what was posthumously described

as chronic stroke disease, in addition to an inoperable inguinal hernia and a variety of other ailments, some of them the result of decades of smoking and often excessive drinking.[2] A broad swath of the history of Western art music had unfolded since his birth, at Oranienbaum (modern-day Lomonosov), near St. Petersburg, on June 17, 1882. At that time, Wagner had been preparing *Parsifal* for its premiere the following month; Brahms had completed only the first two of his four symphonies and Tchaikovsky the first four of his six; Verdi had not yet written *Otello* or *Falstaff*; and Richard Strauss, Debussy, and Mahler, ranging in age from eighteen to twenty-two, were all struggling to find their individual musical voices. By 1964, Stravinsky had outlived not only all of those older masters but nearly all of the most celebrated colleagues of his own generation: Sergei Prokofiev had been dead for eleven years, Arnold Schoenberg for thirteen, Béla Bartók and Anton Webern for nineteen, Maurice Ravel for twenty-seven, and Alban Berg for twenty-nine. When Stravinsky was born, Alexander III was tsar of all the Russias; William Gladstone was Queen Victoria's prime minister; Franz Joseph I reigned over the Austro-Hungarian Empire; Otto von Bismarck was Germany's Iron Chancellor, under Kaiser Wilhelm I; and former vice president Chester A. Arthur had recently become president of the United States following the assassination of James A. Garfield. Now, more than eight decades later, the People's Republic of China, under the leadership of Mao Zedong, was preparing its first nuclear bomb test; Lyndon B. Johnson had recently replaced the assassinated John F. Kennedy in the White House; the Cold War and space race were in full swing; and Nikita Khruschchev was about to be deposed by Alexei Kosygin and Leonid Brezhnev as, respectively, prime minister of the USSR and first secretary of the Soviet Communist Party.

Yet despite his age and ill health, Stravinsky still felt the need to plunge into new creative projects, just as he had done over and over again for sixty years. He was determined to use whatever strength remained in his frail body to rise once again to the challenge of turning music's raw materials into compositions that would meet his terrifyingly self-critical standards. According to his biographer Stephen Walsh, by the mid-1960s the composer "lived in fear of the time—plainly not far distant—when he would no longer be able to conduct" (conducting was a major source of income for him), "while his already grotesque medical bills continued to mount."[3] This explains why he took special care, financial as well as musical, in considering the various requests that came his way for new compositions. And fortunately a different commission—one that met Stravinsky's economic and scheduling requirements—came along at about the same time as Nadia Boulanger's request, although the commissioning party had no personal connection with the composer.

Stanley J. Seeger Jr., an art collector and amateur composer, was the son of the recently deceased Helen Buchanan Seeger, the wealthy daughter of a Texas timber magnate. Mrs. Seeger had been a major benefactor of Princeton University, her son's alma mater, and a member of the university's Friends of Music, and Stanley had stipulated that some of the funds bequeathed by his mother be used to commission a piece of music that would commemorate her. Through some friends—a Mr. and Mrs. Jascha Kajaloff—Seeger asked the composer for an appropriate work.

The ideal commission—Stravinsky reportedly said—came about when the potential commissioning party asked him to write a piece that he had already wanted to write. Sometimes, however, an unanticipated request could either plant a stimulating new idea in his mind or function as a catalyst to an as yet inchoate artistic desire. He showed interest in Seeger's proposal, although he had never met Mrs. Seeger, but he stipulated that he could "only work in my own tempo and under my own pressures."[4] No deadline, in other words. Seeger agreed to the composer's conditions, including the $25,000 fee (over $200,000 in 2020 purchasing power).

Stravinsky seems to have planned—at first and for several months thereafter—a purely instrumental piece: in a letter dated March 21, 1965, to his friend Nicholas Nabokov, he referred to "the symphony I promised the young Princeton orchestra so long ago."[5] But in the end he opted to make the new work a vocal and instrumental setting of parts of the Latin mass for the dead. And indeed, in that same month of March Stravinsky started to compose the new piece, which he called *Requiem Canticles*. Robert Craft, his musical assistant, provided him with a preliminary selection of verses from the Latin mass for the dead, although the composer may have suggested guidelines for the choices and certainly altered some of them. Craft agreed with the music critic Harris Goldsmith's comment that the texts chosen tended to be more menacing than consolatory, and he added his own opinion that this was because Stravinsky "was becoming more defiant and less mellow with age" and because "the octogenarian was naturally somewhat short-winded."[6] Stravinsky's waning energy level may have been relevant, but his presumably increasing defiance was not: in accordance with church doctrine, the violence implicit in many of the verses has to do with God's threatened punishment for sinners, not with any conceivable protest or resistance on the sinners' part.

Stravinsky continued to work sporadically on the *Canticles* for well over a year,* and as he toiled he pasted into his sketchbook obituaries of people he knew who died during that period, including the composer Edgard Varèse, the sculptor Alberto Giacometti, and the writer Evelyn Waugh—the last two his juniors by two decades; perhaps he was reminding himself that little time remained to him. He completed the score on August 13, 1966, and that evening he celebrated by going, with

---

* For a detailed account of the chronology of the *Requiem Canticles'* composition, as well as an analysis of some of the compositional techniques that Stravinsky employed in the work, see Appendix G, "On the Chronology of the REQUIEM CANTICLES," in R. Craft, ed., *Stravinsky: Selected Correspondence*, vol. 2 (New York: Alfred A. Knopf, 1984), pp. 467–71.

his wife, Vera, and with Lillian Libman, his personal manager, to see *Seduced and Abandoned*, a movie directed by Pietro Germi, with Stefania Sandrelli and Aldo Puglisi in the lead roles. According to Libman, Stravinsky laughed uproariously during the movie's comic scenes but also consumed too much popcorn, with results that kept him up all night.[7]

The score of the *Requiem Canticles* calls for soprano, alto, tenor, and bass solos, although only the alto and bass voices have segments in which they sing alone; a four-part chorus; and an orchestra comprised of three standard flutes (with the third flute player doubling on piccolo), alto flute, two bassoons, four horns, two trumpets, three trombones, timpani (two players), xylophone, vibraphone, bells, harp, piano, celesta, and strings. Once the piece was finished, Stravinsky pressed to have it performed as soon as possible, despite the fact that his recent compositions—in which he had adopted personalized versions of Schoenberg's twelve-tone (serial) system—had been criticized not only by conservatives, who accused him of jumping without conviction onto the radicals' bandwagon, but also by the radicals themselves, who thought he was joining their cause when it had already been won. The *Canticles* "will be another big flop,"[8] he told Lawrence Morton, a musicologist and concert organizer in Los Angeles, where Stravinsky and his wife had been living since their emigration from Europe in 1940. But he felt so sure of the composition's value that he cared only tangentially about how it would be received.

The premiere—subsidized by the Seeger bequest and organized by Arthur Mendel, the chairman of Princeton's music department, and by the Chilean-born composer Claudio Spies, a friend of Stravinsky's—took place at the university's McCarter Theatre on October 8, 1966. The instrumental ensemble was made up of New York–based freelance musicians and was dubbed, for the occasion, the New York Concert Symphony Orchestra. As ticket requests far exceeded the number of seats available, Stravinsky allowed students to attend the afternoon dress rehearsal. At the concert proper, he received a standing ovation as he walked slowly and with some difficulty to the podium to begin the program by conducting his *Symphonies of Wind Instruments*, and he returned later to lead *Three Sacred Choruses in Old Slavonic*, which he had composed during the 1930s. Craft led the rest of the program, which included the recent Variations for orchestra and the Mass (1948) as well as, of course, the *Requiem Canticles*, performed once before the intermission and again after it, with soloists Linda Anderson, soprano; Elaine Bonazzi, mezzo-soprano; Charles Bressler, tenor; and Donald Gramm, bass-baritone. The Ithaca College Concert Choir had been prepared by Gregg Smith, an esteemed choral conductor with whom Stravinsky had worked on other occasions.

Present among the capacity audience of 1,100 were the composers Aaron Copland, Elliott Carter, Arthur Berger, and Vladimir Ussachevsky, as well as the violinist Samuel Dushkin, for whom Stravinsky had written his only violin concerto, thirty-five years earlier. A request in the printed program, asking that there be no applause after the *Canticles*, was obeyed following the first playing but disobeyed after the second, which received a standing ovation; Stravinsky acknowledged the latter reaction "with a stiff bow and a smile," according to a report in the *Daily Princetonian*.[9] He was given another standing ovation at the end of the concert.

Few American critics were in attendance, and local reporters seemed somewhat flummoxed by much of what they had heard. But the *Times* of London did send an observer, who reported: "The new *Requiem Canticles*, though brief, are of great originality and invention, variety and contrast, and"—the critic added, presciently—"are likely to prove [Stravinsky's] most impressive and accessible serial work to date."[10]

Three days after the concert, Craft and the other Princeton performers recorded the *Canticles* for Columbia Records at New York's Manhattan Center; for the occasion, the ad hoc instrumental ensemble was redubbed the Columbia Symphony Orchestra. Several of the other pieces that had been played during the concert were also recorded that day—all of them, including the *Canticles*, supposedly under the composer's supervision, whereas in fact Stravinsky put in only a single, brief appearance during the sessions and did not hear the *Canticles* at all.

THE PRESSING NEED TO EARN MONEY, implicit in his above-quoted telegram to Nadia Boulanger, was not new to Stravinsky and was not only the result of old age and infirmity. His three celebrated, pre–First World War ballet scores—*The Firebird*, *Petrushka*, and *The Rite of Spring*—had brought him international fame, but they had been published in tsarist Russia, which had not adhered to the Berne copyright convention; nor did the post-revolutionary Soviet government accept the convention's authority. As a result, Stravinsky received severely diminished royalties for performances of his most popular works.* Although he was paid substantial commission fees for many of his subsequent compositions, which he published under copyright in the West, none of those works achieved the popularity of the three earlier scores. He developed sufficient skill as a conductor and pianist to lead or play in performances and recordings of his works, and his fees as a performer greatly augmented his income. But money worries had plagued him for most of his adult life.

He sometimes carried those worries to extremes. The Italian composer Bruno Bettinelli recounted that once, in Venice, he had noticed Stravinsky, whom he revered, dining with Vera and others at an outdoor café in Piazza San Marco; Bettinelli placed himself behind a potted shrub so that he could observe his idol without being seen. At the end

---

* In the 1940s, Stravinsky made revisions to those three scores, and the revised versions, published in the West under copyright, did bring him royalties. But orchestras and ballet companies were not legally bound to use the revised versions.

of the meal, Vera, who handled the couple's money when they traveled, took out her purse, paid the check, and left a tip on the table. By the time the aged and ailing Stravinsky managed to hoist himself out of his chair, all of the group's other members had begun to move away from the table, and the composer, unobserved except by Bettinelli, picked up the tip, or part of it, and put it in his pocket.

Yet Stravinsky had not grown up in straitened circumstances. His parents, Fyodor Ignatyevich and Anna Kirillovna (*née* Kholodovsky) Stravinsky, were firmly rooted in the Russian bourgeoisie. They and their four sons, of whom Igor was the third, lived in a fine apartment on St. Petersburg's Kryukov Canal, facing the Mariinsky Theater, which, then as today, was the city's and, arguably, the nation's most important lyric theater. Fyodor, a leading basso at the Mariinsky, had sung in the premieres or in early productions of operas by most of the Russian composers of his day, including Mussorgsky, Borodin, Rimsky-Korsakov, and Tchaikovsky—all of whom he knew personally—and he had taken key roles in foreign works as well. Anna, a fine amateur pianist, ran the household with considerable assistance from servants, including a German nanny for her sons, who all grew up speaking Russian, German, and French. Most summers were spent on the country estates of one or another of the elder Stravinskys' various comfortably-off siblings. Although Igor later described his childhood as unhappy, his unhappiness was attributable to his parents' strict disciplinary practices and to his own social awkwardness rather than to any lack of creature comforts.

Music fascinated him from as early as he could remember, but he was not allowed to take piano lessons until he was nine years old, and he was even older when he began to learn something about harmony and counterpoint and to make some attempts at composing. At school he was a mediocre student, yet his parents eventually persuaded or forced him to enroll in the law faculty at St. Petersburg University. There he became friendly with a fellow student, Vladimir Rimsky-Korsakov, through whom he met Vladimir's father, Nikolai Andreyevich Rimsky-Korsakov, the composer of such internationally successful scores as *Scheherazade* and *Capriccio espagnol* and of several operas that were popular in Russia. Finally, at the age of twenty and under Rimsky's tutelage, Stravinsky began to receive serious professional musical instruction. For six years, and especially during the last three of those years, he worked intensively with Rimsky and frequented the musical get-togethers that took place in the Rimsky family's bustling apartment, where he was exposed to some of the new music from Western Europe that was filtering into Russia. Like the young Schumann three-quarters of a century earlier and the young Sibelius in the 1880s, the young Stravinsky eventually dropped any pretense of trying to obtain a law degree.

Rimsky, however, died in 1908, and Stravinsky was left feeling both bereft and adrift. But the following year, two orchestral pieces, *Scherzo fantastique* and *Fireworks*, which he had composed before his mentor's death, were performed on one of the St. Petersburg concerts presented by the famed pianist and conductor Alexander Siloti. Luckily for the aspiring young composer, that concert was attended by a thirty-seven-year-old impresario, Sergei Pavlovich Diaghilev.

Since 1907, Diaghilev had been bringing various Russian works to Paris, and his productions, which included the French premiere of Mussorgsky's opera *Boris Godunov*, had become a virtually unmissable annual cultural festival and social event in the French capital. Diaghilev decided that he would return to Paris in 1909 with his own company of dancers and musicians, which he dubbed the Ballets Russes. After having heard Siloti's performance of Stravinsky's two colorful compositions, Diaghilev invited the young man to orchestrate some piano pieces by Grieg and Chopin for the forthcoming Paris season. Stravinsky's arrangements were well received, and Diaghilev commissioned him to write an entire ballet score for the following year. That work—

The Firebird, with a scenario based on a Russian folktale—opened at the Paris Opéra on June 25, 1910 and brought the composer his first major success, as well as a commission from Diaghilev to write another ballet score, this one to be based on a dream that Stravinsky had had about a primitive, pagan ritual sacrifice.

Four years earlier, in 1906, Stravinsky had married his first cousin Katerina Nossenko, and by the fall of 1910 Katerina had given birth to three children: Fyodor, Lyudmila, and Soulima. (A fourth child, Milena, was born in 1914.) Until *The Firebird* launched Stravinsky's international career, the family had been living most of the year in an apartment in St. Petersburg but spending summers in a new home in Ustilug, a village some eight hundred miles south-southwest of the tsar's capital, in what is now the extreme western part of Ukraine. Now, however, Stravinsky's increasingly close connection with the Paris-based Ballets Russes caused the family to begin to spend more time in France and in nearby French Switzerland.

Not many weeks after the *Firebird* premiere, Diaghilev visited Stravinsky in Lausanne, heard him play parts of a new piece for piano and orchestra—a piece inspired by the idea of a puppet that comes to life—and persuaded him to turn the work into a fully orchestrated ballet. Stravinsky and the set designer Alexandre Benois prepared the scenario; Mikhail (Michel) Fokine created the choreography; and on June 13, 1911, four days before Stravinsky's twenty-ninth birthday, *Petrushka* had its premiere at Paris's Théâtre du Châtelet, with a now-legendary cast: Vaslav Nijinsky in the title role, Tamara Karsavina as the Ballerina, Alexandre Orlov as the Moor, and Enrico Cecchetti—the teacher of Nijinsky and many other star dancers—as the Charlatan. Pierre Monteux, who would become one of the century's most respected conductors, led the enthusiastically received premiere.

In the lushly orchestrated *Firebird*, the influence of Rimsky-Korsakov had loomed large, but in *Petrushka* the full individuality of

Rimsky's pupil exploded into vibrant life. And an even bigger explosion occurred two years later, when Diaghilev presented the world premiere of Stravinsky's *The Rite of Spring* (*Le Sacre du printemps*), the work that had originated with the composer's dream of a pagan sacrifice; its subtitle is *Pictures of Pagan Russia*. That premiere, conducted by Monteux at Paris's new Théâtre des Champs-Elysées on May 29, 1913, was one of the most turbulent first performances in the history of Western music. Nijinsky's startling but ineptly executed choreography drew protests and counterprotests from the audience, and the music itself, with its jagged rhythms, jarring dissonances, overt sensuality, and sheer, savage orchestral power, compounded the negative reaction, to such a point that the police had to intervene. *The Rite of Spring*, more than any other individual composition of the age, transformed European art music.

Try to imagine music's evolution as a river that grows in size as it flows downstream, and then imagine a superhuman force taking that river's bed and turning it suddenly in a different direction. Beethoven's intensely self-referential music had had such an effect a century earlier; Wagner's harmonically and structurally daring music dramas had done something similar a half-century further on; and now Stravinsky, with a single, thirty-five-minute-long composition, was putting an end to German musical domination and setting a new course—or, at the very least, drastically altering the old one—for European and Euro-influenced composers. As Stravinsky authority Richard Taruskin has pointed out, *The Rite of Spring* did not appear out of nowhere: its roots were sunk deep within traditional Russian music. Nevertheless, its effect was enormous. Just as the fast-approaching, cataclysmic First World War would permanently alter Western civilization, so *The Rite* would prove to be a watershed in Western music. In later years, Stravinsky would declare, with a combination of self-awe and a peculiar form of modesty: "I am the vessel through which *The Rite of Spring* passed."

STRAVINSKY'S THREE EARLY TRIUMPHS (the *The Rite* was recognized, relatively quickly, as a masterpiece as great as or greater than *The Firebird* and *Petrushka*) made his name known even among musicians and music lovers who were opposed to him. Yet growing fame and its side benefits did not hamper his own musical evolution. He was, after all, still short of his thirty-first birthday when the meteor-*Rite* slammed into the musical world, and he had been a professional, only occasionally bread-winning composer for barely four of those years—a period during which he had undergone what his early biographer Eric Walter White described, only a bit hyperbolically, as "the most rapid development that any composer has ever experienced."[11] The main issue that confronted Stravinsky after the composition of *The Rite of Spring* was the choice of a logical path forward. He must have understood, or at least sensed, that *The Rite* was, for him, a point of arrival, not a point of departure—the end, not the beginning, of his first major creative phase. *The Firebird* had nearly brought late Russian Romanticism to a close (although the style would continue to thrive for a while in the hands of Rachmaninoff and others); *Petrushka* had gently mocked Romanticism; *The Rite* had pulverized it. Any attempt to compose a work even more massive, and massively violent, than *The Rite* would have led to empty exaggeration and, ultimately, to an artistic dead end. Others could imitate it if they wished, but Stravinsky refused to imitate himself.

As things turned out, the First World War helped him to find new creative paths. Not only did it strand him in Western Europe: it also limited his earning ability, partly as a result of the precarious state of the Ballets Russes' finances. These restrictions compelled him to invent new, more compact forms of musical expression. While living with his family in straitened circumstances in French Switzerland, Stravinsky composed—among much else—songs and short pieces as well as *Reynard* (*Renard*), a one-act barnyard "burlesque for the stage with singing and music" plus acrobatic dancing; *The Soldier's Tale* (*L'Histoire du soldat*), written in collaboration with the Swiss poet Charles-Ferdinand Ramuz), a work "to be read, played, and danced" by the unusual combination of three actor-narrators, clarinet, bassoon, cornet, trombone, percussion, violin, double bass, and a female dancer; and *Rag-Time*, for eleven instruments (woodwind, brass, strings, and percussion). Each of these titled pieces was original in form, and even after the war ended, Stravinsky generally avoided creating scores for gigantic orchestral forces.

He was well aware of the experimentalism that was taking place in German music—the post-Wagnerian trends toward atonality and, a little later, dodecaphony (twelve-tone or serial composition, promulgated by Arnold Schoenberg and his disciples)—but these were not paths that he wished to explore. Not yet, at any rate, or for a long time thereafter. To his way of thinking, the German avant-garde was prolonging Teutonic Romanticism, albeit through harmonically radical means. Stravinsky, taking a very different approach, began to create a bridge that would connect pre-Romantic forms, which he admired, with modern harmonic, melodic, and rhythmic combinations. He saw himself as an anti-Romantic: "Music means itself," he often said, pugnaciously defying others to claim that this or that instrumental passage could be understood to represent or express a specifically identifiable emotion or agglomerate of emotions. The declaration was meant mainly to shock complacent listeners, since Stravinsky was himself deeply moved by music—his own music and the music of others—but he saw himself as an exemplar of the category *homo faber*, man who makes things. To which I would add—as in Prokofiev's case—the category *homo ludens*, man who plays or, more specifically, man who takes pleasure in and is absorbed by the craft of making things.

By the time he turned forty, Stravinsky was heading into what we pigeon-holers call his neoclassical period—a phase that would endure for three decades and would produce a considerable number of outstanding pieces of music, almost every one of which was *sui generis*. Most composers tend to write multiple works in the forms with which they feel most comfortable: a substantial number of symphonies or operas or string quartets or lieder or oratorios or sonatas or concerti. But Stravinsky was musically promiscuous. He would become fascinated by the sound of a certain instrument or combination of instruments, or by a particular musical structure, or even by something he had read or a painting he had seen, and he would work (and play) at extracting something new and entirely his own out of a specific sound or form or text.

Pulcinella (1919–20), a one-act ballet with three voices, largely based on music by early eighteenth-century composers, truly initiated Stravinsky's neoclassical phase, and he later arranged it, or parts of it, for various instrumental combinations. One strikingly original work followed another; I particularly love the brilliant Octet for wind instruments— dedicated (although not publicly, at the time) to his lover and future second wife, Vera de Bosset Soudeikine*—and the long-delayed, pre-neoclassical *The Wedding* (*Les Noces*), his stunning, highly stylized "choreographed scenes" (as he called the work) for four solo voices, four-part chorus, four pianos, percussion, and dancers; this remains one of his greatest masterpieces. Other major works of the interwar years include the Latin-language opera-oratorio *Oedipus Rex*, with a Sophocles-inspired libretto by Jean Cocteau, and the dazzlingly beautiful ballet *Apollon musagète* (later redubbed, simply, *Apollo*), commissioned for performance at the Library of Congress in Washington, DC. When Serge Koussevitzky, the Boston Symphony Orchestra's Russian-born conductor, commissioned Stravinsky to write a piece for the ensemble's fifti-

---

* Vera de Bosset (originally Vera Bosse), a Russian dancer and set designer of German parentage, had left her husband, the painter Serge Soudeikine, after she fell in love with Stravinsky.

eth anniversary, in 1930, the composer, who had recently returned to the Russian Orthodox faith after having lapsed for many years, created the moving *Symphony of Psalms* for chorus and orchestra—an orchestra, however, with no violins, violas, or clarinets.

The list of outstanding works, large and small, grew throughout the 1930s. But several terrible events, personal and world-political, were about to cause another major shake-up in the composer's life.

STRAVINSKY, A POLITICAL CONSERVATIVE from a bourgeois Russian family, had not returned to his homeland since the formation of the Soviet Union. He and his family had officially moved to France in 1920, and he had become a French citizen in 1934. He was fascinated by Benito Mussolini's fascist regime in Italy—he even met and praised the dictator—and he tried to prevent his own music from being banned in Nazi Germany, protesting that he was not Jewish. (His plea was to no avail: the music he wrote was considered "degenerate" in Hitler's Reich, despite its composer's non-Semitic credentials.) But in 1939, with the outbreak of the Second World War, and following the deaths of his elder daughter, his wife, and his mother—the first two of tuberculosis, and all three within a seven-month period—he immigrated to the United States, which he had already visited three times. There he married Vera, with whom he had been living off and on since 1920 (with his first wife's knowledge and acquiescence); they bought a house in Los Angeles—a haven, at the time, to many European exiled and fugitive artists and intellectuals—and became US citizens in 1946.

Probably owing to all of these upheavals, there was a noteworthy diminution in Stravinsky's creativity during the early 1940s, but the mid- to late years of that decade witnessed a fresh upsurge in his output, which included the dramatic Symphony in Three Movements; the *Ebony Concerto* for the jazz clarinetist Woody Herman and his band; the Concerto in D for string orchestra; *Orpheus*, for George Balanchine's Ballet Society (precursor of the New York City Ballet); and the Mass. Although Stravinsky's creative voice is unmistakably present in all of these works, each one is entirely, often startlingly, different from the others. The tremendous *angst* of the first movement of the Symphony in Three Movements, for instance, with its jarring chords (which composers of Hollywood suspense films would imitate for decades), seems worlds away from the elegant chatter of the Concerto in D, which, in turn, appears to have little or nothing in common with the frigidly austere dissonances of the Mass. But then, from 1948 to 1951, Stravinsky focused on creating an opera in which he fused most of these elements and others as well.

The Rake's Progress is a sort of *summa* of the neoclassical style that Stravinsky had been developing over the previous thirty years. Inspired by a series of William Hogarth's paintings and engravings, and set to a brilliant libretto by W. H. Auden and Chester Kallman, the opera is an eighteenth-century work in its form and in the shape of its melodic lines, but it is cloaked in an eclectically twentieth-century harmonic language. Stravinsky intentionally ignored all of the formal innovations of Wagner, Verdi (in his later works), and their successors—Puccini, Strauss, and Berg, among others—and returned to the set-piece style of Mozart and his contemporaries, with its arias, duets, and other ensemble numbers, often separated by harpsichord-accompanied "dry" recitatives or orchestra-accompanied "full" recitatives. Stravinsky, the master orchestrator, deploying a subtle but precise instrumental palette, leads his listeners from arguments about idleness to touching declarations of love, from displays of moral dissolution to hopes for redemption, from pure evil to pure goodness, and from lighthearted comedy to a condition that borders on tragedy. And, as Eric Walter White pointed out, one of the opera's concluding verses—"For idle hands / And hearts and minds / The Devil finds / A work to do"—is also "a succinct and witty statement" of Stravinsky's approach to life and work.[12]

BUT WHERE WAS HE TO GO NOW? In which direction was he to proceed in order to continue to keep his own hands and heart and mind from idleness? The same questions that the thirty-one-year-old Stravinsky had had to ask himself following the creation of *The Rite of Spring* recurred now, nearly four decades later, after the birth of his opera. *The Rake*, like *The Rite*, was a stylistic endpoint, not a beginning.

By an odd coincidence, *The Rake's Progress*'s premiere, at Venice's Teatro La Fenice on September 11, 1951, took place not quite two months after the death of Arnold Schoenberg, who was often seen as Stravinsky's opposite number among twentieth-century music's most notorious iconoclasts. The two had met only once, in 1912, and had carefully avoided each other thereafter, although they both lived for years in adjoining Los Angeles neighborhoods and had occasionally even found themselves in the same room at the same time. Schoenberg—who had immigrated to the United States after the Nazis had forced him out of his position as professor of composition in Berlin—had considered his Russian-born colleague's neoclassical compositions an embarrassing retreat from radical modernism, and Stravinsky had found his Austrian-born colleague's twelve-tone system contrived and off-putting.

The situation had begun to change as early as 1948, when Stravinsky made the acquaintance of Robert Craft, a twenty-four-year-old American musician who was deeply interested in contemporary music. Before long, Craft had become a sort of musical amanuensis to Stravinsky, as well as a live-in helper and companion to both Igor and Vera, and he made an ultimately successful attempt to open the composer's ears and mind to the music of the so-called Second Viennese School, namely Schoenberg, his disciples Anton Webern and Alban Berg, and their followers. Stravinsky, who had long preferred to work within whatever tight formal limits he set for himself, became especially fascinated by

Webern's brief, striking, serialistic musical gems. "In the years between 1952 and 1955 no composer can have lived in closer contact with the music of Webern," Craft wrote of Stravinsky, in 1957. "The challenge of Webern"—who had died in 1945, the accidental victim of a shooting by an American member of the Allied occupying forces in Austria—"has been the strongest in his entire life. It has gradually brought him to the belief that serial technique is a possible means of musical composition."[13] And indeed, in several pieces written during the first half of the 1950s Stravinsky started to experiment with serialism in a highly personal way.

The impulse to change also had extramusical causes. During a performance at a festival of twentieth-century music in Paris in 1952, Stravinsky's *Oedipus Rex* was paired with *Erwartung*, Schoenberg's one-act monodrama, and the young modernists in the audience applauded Schoenberg's work and booed Stravinsky's. Although *Erwartung* was nearly twenty years older than *Oedipus*, the radicals deemed Stravinsky's entire neoclassical output a betrayal of the musical revolution of which he himself had been one of the principal instigators. As Stephen Walsh has put the matter, the composer now recognized that "whatever his prestige as a historic figure and modern-art grandee," he was becoming "a back number to the younger generation."[14] More than half a century later, Pierre Boulez, who had been a leader of those young French radicals (although not one of the booers), recalled: "We all felt that Stravinsky's neoclassical period was a dead-end street, a waste of time." But did Stravinsky's encounters with Boulez and other prominent young musicians influence the older composer's decision to pursue serialism? "Well, he was actually quite independent and open-minded," Boulez said. Stravinsky had simply "decided he didn't want to be left on the side of the street."[15]

Yet an even more important factor than Stravinsky's independence and desire to remain in the front lines was his endless curiosity, which jibed, once again, with his essence as both *homo faber* and *homo ludens*. He wanted, and needed, to plunge his hands into fresh, malleable materials and to play with those substances until he had created something that fascinated him and that could fascinate others as well.

His Cantata (1951–52), a setting of Old English texts, had already made use of series of notes that were deployed and re-deployed in various forms—"extended rows of mostly non-repeating notes," as Alex Ross succinctly described the procedure.[16] But those rows were not made up of twelve notes, nor was the end result atonal. "Twelve-tone composers have to use the twelve tones," Stravinsky explained at the time, in an interview published in the *New York Herald Tribune*. "I can use five, eleven, six—anything I like. . . . I am also able to work in series, like the atonalists. But what is important is that I do not have to."[17]

Yet serialism, often combined with atonality, did become Stravinsky's major compositional occupation and preoccupation. He used the procedure in the engagingly clever Septet of 1952–53, for three winds, three strings, and piano, and further tightened it in the choral-orchestral *Canticum Sacrum* (1955), the ballet *Agon* (1953–57), and the vocal-orchestral *Threni* (1957–58). Up to that point, twelve-tone technique was being approached gradually,* but with *Movements* for piano and orchestra (1959) Stravinsky's conversion to a Webernian form of serialism seemed complete: in this five-movement, ten-minute-long piece, the piano dominates a pointillistic soundscape created by a twelve-piece wind section, twenty-one string instruments, harp, and celesta. And, like so many of Webern's works, Stravinsky's *Movements* combines extreme complexity with equal degrees of lucidity and transparency.

---

* Readers conversant in music theory can find a thorough analysis of Stravinsky's approach to and application of serial techniques in Pieter C. van den Toorn's *The Music of Igor Stravinsky*, published by Yale University Press in 1983, as well as in Joseph N. Straus's *Stravinsky's Late Music*, published by Cambridge University Press in 2001. Van den Toorn's book also includes analyses of Stravinsky's earlier works.

Stravinsky knew that he would be accused of kowtowing to the avant-garde, but he forged ahead as he always had, fascinated by the very process of composing. Through his late seventies and on into his early eighties, he produced one completely worked-out piece after another, all of them connected in some way to serialism—a fact for which Craft was lauded by some and damned by others. The consensus among most Stravinsky scholars today seems to be that the aging composer had found himself at a dead end after having completed *The Rake's Progress*, that he needed a fresh stimulus in order to get his creative juices circulating once more, and that Craft and serialism gave him a new lease on musical life. There can be little doubt that Craft—who died in 2015 at the age of ninety-two—sincerely encouraged Stravinsky's creativity, or that he loved and was devoted to both Igor and Vera, or that the fondness was mutual. (Bizarre gossip about Craft having had a sexual relationship with either or even both members of the Stravinsky couple has been completely and convincingly discounted by everyone close to any or all of the parties involved.) But there can also be little doubt that Craft used the close connection to further his own career. He was a brilliant man and an accomplished musician, but he was not a gifted conductor; what success he had in that field depended largely on the pairing of his name with that of his celebrated mentor. He displayed greater gifts as a writer, but in that area, too, he owed his career to Stravinsky, and specifically to the various books that he published, between 1959 and 1969, in co-authorship with the composer. Stravinsky's famously acerbic wit was on display in all of these books, which served as Craft's literary launchpad, but the general belief today is that, especially in the later volumes, Craft simply invented much of the content that he attributed to Stravinsky, at a time when the composer was ill and fading, no longer the adept conversationalist that he had been in earlier years.

Craft's assistance also allowed Stravinsky to maintain his travels and conducting engagements as long as he did. As an octogenarian, the composer was no longer physically capable of conducting entire concert programs; he shared the podium with Craft, who would lead most of the rehearsals and the first half of each concert before turning over parts of the final rehearsal or rehearsals and the second half of each concert to Stravinsky. One of their joint concert tours, shortly after Stravinsky's eightieth birthday, in 1962, took the composer back to Russia for the first time in fifty years—and the last time in his life.

In short, Craft's part in the Stravinsky story has its share of ambiguities. Yet without the younger man's influence, we would not have had most of the astonishing works of Stravinsky's last active decade and a half—works of which the *Requiem Canticles* may well count as the most astonishing of all.

REQUIEM CANTICLES
PRELUDE

ExAUDI orationem meam, ad te omnis caro veniet.

DIES IRAE, dies illa,
Solvet saeclum in favilla,
Teste David cum Sibylla.

Quantus tremor est futurus,
Quando Judex est venturus,
Cuncta stricte discussurus!

TUBA MIRUM spargens sonum
Per sepulchra regionum
Coget omnes ante thronum.

INTERLUDE

REX TREMENDAE majestatis,

Qui salvandos salvas gratis,

Salva me, fons pietatis.

LACRIMOSA dies illa,

Qua resurget ex favilla,

Judicandus homo reus,

Huic ergo parce Deus:

Pie Jesu Domine,

Dona eis requiem. Amen.

LIBERA ME, Domine, de morte aeterna, in die illa tremenda:

Quando coeli movendi sunt et terra:

Dum veneris judicare saeculum per ignem.

Tremens factus sum ego, et timeo, dum discussio venerit, atque ventura ira.

Quando coeli movendi sunt et terra.

Dies illa, dies irae, calamitatis et miseriae, dies magna et amara valde.

Libera me.

POSTLUDE

IN MY OPINION, the *Requiem Canticles*, written in 1965 and 1966, are not only the crowning glory of Stravinsky's last compositional phase: they are also one of the most striking of all-serial or partially serial compositions by any composer, and among the most intensely spiritual pieces of the twentieth century, for religious and nonreligious people alike. Yet the element that unites the *Canticles* and Stravinsky's other specifically spiritual and/or liturgical works with almost all of his other compositions is their pungent physicality. No matter how abstruse some of the later pieces may sound to ears unaccustomed to post-tonal music, they, like their predecessors, grew out of a dynamic, entirely individual approach to rhythmic energy. We feel Stravinsky's pulse throughout his music—which explains why so many of his works, including those of a religious nature, have been choreographed: they seem to demand movement!

It comes as no surprise, then, that the *Requiem Canticles'* Prelude begins with rapid, driving, repetitive groups of notes in the strings—notes that could almost be an accelerated version of the "Adolescents' Dance" from *The Rite of Spring*. This jagged, relentless pulsation, frequently but irregularly punctuated by short rests, immediately creates an atmosphere of panic; Stravinsky indicates that these notes are to be played *non f[orte] ma ben marc[ato]* (not loud but well emphasized). Then, only a few seconds into the piece, a wailing, strident, perhaps pleading cry is superimposed over the driving rhythm, first by one violin, later by two, and eventually with the addition of a viola, a cello, and a double bass. During the Prelude's last few seconds, however, the cry disappears, and only the driving, repetitive notes remain. The entire segment—a shattering onslaught that lasts only one minute—replaces the somber but consoling words, Requiem aeternam dona eis Domine (Lord, grant them eternal rest), with which the mass for the dead is meant to begin. In Stravinsky's version, there is anguish but no rest.

The first vocal canticle sets only the words (in Latin), "Hear my prayer, to you all flesh shall come," a very small part of the requiem's entire, eight-line Introitus. A few somber notes, played first by the harp and then by a flute, introduce the piece; they are followed by a long chord for bassoon and strings and then by the chorus's mystical entry. For the aged and unwell Stravinsky, this simple plea may well have constituted the raison d'être of the entire segment, or even the entire work.

(The same words also opened Stravinsky's *Symphony of Psalms*, written thirty-six years earlier. And there is something about the single-note-by-single-note solitude of the harp in this section of the *Requiem Canticles* that makes this listener think of the oboe's detached notes that begin the introductory fugue of the *Symphony of Psalms'* second movement.) The *Exaudi's* main choral section lasts about one minute and ends on what sounds like part of a simple, expectant, tonal dominant seventh chord. But that chord resolves, or dissolves, into a group of quiet, concluding dissonances for the strings.

Stravinsky chose to set only six of the Dies irae's nineteen three-line verses; in this case, however, it seems legitimate to speculate that the lines he chose had at least as much to do with their dramatic possibilities as with any special personal significance. The Dies irae canticle proper, which contains the first two of those verses, begins with a violent fortissimo played by the strings plus piano and timpani, followed by the brass-accompanied chorus, which loudly intones "Dies irae" (Day of wrath) and then fearfully whispers only "irae." There is a similarly dramatic outburst on the words "dies illa" (that day), but the canticle then proceeds with the chorus quietly speaking, not singing, the remaining text, which translates as: "the world will dissolve in ashes, as foretold by David and the Sibyl. There will be great trembling when the judge has come, shattering everything." This occurs over an accompaniment dominated first by the piano and then by the trombones. An altered version of the violent and then frightened (not frightening) opening bars brings this less-than-one-minute-long canticle to a close.

A two-trumpet fanfare, reminiscent of the one that announces Jocasta's death in Stravinsky's *Oedipus Rex*, opens the Tuba mirum canticle's single verse, sung by the solo bass: "The trumpet, spreading its wondrous sound through sepulchral regions, will gather all before the throne." Stravinsky uses the bass's voice as if it were a trombone underlining a portentous announcement, and he accompanies the vocal line first by trumpets (initially also trombone) and then, at the end, with two rather subdued (*mezzo forte*) bassoons.

Like the Dies irae, the Tuba mirum lasts slightly less than a minute, but it is followed by a nearly three-minute-long instrumental Interlude—the *Requiem Canticles'* centerpiece and longest segment. The volume level of this hauntingly solemn, hieratic funeral march, played only by flutes, bassoons, horns, and timpani, never rises above a *mezzo forte*. Three standard flutes plus one alto flute converse with each other through the entire central portion of the piece; their sound dominates most of the rest of the Interlude as well, although Stravinsky has the two bassoons bring it to a quiet close. The Interlude's general tone recalls the choral "Mourn for Adonis" dirge in *The Rake's Progress*, but it is wordless, and it trails off into a cosmic vacuum.

Bringing us back to earth, and to worldly fears, the chorus forcefully intones the Rex tremendae's single verse: "King of dreadful majesty, who freely saves those who must be saved: save me, fount of mercy." Stravinsky's eighty-second-long canticle is enveloped in a mystical aura, in contrast to the stark drama expressed at this point in the requiem masses of Mozart and Berlioz, or the battle that Verdi, in *his* requiem, creates between the crushing weight of the words "Rex tremendae majestatis" and the generous, warm "Salva me fons pietatis." Three times, the flutes and lower strings play repeated notes, to punctuate the chorus's words, and the composer uses the same instruments in the same way to bring the piece to a close.

The Lacrimosa opens with a mournful, melismatic contralto solo on that single word, with fifteen notes spread across a long-held chord played by piccolo, two flutes, alto flute, double bass, and harp. The tone of this brief, vocal preamble is closer to that of a muezzin summoning Muslim worshipers to prayer or a cantor chanting in a Jewish synagogue than to anything one would be likely to hear in most Christian church services. But the piece then proceeds in a more measured, less overtly dramatic way. Stravinsky set both verses (six lines) of the text: "That day is one of weeping, on which the guilty man shall rise from the ashes, to be judged. Therefore, spare this one, o God. Merciful Lord Jesus, grant them peace. Amen." There is no breast-beating here—only a humble, simply sung request.

Over an accompaniment of long notes played softly by four horns, the four vocal soloists—singing as a mini-chorus—intone the text of the extraordinary, one-minute-long Libera me in a calm, liturgical flow. At the same time, however, the real chorus frantically but quietly *speaks* the same words: "Free me, Lord, from eternal death, on that terrible day, when heavens and earth are moved, while you come to judge the world by fire. I tremble and fear while the accounting takes place, and the wrath to come, when heavens and earth are moved. That day, day of wrath, calamity, and misery, that great and most bitter day." This final vocal canticle would seem a jumble if Stravinsky had not defined the three strands of sound with what seems to me absolute, unmistakable clarity: the supplicant masses speak their prayer fearfully; the chanting voices are those of the intermediating clergy; and the horns' slow, underlying chords are the impassive, inscrutable voice of Stravinsky's omniscient God.

Most extraordinary of all, however, is the Postlude—an intense, two-minute-long anticipation of infinite finality. In this last of the work's three purely instrumental movements, the drama of the Prelude and the dirgelike formality of the Interlude are replaced by a frozen calm. The pace (quarter note = 40) is so slow as to be nearly static, yet the atmosphere is highly charged. Piccolo, flute, alto flute, piano, and harp play long, sustained *mezzo forte* whole-note chords, which Craft described as "chords of Death," and which alternate with series of somber quarter notes played by the celesta, bells, and vibraphone (an instrument that Stravinsky used here for the first and last time), while a single horn intones long, middle-to-low-register notes underneath both groups. Nearly one-sixth of the piece consists of rests: pure silence.

The composer Louis Andriessen and composer-musicologist Elmer Schönberger—co-authors of the book *The Apollonian Clockwork: On Stravinsky*—point out that the entire Postlude is made up of only seventy-seven quarter-note beats, all of them in a slow, unchanging tempo, and that the Postlude can be divided into three sections, each initiated by the "chord of Death." The first two sections consist of twenty-two beats each (two times eleven), the third of thirty-three (three times eleven). The endgame chords, tolled by the celesta, bells, and vibraphone, strike eleven times in each section and then a twelfth, final time when they bring the piece to an end by chiming in tandem with the lonely horn and the instruments that are playing the "chord of Death."[*18] We are left not knowing whether we are saved, condemned, or simply dangling from the dot under an ice-cold question mark.

THERE IS LITTLE DOUBT in my mind that Stravinsky was thinking of his own approaching death, as well as the deaths of people dear to him who had died before him, when he wrote the *Requiem Canticles*. This notion was opposed by Lillian Libman, who wrote: "nowhere is there any indication, nor did I ever hear the composer express the idea, that he intended this work . . . for himself."[19] Yet it seems impossible that a deeply religious, physically frail, eighty-three-year-old composer would not have reflected on the end of his own life as he composed parts of a mass for the dead. Readers may recall Saul Bel-

---

* I refer readers also to Jeffrey Perry's article, "A 'Requiem for the Requiem': On Stravinsky's *Requiem Canticles*," in *College Music Symposium*, October 1, 1993 (https://symposium .music.org/index.php?option=com_k2&view=item&id=2108:a-requiem-for-the-requiem -on-stravinskys-requiem-canticles&Itemid=124). The article draws on the Andriessen-Schönberger book but also offers a personal interpretation of the *Requiem Canticles*.

low's comment, quoted near the very beginning of this book, about Mozart's music expressing "our sense of the radical mystery of our being." I would go so far as to say that Stravinsky's *Requiem Canticles* express our sense of the radical mystery of our unbeing.

The *Requiem Canticles* have never found their way onto the list of Stravinsky's greatest hits. For one thing, the work's general tone can seem hard to penetrate, on first or second hearing, to those unaccustomed to or simply uncomfortable with a mainly post-tonal musical language. For another, putting together a fully competent ensemble made up of a somewhat odd instrumental combination plus vocal soloists and a chorus, for a difficult piece that lasts barely fifteen minutes, can be an expensive investment for a concert organization. And perhaps the unpolished and somewhat bland quality of Craft's recorded performance, which was incorrectly assumed to have won Stravinsky's enthusiastic approval, has put off some potential conductors who ought instead to study the score thoroughly before deciding whether or not to add the piece to their own and their orchestras' repertoires. (Stravinsky himself may not have been happy with Craft's premiere performance and recording of the *Requiem Canticles*. In a letter of December 10, 1966— two months after both the performance and the recording session—the composer wrote to Rufina Ampenoff of Boosey & Hawkes, the publishing company that would issue the score: "The question about the *Requiem* is simple. I will not allow it to be played [again] until it has been published. I was at all of Bob's rehearsals and can see that this delicate music can be performed properly only if the orchestra and choral scores are presented in a *complete and orderly form*. To achieve this, proofs and more proofs."[20] Since, at the time of the premiere and the recording, the scores had not yet been made available in the form that Stravinsky demanded, the implication is that the "delicate music" had not yet been performed "properly.")

Despite his eighty-four years at the time of the *Canticles*' premiere,

Stravinsky wanted to continue to create music. Most of *The Owl and the Pussy-Cat*, a setting for soprano and piano of a poem by Edward Lear, may have been written before the *Canticles*, but it was probably completed after them, and Stravinsky continued to think about and sometimes even to sketch other pieces as well, and to make arrangements of music by other composers. Walsh reports that following the assassination, in April 1968, of Martin Luther King Jr., Stravinsky began to write an additional prelude to be performed in "a choreographed version of the *Requiem Canticles* that Balanchine was staging with the New York City Ballet in King's memory,"[21] but that he gave it up for lack of time.

The last four years of Stravinsky's life were marked by increasing infirmity. After Vera turned eighty, in 1968, the couple moved from their full-sized house in Los Angeles to a rented suite in the elegant Essex House, on New York's Central Park South. Igor's health continued to deteriorate; hospitalizations became more frequent and more serious. Vera bought an apartment for them, on Fifth Avenue, but by March 29, 1971, when Igor was at last able to move into the new home—following yet another prolonged hospital stay—he was too ill to appreciate his new surroundings. Eight days later, on April 6, a little over two months before his eighty-ninth birthday, he died there, in his sleep. His body was flown to Venice, where, during the funeral in the church of Santi Giovanni e Paolo, Craft conducted the *Requiem Canticles*, Stravinsky's final complete, major, original work—the endpoint of a sixty year-long career. He was buried on the city's cemetery island, San Michele, in a grave next to that of Sergei Diaghilev. Vera died eleven years later and was interred next to her husband.

ONE IMAGE ALWAYS COMES immediately to my mind when I think of Stravinsky: I see his small, aged, bent frame wrapped in a *shuba*—a

Russian-style fur coat—and his large eyes and nose sticking out from beneath a black homburg hat.

In March 1964, Stravinsky was in Cleveland, my home town, to conduct the Cleveland Orchestra in some of his own compositions. I was nearly eighteen, consumed by music, and excited by the chance to see the octogenarian master lead performances of his own works—although, at the time, I was not familiar with any of the pieces that he was to perform: the early *Fireworks*, the rarely heard *Ode: Elegiacal Chant for orchestra*, and the ballet music *Jeu de cartes (Card Game)*, composed in 1937.

At Severance Hall that Saturday evening, Stravinsky looked frail as he made his way slowly and cautiously from the stage entrance to the podium, but once he stood before the orchestra he appeared to be fully in command. After the concert, a friend and I rushed to the conductor's room and waited for several minutes, in front of the closed door, with two or three other young people. When Stravinsky finally emerged, wearing the *shuba* and the homburg, Craft, who had conducted the first part of the concert, and A. Beverly Barksdale, the orchestra's manager, were each holding one of his arms; Vera Stravinsky walked behind them. Upon seeing us kids, Stravinsky stopped, smiled charmingly, and said, in heavily accented English: "I am sorry I cannot sign your programs, but I take off my hat to you." He briefly tipped the homburg and slowly moved away; we followed him down the steps and out the door to the car that awaited him, and we watched him climb carefully into the back seat. As the car began to move away, he turned to look out the rear window, and he smiled and waved at us. That was well over half a century ago, but I still remember the feeling of standing within three feet of the man who was, to me, the greatest living link in the centuries-long chain of Western art-music.

I HAVE NOT CHOSEN TO END this book with fragments from a mass for the dead either because I believe that "classical" music is dying (I most fervently do not) or because I am in my mid-seventies and want to make my peace with the Lord (I am a non-believer). I have chosen it because I love and admire it and because it was the last brilliant and substantial work of one of the last masters of a particular cycle in the history of music. I don't doubt that other cycles will follow, if we as a species don't in the meantime destroy ourselves and, coincidentally, our planet. But *that* subject far exceeds this book's scope.

Writing this book has been an enlightening experience for me, because the very act of analyzing ten discrete pieces resulted in, among other things, a clearer vision of some of the connective tissue, tenuous or otherwise, that leads from one composer to another and from one work to another, all under the embracing arc of Western art-music. My aim, from the start, has been to bring ten works and their composers a little more vividly to life through the perspective of someone who has lived with them for many decades, and my best hope—as I mentioned in my foreword—is to have been able to communicate my love for these creations not only to people who were already receptive to them but also to others, especially young people, whose lives could be as immeasurably enriched by this music as mine has been.

ACKNOWLEDGMENTS

I OFFER MY SINCERE THANKS to the following individuals:
Robert Weil, my editor at Liveright; Haley Bracken and Gabriel Kachuck, his assistants; Don Rifkin and Rebecca Homiski, my project editors; Jodi Beder, my copyeditor; Cordelia Calvert, my publicist; and the other members of the Liveright staff

Denise Shannon, my endlessly encouraging and patient literary agent, and her assistants

For help with translations (see my preface): Claire Catenaccio, Mark Ebers, and Yola Schabenbeck-Ebers

For research assistance (in alphabetical order): Natalia Ermolaev, Project Archivist, the Prokofiev Archive, Butler Library, Columbia University; Amanda Ferrara, Public Services Projects Archivist, Seeley G. Mudd Manuscript Library, Princeton, University; Andria Hoy, Archivist, The Cleveland Orchestra; Professor Seow-Chin Ong, of the University of Louisville; and Michelle Oswell, formerly with The John de Lancie Library, The Curtis Institute of Music

For having read each chapter in draft form and offered extremely useful comments: Jeffrey Karp and Jeffrey Siegel

My love goes, as always, to Eve Wolf and to my children, Julian and Lyuba Sachs.

NOTES

CHAPTER 1: "IL CATALOGO È QUESTO"

1 *Mozart's Thematic Catalogue: A Facsimile* (London: The British Library Board, 1990), p. 5.
2 S. Bellow, "Mozart: An Overture," in *It All Adds Up* (New York: Viking Penguin, 1994), pp. 12 and 14.
3 *Mozart Briefe und Dokumente,* Online Edition, http://dme.mozarteum.at/DME/briefe/doclist.php, May 9, 1781.
4 *Mozart Briefe und Dokumente,* June 9, 1781.
5 *Mozart Briefe und Dokumente,* December 15, 1781.
6 *Mozart Briefe und Dokumente,* December 15, 1781.
7 H. C. Robbins Landon, *Mozart: The Golden Years* (London and New York: Thames & Hudson, 1989), p. 88.
8 *Mozart Briefe und Dokumente,* March 3, 1784.
9 *Mozart Briefe und Dokumente,* March 3, 1784.
10 *Mozart Briefe und Dokumente,* March 20, 1784.
11 *Mozart Briefe und Dokumente,* April 10, 1784.
12 *Mozart Briefe und Dokumente,* June 12, 1784.
13 *Mozart Briefe und Dokumente,* May 26, 1784.
14 *Mozart Briefe und Dokumente,* July 21, 1784.
15 *Mozart Briefe und Dokumente,* June 9–12, 1784.
16 Landon, *Mozart: The Golden Years,* p. 119.
17 *Mozart's Thematic Catalogue: A Facsimile.*
18 *Mozart Briefe und Dokumente,* April 4, 1787.
19 Landon, *Mozart: The Golden Years,* p. 85.

CHAPTER 2: HIS IMPERIAL HIGHNESS'S SORE FINGER

1 *Ludwig van Beethovens sämtliche Briefe,* ed. E. Kastner (Tutzing: Hans Schneider, 1975; reprint of 1923 Leipzig edition), p. 184.
2 *Beethovens Briefe,* p. 186.

3   L. van Beethoven, *Heiligenstädter Testament*, ed. H. M. von Asow (Vienna and Wiesbaden: Doblinger, 1957) pp. 9–13.

4   https://da.beethoven.de/sixcms/list.php?page=museum_internetausstellung_seiten_en&sv%5binternetausstellung.id%5d=31561&skip=2#bild1.

5   *Beethovens Briefe*, p. 187.

6   *Beethovens Briefe*, p. 187.

7   *Beethovens Briefe*, p. 189.

8   E. Forbes, ed., *Thayer's Life of Beethoven* (Princeton: Princeton University Press, 1973), pp. 577–78 (translation of excerpt from L. Spohr, *Selbstbiographie*, Kassel und Göttingen, 1860–61).

9   Forbes, *Thayer's Life of Beethoven*, p. 578.

10   H. C. Robbins Landon, *Beethoven: Sein Leben und seine Welt in zeitgenössischen Bildern und Texten* (Zurich: Universal Edition, 1970), p. 352.

PART II: THE ROMANTIC CENTURY

1   W. C. Langsam, *Francis the Good* (New York: Macmillan, 1949), p. 12.

2   Quoted in G. Servadio, *Rossini* (New York: Carroll and Graf, 2003), p. 97.

CHAPTER 3: A QUARTET THAT'S ABOUT NOTHING

3   O. E. Deutsch, ed., *Franz Schubert: Die Dokumente seines Lebens und Schaffens* (Munich and Leipzig: Georg Müller, 1914), p. 330.

4   Quoted in J. A. Westrup, *Schubert Chamber Music* (Seattle: University of Washington Press, 1969).

5   Deutsch, *Franz Schubert: Die Dokumente*, p. 167.

6   Deutsch, *Franz Schubert: Die Dokumente*, p. 168.

7   Deutsch, *Franz Schubert: Die Dokumente*, p. 201.

8   Deutsch, *Franz Schubert: Die Dokumente*, p. 335.

9   J. Reed, *Schubert* (Oxford: Oxford University Press, 1997), p. 130.

10   M. J. E. Brown, *Schubert: A Critical Biography* (London: Macmillan, 1958), p. 181.

11   G. von Breuning, quoted in W. Reich, *Franz Schubert aus Briefen und Schriften* (Zürich: Werner Classen, 1949), p. 73.

12   Quoted in J. Chernaik, *Schumann: The Faces and the Masks* (New York: Knopf, 2018), p. 109.

CHAPTER 4: IN THE WONDROUSLY DISTURBING MONTH OF MAY

1   R. Schumann, letter to Clara Wieck, in *Early Letters*, April 13, 1838, pp. 271–72.

2   M. Musgrave, *The Life of Schumann* (Cambridge: Cambridge University Press, 2011), p. 60.

3   R. Schumann, *Tagebücher*, https://archive.org/details/RobertSchumannTagebcherBd1/page/n63.

4   Musgrave, *Life of Schumann*, pp. 25–26.

5   H. Heine, *Selected Works*, trans. and ed. H. M. Mustard (New York: Random House, 1973), p. 281.

6   F. M. Ford, *The March of Literature* (Normal, IL: Dalkey Archive Press, 1994; orig. ed. 1938), pp. 698, 719–20.

7   E. Sams, *The Songs of Robert Schumann* (London: Eulenburg, 1975), p. 1.

8   Sams, *Songs of Schumann*, p. 5.

9   C. Gerhaher, "Schumanns *Myrthen*—Ein 'Kaleidoskop der Ehe,'" liner notes to Schumann *Myrthen*, Sony Classical CD 19075945362, 2019.

10   R. Schumann, *Dichterliebe Op. 48*, ed. H. Ewert (Kassel: Bärenreiter, 2011), p. vi.

CHAPTER 5: A MONUMENT REIMAGINED

1   H. Berlioz, *La Damnation de Faust*, foreword, miniature score (London: Eulenburg, 1964), p. v.

2   H. Berlioz, *Mémoires de Hector Berlioz* (Paris: Calmann-Lévy, n.d.), vol. 1, p. 145.

3   D. K. Holoman, *Berlioz* (London: Faber and Faber, 1989), p. 53.

4   Berlioz, *Mémoires*, vol. 1, pp. 145–46.

5   Berlioz, *Mémoires*, vol. 2, pp. 258–65 for this and the quotations in the next few paragraphs.

6   Berlioz, *Mémoires*, vol. 1, p. 2.

7   Berlioz, *Mémoires*, vol. 1, p. 97.

8   All of the Berlioz quotes in this paragraph come from H. Berlioz, *Correspondance générale*, ed. P. Citron (Paris: Flammarion, 1972), vol. 2, pp. 168, 229, 244.

9   H. Berlioz. *Fantastic Symphony*, ed. E. T. Cone (New York: W. W. Norton, 1971), pp. 30–32 (my translation).

10   Quotations in this paragraph from Holoman, *Berlioz*, pp. 352–53.

11   H. Berlioz, *Mémoires*, vol. 2, pp. 391–92.

12   H. Berlioz, *Correspondance inédite* (Paris, 1879), p. 229.

13   A. Luzio, ed., *Carteggi verdiani* (Rome, 1935), vol. 2, p. 194 (also quotes in the next paragraph).

CHAPTER 6: THE CROWN, THE CROSS, AND THE CRUELTY OF LOVE

1   *Verdi intimo. Carteggio di Giuseppe Verdi con il conte Opprandino Arrivabene* (Milan: Mondadori, 1931), p. 24.

2   J. Budden, *The Operas of Verdi* (New York: Oxford University Press, 1976), p. 7.

3   Budden, *Operas of Verdi*, p. 8 (also the subsequent quotation).

4   This and three subsequent quotations: A. Turba, ed., *Lettere di Giuseppe Verdi a Opprandino Arrivabene* (Lucca: Libreria Musicale Italiana, 2018); letters of February 16, March 14, and December 10, 1866, and March 12, 1867.

5   F. Abbiati, *Giuseppe Verdi* (Milano, 1959), vol. 2, p. 272.

6   M. Elizabeth C. Bertlet, "Grand Opéra," in *The New Grove Dictionary of Opera*, ed. S. Sadie (London and New York: Macmillan, 1992), vol. 2, p. 512.

7   A. Ross, "The Dark, Prophetic Vision of Giacomo Meyerbeer," *The New Yorker*, October 15, 2018.

8   P. Domingo, *My First Forty Years* (New York: Knopf, 1983), p. 98.

9   M. Mila, *Verdi* (Milan: Rizzoli, 2000), p. 574.

10   Turba, *Lettere di Verdi*, letter of March 12, 1867.

11   I. Stravinsky and R. Craft, *Themes and Episodes* (New York: Knopf, 1967), p. 236.

12   C. E. Passage, introduction to Friedrich von Schiller's *Don Carlos, Infante of Spain* (New York: Frederick Ungar, 1959), pp. x–xi.

CHAPTER 7: ALMOST A TALE OF JOY

1   J. Swafford, *Johannes Brahms* (New York: Knopf, 1997), p. 566.

2   Swafford, *Brahms*, p. 569.

3   Quoted in W. Altmann, foreword, *Brahms Quintet in G Major, Op. 111*, miniature score (Mainz: Eulenburg, 2017), pp. v–vi.

4   Swafford, *Brahms*, p. 77.

5   H. Gál, *Johannes Brahms* (Frankfurt am Main: Fischer Bücherei, 1961), p. 132.

6   P. Gauguin, *Intimate Journals*, trans. Van Wyck Brooks (New York: Crown Publishers, 1936).

7   Swafford, *Brahms*, p. 317.

8   *J. Brahms im Briefwechsel mit Karl Reinthaler et al.* (Verlag der deutschen Brahms-Gesellschaft, 1908), p. 10.

9   Swafford, *Brahms*, p. 606.

10   S. Avins, *Johannes Brahms: Life and Letters* (Oxford and New York: Oxford University Press, 1997), p. 678.

11   A. Moser, ed., *Johannes Brahms im Briefwechsel mit Joseph Joachim* (Verlag der deutschen Brahms-Gesellschaft, 1908), vol. 2, p. 240.

12   R. W. Emerson, *Essays*, First Series (1841): "Self-Reliance," American Transcendentalism Web, https://archive.vcu.edu/english/engweb/transcendentalism/authors/emerson/essays/selfreliance.html.

13   M. Notley, in L. Botstein, ed., *The Compleat Brahms* (New York and London: W. W. Norton, 1999), p. 138.

14   Moser, *Brahms im Briefwechsel*, vol. 2, p. 240.

15   M. Kalbeck, ed., *Johannes Brahms Briefe an P. J. Simrock und Fritz Simrock* (Berlin: Verlag der deutschen Brahms-Gesellschaft, 1919), p. 35.

16   Michelangiolo Buonarroti, *Rime,* ed. E. N. Girardi (Bari: Laterza, 1967), no. 241, p. 251.

17   N. Grimes, *Brahms's Elegies: The Poetics of Loss in Nineteenth-Century German Culture* (Cambridge: Cambridge University Press, 2019), p. 2.

18   Swafford, *Brahms*, p. 607.

19   K. Ekman, *Jean Sibelius: His Life and Personality*, trans. E. Birse (New York: Tudor Publishing Co., 1938).

20   S. Levas, *Sibelius: A Personal Portrait*, trans. P. M. Young (London: J. M. Dent & Sons Ltd., 1972).

CHAPTER 8: EUROPE, A PROPHECY?

1   E. Tawaststjerna, *Sibelius*, trans. R. Layton (London: Faber and Faber 1976–97), vol. 2, p. 159.

2   Tawaststjerna, *Sibelius*, vol. 2, pp. 139, 141, 143, 161, 163.

3   Tawaststjerna, *Sibelius*, vol. 2, p. 170.

4   R. Layton, entry on Jean Sibelius in *The New Grove Dictionary of Music and Musicians*, ed. S. Sadie (London and New York: Macmillan, 1980), vol. 17, p. 280.

5   *Vladimir Ashkenazy on the Path of Sibelius* (2015): https://www.youtube.com/watch?v=VnPFI3Yf5dY.

6   Tawaststjerna, *Sibelius*, vol. 2, pp. 93, 104, 106.

7   P. R. Bullock, ed., *The Correspondence of Jean Sibelius and Rosa Newmarch 1906–1939,* (Woodridge, UK: The Boydell Press, 2011), pp. 128, 130.

8   Ekman, *Sibelius*, pp. 204–8.

9   Tawaststjerna, *Sibelius*, vol. 2, p. 180.

10   Tawaststjerna, *Sibelius*, vol. 2, pp. 141, 145.

11   Ekman, *Sibelius*, pp. 204–8.

12   Bullock, *Correspondence of Sibelius and Newmarch*, p. 85.

13   Bullock, *Correspondence of Sibelius and Newmarch*, pp. 161–62.

14   Bullock, *Correspondence of Sibelius and Newmarch*, p. 163.
15   J. Stalworthy, ed., *The Poems of Wilfred Owen* (New York: W. W. Norton, 1986).
16   Ekman, *Sibelius*, p. 256.
17   A. Barnett, *Sibelius* (New Haven, CT: Yale University Press, 2007), pp. 301–2.
18   Tawaststjerna, *Sibelius*, vol. 2, p. 80.

CHAPTER 9: CREATIVE SUFFERING

1   https://www.nobelprize.org/prizes/literature/1957/camus/25232-albert-camus
      -banquet-speech-1957/
2   H. Robinson, *Sergei Prokofiev* (New York: Viking 1987), p. 103.
3   Robinson, *Prokofiev*, p. 137.
4   S. Morrison, *The People's Artist: Prokofiev's Soviet Years* (Oxford and New York: Oxford
      University Press, 2009), pp. 162–63.
5   Morrison, *The People's Artist*, p. 162.
6   D. Gutman, liner notes to Decca CD 444 408-2, Prokofiev's Piano Sonatas Nos. 4, 5, and
      6 performed by Vladimir Ashkenazy.
7   Liner notes, Decca CD 444 408-2.
8   Morrison, *The People's Artist*, p. 164.
9   B. Monsaingeon, *Sviatoslav Richter: Notebooks and Conversation*, trans. Stewart Spencer
      (London: Faber and Faber, 2001), p. 82.
10   Monsaingeon, *Richter*, pp. 30 and 56.
11   Liner notes, Decca CD 444 408-2.
12   Liner notes, Decca CD 444 408-2.
13   M. Murray, ed., *A Jacques Barzun Reader* (New York: HarperCollins, 2002), pp. 325–29.
14   Morrison, *The People's Artist*, p. 307.
15   Robinson, *Prokofiev*, p. 199.
16   Robinson, *Prokofiev*, p. 199.
17   Robinson, *Prokofiev*, p. 199.

CHAPTER 10: AN ICE-COLD QUESTION MARK

1   I. Stravinsky (R. Craft, ed.), *Selected Correspondence*, vol. 1 (New York: Alfred A. Knopf,
      1982), p. 261.
2   D. O'Neill, C. A. Macsweeney, A. Cornell, H. Moss, "Stravinsky Syndrome: Giving
      Voice to Chronic Stroke Disease," *QJM: An International Journal of Medicine*, vol. 107, no.
      6 (June 2014), pp. 489–93.
3   S. Walsh, *Stravinsky: The Second Exile: France and America, 1934–1971* (New York: Alfred
      A. Knopf, 2006), p. 497.
4   Walsh, *Stravinsky: The Second Exile*, p. 663.
5   Stravinsky, *Selected Correspondence*, vol. 2 (1984), p. 417.
6   R. Craft, *Stravinsky: Glimpses of a Life* (New York: St. Martin's Press, 1992), p. 10.
7   L. Libman, *And Music at the Close: Stravinsky's Last Years* (New York: W. W. Norton, 1972),
      p. 277.
8   Walsh, *Stravinsky: The Second Exile*, p. 522.
9   S. Fager, "'Requiem' Premieres," *Daily Princetonian*, October 10, 1966.
10   *Times* of London, October 11, 1966, quoted in V. Stravinsky and R. Craft, *Stravinsky in
      Pictures and Documents* (New York: Simon & Schuster, 1978), p. 479.

11   E. W. White, "Stravinsky, Igor (Fyodorovich)," in *The New Grove Dictionary of Music and Musicians* (London: Macmillan, 1980), vol. 18, p. 247.

12   White, "Stravinsky," p. 257.

13   R. Craft, "A Personal Preface," in *Score* No. 20, 1957, p. 7, quoted in Pieter C. van den Toorn, *The Music of Igor Stravinsky* (New Haven and London: Yale University Press, 1983), p. 374.

14   Walsh, *Stravinsky: The Second Exile*, p. 290.

15   Peter Culshaw, "Pierre Boulez: 'I was a bully, I'm not ashamed," in *The Telegraph*, London, December 10, 1908.

16   A. Ross, *The Rest Is Noise* (New York: Farrar, Straus and Giroux, 2007), p. 419.

17   Walsh, *Stravinsky: The Second Exile*, p. 294.

18   L. Andriessen and E. Schönberger, *The Apollonian Clockwork: On Stravinsky*, trans. by J. Hamburg (Oxford and New York: Oxford University Press, 1989), pp. 9–10.

19   Libman, *And Music at the Close*, p. 23.

20   Stravinsky, *Selected Correspondence*, vol. 3 (1985), p. 456.

21   Walsh, *Stravinsky: The Second Exile*, p. 540.

SOME RECORDINGS

IN A BOOK (*Virtuoso*) that I wrote decades ago, I joked that some mysterious process causes recordings to change as they lie unplayed on our shelves, and that when we return to them after having set them aside for a few years we discover details great and small that could not possibly have sounded the same a few years earlier.

Of course the changes take place in us, the listeners—in our overall life-experience, our psyches, and our thoughts and feelings about individual pieces of music and their composers and interpreters. For that matter, if you ask any self-respecting performing musician about a recording that she or he made more than a few months earlier, you will likely get an earful about everything that's wrong with that interpretation, plus a list of those details that ought to have been done differently. Composers, too, change their interpretations of their own works, as we can hear in the case of Stravinsky's and other twentieth- and twenty-first-century composers' multiple recordings of certain pieces.

All of this is to explain that what I offer below is a selection of recordings with which I am or have been familiar, of the ten works that are the focal points of this book. I certainly don't love them all, but I find each of them worth hearing.

My lists are in alphabetical order by the performers' surnames, not in order of preference.

Wolfgang Amadeus Mozart: Piano Concerto No. 17 in G Major, K. 453

Leif Ove Andsnes, soloist and conductor; Norwegian Chamber Orchestra

Vladimir Ashkenazy, soloist and conductor; Philharmonia Orchestra

Malcolm Bilson; English Baroque Soloists conducted by John Eliot Gardiner

Alfred Brendel; Scottish Chamber Orchestra conducted by Sir Charles Mackerras

Murray Perahia, soloist and conductor; English Chamber Orchestra

Arthur Rubinstein; RCA Victor Symphony Orchestra conducted by Alfred Wallenstein

András Schiff; Camerata Academica des Mozarteums Salzburg conducted by Sándor Végh

Here we have a substantial panoply of interpretations, from Rubinstein's well-thought-out but often overly nuanced version, by today's standards, to the dry interpretation of Bilson, who, however, plays on a replica of a Mozart-era fortepiano. (The other versions are all performed on modern grand pianos.) I greatly admire Brendel's highly intelligent and stunningly realized interpretation, seconded by Mackerras and his ensemble. Ashkenazy and Perahia each conduct a beautifully conceived performance from the keyboard; so does Andsnes, but his version is more in keeping with modern ideas of eighteenth-century performance practices, especially with respect to the strings' bowings and articulations. The young Schiff—he was thirty when this recording was made—is in complete accord with the outstanding musicality of violinist-conductor Sándor Végh and his ensemble, lovingly dedicated to Mozart.

Ludwig van Beethoven: Trio in B-flat Major for Piano, Violin, and Cello, Op. 97, "Archduke"

Vladimir Ashkenazy, piano; Itzhak Perlman, violin; Lynn Harrell, cello

Alfred Cortot, piano; Jacques Thibaud, violin; Pablo Casals, cello

Alexander Melnikov, piano; Isabelle Faust, violin; Jean-Guihen Queyras, cello

Arthur Rubinstein, piano; Jascha Heifetz, violin; Emanuel Feuermann, cello

These four performances, recorded over a period of eighty-three years by artists separated in age by nearly a century, could hardly differ more from each other. The Cortot-Thibaud-Casals version (1928) is a wild ride, with some rough playing by both Thibaud and Cortot—the latter can't seem to execute a scale passage in a single tempo or to hold a rest for its full duration—but there is great vitality to the performance. Rubinstein, Heifetz, and Feuermann (1941), on the contrary, play beautifully throughout, especially in the third, *Andante cantabile* movement, but the three quick-tempo movements all feel strait-jacketed. With Ashkenazy-Perlman-Harrell (1982) we have a thoroughly beautiful, well-thought-out "Archduke" recording; the first movement feels a little too careful for my taste, but all the playfulness of the scherzo, earthly and unearthly beauty of the third movement, and exuberance of the finale are fully present. Finally, in the Melnikov-Faust-Queyras recording (2011), Melnikov plays an 1828 Alois Graf piano and the two string players limit their use of vibrato, although they don't dispense with it. Altogether, their approach to tempo is somewhat freer than that of any of the others, and they have obviously given a great deal of thought to phrasing and articulation. The finale's coda is particularly dazzling, and all in all the performance is very effective.

Franz Schubert: String Quartet No. 15 in G Major, Op. posth. 161, D. 887

Belcea Quartet

Busch Quartet

Emerson String Quartet

I mentioned aspects of these recordings in my Schubert chapter. I admire all three ensembles, but in the case of this work I find the Emerson's version the most satisfying, all aspects considered.

Robert Schumann: *Dichterliebe* (Poet's Love), Op. 48

Dietrich Fischer-Dieskau, baritone: various recordings with various pianists, including Alfred Brendel, Jörg Demus, Christoph Eschenbach, Hartmut Höll

Christian Gerhaher, baritone; Gerold Huber, piano

Christine Schäfer, soprano; Natascha Osterkorn, piano

I can't help it: I grew up with Fischer-Dieskau's recordings of this work—recordings made over several decades—and they remain the standard for me. His closest musical heir, in my opinion, is Gerhaher, certainly with respect to attention to text, and the beauty of this baritone's voice is remarkable. But, at least in *Dichterliebe*, Fischer-Dieskau did not let the detail overwhelm the overall movement from phrase to phrase and within each phrase, whereas Gerhaher sometimes doesn't let us see the forest for the trees. Still, his recording is very fine. Also fascinating, from the musical point of view, is a bizarre, distracting video of the work with the soprano Christine Schäfer: the clarity of her sound is enchanting—and don't forget that Schumann wrote *Dichterliebe* for the soprano voice.

Hector Berlioz: *La Damnation de Faust*

Pierre Monteux, conductor; London Symphony Orchestra;
  Régine Crespin (Marguerite); André Turp (Faust); Michel Roux
  (Méphistophélès)

Sir Georg Solti, conductor; Chicago Symphony Orchestra; Frederica
  von Stade (Marguerite); Kenneth Riegel (Faust); José van Dam
  (Méphistophélès)

I wish that there were a generally available recording of one of the Metropolitan Opera's performances of this work in its 2008–9 season, with James Levine conducting and Susan Graham, Marcello Giordani, and Gary Relyea in the principal roles, or in the 2009–10 season, with James Conlon conducting and Olga Borodina, Ramón Vargas, and Ildar Abdrazakov in the principal roles. I heard several of those performances and remember them as particularly powerful. Another wish would be for a recording of the work by Riccardo Muti, who is an especially fine Berlioz conductor. Solti's recording is very good, but I don't feel that he was entirely at home in this repertoire. An occasionally flawed but wholly remarkable recording captures a live public performance conducted by the great Pierre Monteux in 1962, just short of his eighty-seventh birthday.

Giuseppe Verdi: *Don Carlo* (five-act Italian version)

Carlo Maria Giulini, conductor; Royal Opera, Covent Garden,
  London; Montserrat Caballé (Elisabetta); Shirley Verrett (Eboli);
  Plácido Domingo (Don Carlo); Sherrill Milnes (Rodrigo);
  Ruggero Raimondi (Filippo)

James Levine, conductor; Metropolitan Opera, New York; Mirella
    Freni (Elisabetta); Grace Bumbry (Eboli); Plácido Domingo (Don
    Carlo); Louis Quilico (Rodrigo); Nicolai Ghiaurov (Filippo)—
    DVD

Both of these versions are intelligently conducted and beautifully sung
by outstanding casts. Giulini (1970 studio recording) is at times heavy-
handed, which Levine (1983 live performance) never is. Levine's version
also contains the rediscovered, prologue-like material at the beginning
of Act One. There is also a fine, live performance of the four-act version
at La Scala (1992) conducted by Riccardo Muti and with Daniela Dessì
(Elisabetta), Luciana D'Intino (Eboli), Luciano Pavarotti (Don Carlo),
Paolo Coni (Rodrigo), and Samuel Ramey (Filippo).

Johannes Brahms: String Quintet No. 2 in G Major, Op. 111
Belcea Quartet with Thomas Kakuska, second viola

I do not know all of the recordings of this work, but of the many that I
know this is the only one that I love throughout every movement.

Jean Sibelius: Symphony No. 4 in A Minor, Op. 63
Vladimir Ashkenazy, conductor; Philharmonia Orchestra
Sir Thomas Beecham, conductor; London Philharmonic Orchestra
Esa-Pekka Salonen, conductor; Swedish Radio Symphony
    Orchestra—**video**
Leopold Stokowski, conductor; Philadelphia Orchestra
George Szell, conductor; Cleveland Orchestra
Arturo Toscanini, conductor; NBC Symphony Orchestra

The Beecham (1937), Stokowski (1932), and Toscanini (1940—live performance) recordings are worth hearing because those three men were

among the earliest major, non-Scandinavian conductors to perform Sibelius's music. Szell's live concert performance is powerful, and Ashkenazy and Salonen both conduct the work with great conviction.

Sergei Prokofiev: Piano Sonata No. 8 in B-flat Major, Op. 84

Vladimir Ashkenazy (1993)

Yefim Bronfman (1988)

Emil Gilels

Boris Giltburg

Sviatoslav Richter (1974)

See my comments on these recordings in my chapter on Prokofiev.

Igor Stravinsky: *Requiem Canticles*

Robert Craft, conductor; Columbia Symphony Orchestra (1966)

Robert Craft, conductor; Philharmonia Orchestra (2005)

As mentioned in my chapter on Stravinsky, Craft's 1966 recording, made a few days after the work's premiere and with the same performers, seems to me unsatisfactory, and so do the few other versions that I've been able to find. Craft's 2005 version, however, made when he was eighty-one, is much better than any of the others.

BIBLIOGRAPHY

MOZART

Badura-Skoda, Eva. Preface to the score of *Mozart: Konzert in G für Klavier und Orchester.* Kassel: Bärenreiter, 1979.

Bellow, Saul. "Mozart: An Overture." In *It All Adds Up.* New York: Viking Penguin, 1994.

Landon, H. C. Robbins. *Mozart: The Golden Years, 1781–1791.* London and New York: Thames and Hudson, 1989.

Mozart Briefe und Dokumente. Online Edition: http://dme.mozarteum.at/DME/briefe/doclist .php.

Mozart's Thematic Catalogue: A Facsimile. London: The British Library Board, 1990.

Sadie, Stanley. "Mozart, (Johann Chrysostom) Wolfgang Amadeus," In *The New Grove Dictionary of Music and Musicians,* ed. Stanley Sadie, vol. 12. London and New York: Macmillan, 1980.

BEETHOVEN

Beethoven, Ludwig van. *Heiligenstädter Testament,* ed. Hedwig M. von Asow. Vienna and Wiesbaden: Doblinger, 1957.

Beethoven, Ludwig van. *Ludwig van Beethovens sämtliche Briefe,* ed. Emerich Kastner. Tutzing: Hans Schneider, 1975 (reprint of the 1923 Leipzig edition).

Beethoven-Haus Bonn website: https://da.beethoven.de/sixcms/list.php?page=museum_ internetausstellung_seiten_en&sv%5binternetausstellung.id%5d=31561&skip=2#bild1.

Fortune, Nigel. "The Chamber Music with Piano." In *The Beethoven Companion,* ed. Denis Arnold and Nigel Fortune. London: Faber & Faber, 1971.

Kerman, Joseph, and Alan Tyson. "Beethoven, Ludwig van." In *The New Grove Dictionary of Music and Musicians,* ed. Stanley Sadie, vol. 2. London and New York: Macmillan, 1980.

Landon, H. C. Robbins. *Beethoven: Sein Leben und seine Welt in zeitgenössischen Bildern und Texten.* Zurich: Universal Edition, 1970.

Ong, Seow-Chin. "The Autograph of Beethoven's 'Archduke' Trio, Op.97." In *Beethoven Forum,* vol. 11, no. 2 (2004), pp. 181–208.

Raphael, Günter, ed. *Beethoven: Trios für Klavier, Violine und Violoncello*, vol. 2. Munich-Duisburg: G. Henle, 1967.

Spohr, Louis. *Selbstbiographie*. Kassel and Göttingen 1860–61; quoted in Thayer/Forbes (see below).

Forbes, Elliot, ed. *Thayer's Life of Beethoven*. Princeton: Princeton University Press, 1967.

Watson, Angus. *Beethoven's Chamber Music in Context*. Woodbridge, Suffolk, UK: Boydell Press, 2010.

SCHUBERT

Aderhold, Werner. Preface to the score of *Schubert: Streichquartett in G*. Kassel: Bärenreiter, 1989.

Brown, Maurice J. E. *Schubert: A Critical Biography*. London: Macmillan, 1958.

Brown, Maurice J. E. "Schubert, Franz (Peter)." In *The New Grove Dictionary of Music and Musicians*, ed. Stanley Sadie, vol. 16. London and New York: Macmillan 1980.

Deutsch, Otto Erich, ed. *Franz Schubert: Die Dokumente seines Lebens und Schaffens*, vol. 2. Munich and Leipzig: Georg Müller, 1914.

Erickson, Raymond, ed. *Schubert's Vienna*. New Haven and London: Yale University Press, 1997.

Fischer-Dieskau, Dietrich *Schubert: A Biographical Study of His Songs*, trans. and ed. Kenneth S. Whitton. London: Cassell, 1976.

Frisch, Walter, ed. *Schubert: Critical and Analytical Studies*. Lincoln and London: University of Nebraska Press, 1987.

Gibbs, Christopher H. *The Life of Schubert*. Cambridge: Cambridge University Press, 2000.

Gibbs, Christopher H., and Morton Solvik, eds. *Franz Schubert and his World*. Princeton and Oxford: Princeton University Press, 2014.

Newbould, Brian. *Schubert: The Music and the Man*. Berkeley and Los Angeles: University of California Press, 1997.

Reed, John. *Schubert*. Oxford: Oxford University Press, 1997.

Reed, John. *Schubert* (in the Master Musicians series). Oxford: Oxford University Press, 1987 (rev. 1997).

Reed, John. *Schubert: The Final Years*. New York: St. Martin's Press, 1972.

Voss, Egon. Preface to the score of *Franz Schubert: Streichquartett G-dur*. Munich: G. Henle, 2009.

SCHUMANN

Abraham, Gerald. "Schumann, Robert Alexander," In *The New Grove Dictionary of Music and Musicians*, ed. Stanley Sadie, vol. 16. London and New York: Macmillan, 1980.

Arnold, Matthew. *Heinrich Heine*. Philadelphia: Frederick Leypoldt, 1863.

Chernaik, Judith. *Schumann: The Faces and the Masks*. New York: Alfred A. Knopf, 2018.

Ewert, Hansjörg. Preface to the score *Schumann: Dichterliebe, op. 48*. Kassel etc.: Bärenreiter, 2011.

Ford, Ford Madox. *The March of Literature*. Normal, IL: Dalkey Archive Press, 1994 (orig. ed. 1938).

Heine, Heinrich. *Selected Works*, trans. and ed. H. M. Mustard. New York: Random House, 1973.

Musgrave, Michael. *The Life of Schumann*. Cambridge: Cambridge University Press, 2011.

Predota, Georg. "Heinrich Heine's Favorite Song Composer," in *Interlude*, April 22, 2019, https://interlude.hk/heinrich-heines-favorite-song-composer/.

Sachs, Harvey. *The Ninth: Beethoven and the World in 1824*. New York: Random House, 2010.

Sams, Eric. *The Songs of Robert Schumann*, 2nd edition. London: Eulenburg Books, 1975.

Schumann, Robert. *Early Letters of Robert Schumann*, ed. Clara Schumann, trans. May Herbert. London: G. Bell, 1888.

Schumann, Robert. *Tagebücher*. https://archive.org/details/RobertSchumannTagebcherBd1/page/n63.

BERLIOZ

Berlioz, Hector. *Beethoven*. Paris: Corréa, 1941.

Berlioz, Hector *Evenings with the Orchestra*, ed. Jacques Barzun. Chicago and London: University of Chicago Press, 1973.

Berlioz, Hector. *Mémoires*, vols. I and II. Paris: Calmann-Lévy (undated, early edition).

Berlioz, Hector *The Memoirs of Hector Berlioz*, ed. David Cairns. London: Panther Books, 1970.

Bloom, Peter. *The Life of Berlioz*. Cambridge: Cambridge University Press, 1998.

Bloom, Peter, ed. *The Cambridge Companion to Berlioz*. Cambridge: Cambridge University Press, 2000.

Cairns, David. *Berlioz*, vol. 1, *The Making of an Artist*. London: André Deutsch, 1989.

Cairns, David. *Berlioz*, vol. 2, *Servitude and Greatness*. London: Penguin Press, 1999.

Holoman, D. Kern. *Berlioz*. London: Faber & Faber, 1989.

Macdonald, Hugh, ed. *Selected Letters of Berlioz*, trans. Roger Nichols. New York and London: W. W. Norton, 1995.

Searle, Humphrey, trans. and ed. *Hector Berlioz: A Selection from His Letters*. New York: Harcourt, Brace & World, 1966.

Turner, W. J. *Berlioz: The Man and His Work*. London: J. M. Dent & Sons, 1939.

VERDI

Budden, Julian. *The Operas of Giuseppe Verdi*, vol. 1, *From "Oberto" to "Rigoletto."* London: Cassell, 1973; vol. 2, *From "Il Trovatore" to "La Forza del Destino."* London: Cassell, 1978; Vol. 3, *From "Don Carlos" to "Falstaff,"* New York: Oxford University Press, 1981.

Budden, Julian. *Verdi*. London and Melbourne: J. M. Dent & Sons, 1985.

Luzio, Alessandro, ed., *Carteggi verdiani*. Rome: Reale Accademia d'Italia, 1935–47.

Mila, Massimo. *Verdi*, ed. Piero Gelli. Milan: Rizzoli, 2000.

Phillips-Matz, Mary Jane. *Verdi: A Biography*. Oxford and New York: Oxford University Press, 1993.

Turba, Alessandro, ed. *Lettere di Giuseppe Verdi a Opprandino Arrivabene*. Lucca: Libreria Musicale Italiana, 2018.

Verdi, Giuseppe. *Autobiografia dalle lettere*, ed. Aldo Oberdorfer. Milan: Rizzoli, 1951.

BRAHMS

Avins, Styra, ed. *Johannes Brahms: Life and Letters*. Oxford and New York: Oxford University Press, 1997.

Barkan, Hans, ed. *Johannes Brahms and Theodor Billroth: Letters from a Musical Friendship*, Norman: University of Oklahoma Press, 1957.

Botstein, Leon, ed. *The Compleat Brahms*. New York and London: W. W. Norton, 1999.

Frisch, Walter, and Kevin C. Karnes. *Brahms and His World*. Princeton and Oxford: Princeton University Press, 2009.

Gál, Hans. *Brahms: Werk und Persönlichkeit.* Frankfurt am Main: Fischer, 1961.

Geiringer, Karl. *Brahms: His Life and Work.* Garden City, NY: Doubleday, 1961.

Grimes, Nicole. *Brahms's Elegies: The Poetics of Loss in Nineteenth-Century German Culture.* Cambridge: Cambridge University Press, 2019.

Kalbeck, Max, ed. *Johannes Brahms: The Herzogenberg Correspondence.* London: John Murray, 1909 (reprinted Miami: HardPress Publishing, n.d.).

Loges, Natasha, and Katy Hamilton, eds. *Brahms in Context.* Cambridge: Cambridge University Press, 2019.

MacDonald, Malcolm. *Brahms.* New York: Schirmer, 1990.

Musgrave, Michael. *A Brahms Reader.* New Haven and London: Yale University Press, 2000.

Notley, Margaret. *Lateness and Brahms.* Oxford and New York: Oxford University Press, 2007.

Swafford, Jan. *Johannes Brahms: A Biography.* New York: Knopf, 1997.

SIBELIUS

Barnet, Andrew. *Sibelius.* New Haven: Yale University Press, 2007.

Bullock, Philip Ross, ed. *The Correspondence of Jean Sibelius and Rosa Newmarch, 1906–1939.* Woodbridge: Boydell Press, 2011.

Ekman, Karl. *Jean Sibelius: His Life and Personality*, trans. Edward Birse. New York: Tudor Publishing Co., 1938.

Layton, Robert. "Sibelius, Jean." In *The New Grove Dictionary of Music and Musicians*, vol. 17. London and New York: Macmillan, 1980.

Levas, Santeri. *Sibelius: A Personal Portrait*, trans. Percy M. Young. London: J. M. Dent & Sons Ltd., 1972.

Mäkelä, Tomi. *Jean Sibelius*, trans. Steven Lindberg. Woodbridge, UK: Boydell Press, 2011.

Tawaststjerna, Erik. *Sibelius*, trans. Robert Layton. Vol. 1: 1865–1905; vol. 2: 1904–1914; vol. 3: 1914–1957. London: Faber and Faber, 1976–97.

Vignal, Marc. *Sibelius.* Paris: Editions Seghers, 1965.

PROKOFIEV

McAllister, Rita. "Prokofiev, Sergey (Sergeyevich)." In *The New Grove Dictionary of Music and Musicians*, ed. Stanley Sadie, vol. 15. London and New York: Macmillan, 1980.

Monsaingeon, Bruno. *Sviatoslav Richter: Notebooks and Conversations*, trans. Stewart Spencer. London: Faber and Faber, 2001.

Morrison, Simon. *The Love and Wars of Lina Prokofiev.* London: Harvill Secker, 2013.

Morrison, Simon. *The People's Artist: Prokofiev's Soviet Years.* Oxford and New York: Oxford University Press, 2009.

Robinson, Harlow. *Sergei Prokofiev.* New York: Viking, 1987.

STRAVINSKY

Andriessen, Louis, and Elmer Schönberger. *The Apollonian Clockwork: On Stravinsky*, trans. from the Dutch by Jeff Hamburg. Oxford and New York: Oxford University Press, 1989.

Craft, Robert. *Stravinsky: Glimpses of a Life.* New York: St. Martin's Press, 1992.

Culshaw, Peter. "Pierre Boulez: 'I Was a Bully, I'm Not Ashamed.'" *The [London] Telegraph*, December 10, 2008.

Delan, Donald. "Stravinsky, At 84, Still Innovating." *Princeton Evening Times*, October 11, 1966.

Fager, Sam. " 'Requiem' Premieres." *Daily Princetonian*, October 10, 1966.

Libman, Lillian. *And Music at the Close: Stravinsky's Last Years*. New York: W. W. Norton, 1972.

O'Neill, D. C. A., A. Macsweeney, and H. Moss Cornell. "Stravinsky Syndrome: Giving Voice to Chronic Stroke Disease" *QJM: An International Journal of Medicine*, vol. 107, no. 6, June 2014.

Perry, Jeffrey. "A 'Requiem for the Requiem': On Stravinsky's Requiem Canticles." *College Music Symposium*, October 1, 1993, https://symposium.music.org/index .php?option=com_k2&view=item&id=2108:a-requiem-for-the-requiem-on-stravinskys -requiem-canticles&Itemid=124.

Ross, Alex. *The Rest Is Noise*. New York: Farrar, Straus and Giroux, 2007.

Straus, Joseph N. *Stravinsky's Late Music*. Cambridge: Cambridge University Press, 2001.

Stravinsky, Igor. *Requiem Canticles for Contralto and Bass Soli, Chorus and Orchestra*. London: Boosey & Hawkes, 1967.

Stravinsky, Igor. *Selected Correspondence*, ed. Robert Craft, 3 vols. New York: Alfred A. Knopf, 1982–85.

Stravinsky, Igor, and Robert Craft. *Conversations with Igor Stravinsky*. New York: Alfred A. Knopf, 1959.

Stravinsky, Igor, and Robert Craft. *Dialogues and a Diary*. London: Faber & Faber, 1963.

Stravinsky, Igor, and Robert Craft. *Expositions and Developments*. London: Faber & Faber, 1962.

Stravinsky, Igor, and Robert Craft. *Retrospectives and Conclusions*. New York: Alfred A. Knopf, 1969.

Stravinsky, Igor, and Robert Craft. *Themes and Episodes*. New York: Alfred A. Knopf, 1966.

Stravinsky, Vera, and Robert Craft. *Stravinsky in Pictures and Documents*. New York: Simon & Schuster, 1978.

van den Toorn, Pieter C. *The Music of Igor Stravinsky*. New Haven and London: Yale University Press, 1983.

Walsh, Stephen. *Stravinsky: The Second Exile: France and America, 1934–1971*. New York: Alfred A. Knopf, 2006.

White, E. W. "Stravinsky, Igor (Fyodorovich)." In *The New Grove Dictionary of Music and Musicians*, ed. Stanley Sadie, vol. 18. London and New York: Macmillan, 1980.

INDEX

Page numbers in *italics* refer to illustrations.